T0279066

"*Money on Your Mind* is essential reading for anyone who has ever earned, spent, or saved money. As a financial psychotherapist, Reynal explains how the experiences we had yesterday shape our relationships with money today, and how we can improve our interactions not just with money but also with the partners and loved ones who share our financial resources and shape our financial decisions. Highly recommended."

—Adam Alter, *New York Times*–bestselling author of *Irresistible, Anatomy of a Breakthrough,* and *Drunk Tank Pink*

"As a *Financial Times* journalist, I have long been a fan of Vicky's work as a therapist, and how she's able to unlock deep-seated emotional problems with money that can hold us back in ways we simply don't realize. In this intriguing book, Vicky leads her readers on an incredible voyage of financial self-discovery with plenty of aha moments about how we could make more mindful choices with our money. Think of this as financial therapy with feeling."

—Claer Barrett, *Financial Times*

"In *Money on Your Mind*, Vicky Reynal shares a clear and substantiated road map for the reader who wants to not only improve their finances but also better understand their financial life. The relatable stories she shares will help readers create strategies to build financial wellness and a healthy relationship with money. This one is a keeper!"

—Bobbi Rebell, CFP, founder of Financial Wellness Strategies and author of *Launching Financial Grownups*

"Our relationship with money runs deeper than we think, and Vicky Reynal is uniquely able to bring together real-life stories and research to show us just how deep our issues with money can go. She also offers tangible steps for improving your relationship with money now and into the future."

—Jessica Moorhouse, author of *Everything But Money* and host of the *More Money* podcast

"This book is a must-read for anyone struggling to overcome unhelpful money habits, and especially for anyone in an intimate relationship, since money continues to a be top stressor for couples. I wish I had read this book when I was first married; it would have saved years of financially driven anguish and confusion."

—Ed Coambs, former president of the Financial Therapy Association and host of the *Healthy Love and Money* podcast

"Vicky offers a clear understanding of common, and some less obvious, financial issues with her insightful exploration of our complex relationship with money. . . . I consider it a crucial resource for anyone wishing to understand and manage their money psychology, especially when it comes to personal relationships."

—Michael Aitken, founder and chairman of Magus Wealth and author of *The Levelheaded Investor*

Money on Your Mind

The Unconscious Beliefs That
Sabotage Your Financial Well-Being—
and How to Break Free

VICKY REYNAL, MBA

THE EXPERIMENT

NEW YORK

MONEY ON YOUR MIND: *The Unconscious Beliefs That Sabotage Your Financial Well-Being—and How to Break Free*
Copyright © 2024 by Vicky Reynal, MBA

Originally published in the UK by Lagom, an imprint of the Zaffre Publishing Group, a Bonnier Books UK company, in 2024. First published in North America in revised form by The Experiment, LLC, in 2025.

The Experiment, LLC
220 East 23rd Street, Suite 600
New York, NY 10010-4658
theexperimentpublishing.com

This book contains the opinions and ideas of its author. It is intended to provide helpful and informative material on the subjects addressed in the book. It is sold with the understanding that the author and publisher are not engaged in rendering financial or any other kind of personal professional services in the book. The author and publisher specifically disclaim all responsibility for any liability, loss, or risk—personal or otherwise—that is incurred as a consequence, directly or indirectly, of the use and application of any of the contents of this book.

The Experiment's books are available at special discounts when purchased in bulk for premiums and sales promotions as well as for fundraising or educational use. For details, contact us at info@theexperimentpublishing.com.

Library of Congress Cataloging-in-Publication Data available upon request

ISBN 979-8-89303-008-2
Ebook ISBN 979-8-89303-009-9

Cover and text design by Beth Bugler

Manufactured in the United States of America

First printing January 2025
10 9 8 7 6 5 4 3 2 1

To Ire

Contents

Introduction

You might think that psychotherapists are comfortable talking about anything. Dark secrets, embarrassing memories, shameful thoughts, sexual fantasies . . . these are all part of the material that clients confess in therapy. As therapists we spend years training to equip ourselves with the curiosity and resilience needed to accompany our clients in the exploration of difficult topics. But one area that was, until recently, hardly covered in psychotherapy training is the topic of money.

For reasons I will come to, I made it a personal quest to understand and delve deep into my own relationship with money. Not because money is important, but because money is an object that carries all sorts of connotations, and exploring these helps us better understand who we are.

Sandwiched between a psychology degree and a psycho-therapy postgraduate, I obtained a master's degree in business administration (MBA). I wasn't surprised that the MBA would include a seminar on behavioral finance, which applies psychological theories to explain why people sometimes make irrational choices when it comes to money. But I was surprised when in my psychotherapy studies, which teach you to explore the meaning in everything, the subject of money was generally avoided.

I have been curious to explore questions such as the following.

- Why is money never enough for some people, yet others seem content with much less?

- Why are some people tormented with guilt when they spend on themselves, yet others almost waste away their fortunes?

- Why do some couples argue incessantly about money, yet others seem to agree on most financial matters?

- When is money used to control, to ask for love, to show love, to show off, to compensate, to rebel?

It isn't purely a professional interest for me. It's a personal one too. My father wrote his own book about the financial tragedy that ruined his wealth, hopes, dreams, and so much more than that. It is a story of deceit, betrayal, and loss that left him with a deep sense of injustice, anger, and regret. There is no doubt in my mind that my family's experiences with money colored my views of what it stands for and its importance. It's not just the impact of my father's experience, it's everything that it was imbued with. Money as a measure of achievement (but also self-worth). Money as an instrument of generosity and help (but also of pride). Money as a means to move up a social ladder (but with the inadequacy and even shame that sometimes comes with it). Money as something that can vanish from one day to another (stripping you of opportunities, aspirations, and hopes). I won't speak about my personal story in this book (psychotherapists don't disclose much about themselves) but I mention it here to explain my passion for this subject.

Money is still a taboo

Sigmund Freud, the founder of psychoanalysis (whom I will refer to a fair bit in this book), was the first to observe the taboo aspect of money. He wrote, "Money matters are treated by civilized people in the same way as sexual matters—with the same inconsistency, prudishness and hypocrisy."[1] More than a century later, his statement is still relevant. In multiple surveys, people have said they would rather talk about sex than money with friends and family.[2] Half of people say that talking about personal money matters is taboo in everyday conversation, higher than sex, religion, and politics. More than two fifths (44 percent) of people have avoided discussions about money. Even in therapy, it's brought up with reluctance, as the Jungian analyst James Hillman said: "Patients more readily reveal what's concealed by their pants than what's hidden in their pants' pocket."[3] Which is why, I think, calling myself a "financial psychotherapist" has helped many of my clients feel like they enter a space in which talking and thinking about money is allowed and free of judgment.

Money remains a taboo topic and a great cause of stress, shame, and conflict. When conversations about money do happen, they stir up a range of emotions. When polled, almost a third (32 percent) of people said they find it stressful talking about their finances with family and friends and over two fifths (43 percent) said they had felt embarrassed.[4] Shame or embarrassment seems to be particularly high in younger people facing money conversations.[5]

It is also the case that many of us were raised being taught that talking about money is not polite or appropriate, so there is the additional worry that we might come off as poorly mannered by raising the topic among a group of friends. On top of that, you add pay secrecy clauses, which discourage employees from disclosing their salary to colleagues, and you can see how there are plenty of messages encouraging us to keep our money matters to ourselves. Even when such demands are not verbalized, company cultures that frown upon the discussion of remuneration are not uncommon and perpetuate the idea of money as a taboo.

The link between money and mental health

We avoid the topic of money not because it's unimportant but because of how emotionally loaded it sometimes feels. Some of us give money the power to influence our relationships, our mental and physical health, and our performance at work. If you have stayed up at night, worried about finances, you are certainly not alone. Global studies confirm that close to half of adults feel anxious about finances, and in countries like the US it is more than half.[6]

Money worries can preoccupy anyone, but some people live from paycheck to paycheck, which feels like a daily struggle. It can bring people to dark places in their minds, which is why it is vital for the money taboo to be tackled. Shame, fear, and sadness related to finances can leave people with a deep sense of hopelessness and helplessness. Suppressing emotions, hiding them, and leaving them unexplored and undiscussed can make them overwhelming.

Financial stress, particularly related to debt, has been linked to poor physical health too. A 2010 meta-analysis of over 60 papers on the subject confirmed the link between debt and worse health.[7] Looking at the common health issues affecting those facing financial stress, one study (conducted by the Associated Press–AOL Health Poll in 2008)[8] determined that when people are dealing with substantial debt, they are significantly more likely to have ulcers or digestive tract problems, headaches/migraines, and they were more than six times more likely to suffer from anxiety and depression. They were also twice as likely to have had a heart attack and over half suffered from muscle tension and lower back pain. Also, and consistent with chronic stress symptoms, they had trouble concentrating and sleeping, and reported feeling upset for no good reason.

Our performance at work is also impacted by financial stress. Nearly seven in ten UK employers believe that their staff's performance is negatively affected when employees are under financial pressures, and in fact 10 percent of employees missed days of work as a result (almost five days on average per year for these employees), according to a report by the Centre for Economics and Business Research.[9] The report found that 18 percent of workers noticed a decline in productivity as a result of their financial worries.

There is no doubt that the relationship is two-way: We saw how financial difficulties can cause mental health deterioration, but mental illness too can influence people's ability to make rational and self-enhancing financial choices. It also influences their ability to keep a job.

Money can also interfere with the harmony of our relationships directly or indirectly: We might find that money conflicts plague some of our most important relationships, or simply that our money worries cause such emotional strain that they make us more tense, irritable, and unable to manage our feelings and our communication with our loved ones. Understanding the role that money plays in our minds can help improve more than just our bank balance: It can help improve our relationships.

Wealth is no guarantee for happiness

Even though the absence of wealth presents a risk to our well-being, the presence of wealth and financial success do not guarantee happiness either. Plenty of studies have tried to determine whether happiness increases along with income or wealth. Results are mixed, and academic debates abound on whether one should measure "evaluative well-being" (how we evaluate our lives) or "experienced well-being" (how we feel in the day-to-day). However, evaluative well-being has been proven to be more related to wealth than experienced well-being, indicating that wealth seems to influence how we feel about our lives in general, but in the day-to-day, wealthy people struggle no less than everyone else with their happiness.

Now, as I will repeat more than once in this book, we are complex beings, so trying to rate happiness through a questionnaire has its limitations. And as much comfort and reassurance as we find in reading psychologists' conclusions that the 100 wealthiest Americans are only slightly happier than the average American,[10] there are studies that contradict these findings, too.[11]

My practice and that of many colleagues confirms that many wealthy people struggle to find joy and fulfillment. If anything, they harbor more guilt and shame about their sadness because our society ingrains in us the misleading assumption that more money *will* make us happier. Money, if we allow it to, can be an enabler for happiness, but it isn't a driver of it.

Allowing money to facilitate happiness, however, seems to be harder to do than one would imagine. We can be emotional, irrational, unrealistic, even deluded about what money can get us and so we sometimes let it be a source of conflict or a tool for acting out our self-destruction and self-deprivation, rather than a life-enhancing one.

It is no news that people can be irrational about money

Although the thinking on money in psychoanalytic literature has been scarce at best (with the exception of gambling), the field of behavioral finance has on the contrary been investigating for years the impact of psychology on financial markets and financial decisions.

Research in the field of behavioral finance has demonstrated that people can be irrational with money. For example, looking at how humans make decisions, they found we are prone to certain so-called cognitive biases: the "sunk cost fallacy," "anchoring bias," and "recency bias" distort our rationality and trick our minds into making bad financial choices.

As an example, from the biases listed above, let's take the sunk cost fallacy. Imagine you purchased concert tickets for $150 and theater tickets for $75, without realizing they are both scheduled for the same night. Which one should you attend? You might choose the concert because you have paid a higher price for it. However, the ticket money is lost either way: A rational decision-maker would only look at the future value. Which event will give you greater enjoyment and satisfaction to attend? The money spent should not be a factor in this decision.

This book, however, is not about the irrational tendencies that we *all* face; it is about equipping you with the tools to explore your own, individual attitude toward money, based on the unique mapping of your internal world.

While a psychotherapist might help you see the fallacy in your thinking, they will be more interested in why you got in such a muddle in the first place (booking two events on the same night). If this is something that happens often there might be reasons behind these mistakes. Maybe you feel guilty about spending money on yourself and to avoid this guilt you rush through money decisions without much thinking (or checking dates). Maybe your insecurities about being alone on a Saturday night (rooted in difficulties socializing in school years) makes you rush to book plans without much thought. Or is this a reflection of a chaotic way of being, something that you see in other areas of your life? What I am interested in is the unique emotional imprint that predisposes you to certain patterns of thought and behavior.

By guiding you through a different way of thinking I hope to equip you with a new lens to explore your relationship with money. I remember a client once, who struggled with money anxiety, taking a deep breath after having just recounted in detail the painful early memory of his parents' bankruptcy. The deep breath was followed by a silence, then he asked me, looking hopeful: "Is this it?" What he meant was, "Have we unlocked the mystery? Have we found *the* answer?" or in other words, could this one experience account for everything? Unfortunately, there is never an "it." Some readers might be disappointed to read that there is hardly ever *one* thing, *one* experience or thought that accounts for the way we act in the here and now. This doesn't make the quest less valuable, and I am now convinced of that. In fact, opening your mind to a different approach to self-inquiry and reflection will help you understand yourself in a multifaceted and multidimensional way that will enrich your understanding of yourself (and not just with money).

I will use examples from life, from my own clinical practice and published examples from the clinical practice of colleagues, as well as public figures and popular culture. If I ever draw from work with my own clients this will be done in a disguised and anonymized way to protect their privacy and my oath of confidentiality.

Financial well-being and Financial Emotional Awareness

Financial well-being is generally described as being happy about and in control of one's financial situation. It is not related to the amount of money you have, but rather it's about your ability to feel a good-enough level of control over your financial situation, having a sense that you understand the choices you make (rather than acting irrationally or going against your best interest). The

Money and Pensions Service (MaPS), an independent organization providing free money advice, says, "Financial well-being is about feeling secure and in control. It's about making the most of your money from day to day, dealing with the unexpected, and being on track for a healthy financial future. In short: financially resilient, confident, and empowered."

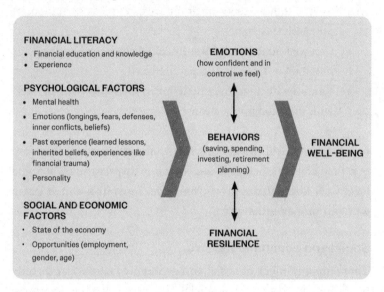

Generally speaking, there are a number of factors that can impact our financial well-being. These include the following.

- Social and economic factors
- Financial literacy
- Psychological factors

All of these influence our financial well-being because they have an impact on how confident and in control we *feel* about our finances. They also influence one another: If we don't feel confident about our finances, we are more likely to make poor financial choices, so we end up in a cycle of deteriorating financial circumstance and poor mental health.

So even though financial well-being isn't necessarily about the amount of money we have in our bank account, the reality of our financial resilience is important.

- Do we have an emergency fund to manage unforeseen expenses?
- Can we access them if needed, or are all our savings tied up in illiquid assets—meaning we can't easily turn them into cash if needed?
- Can we bounce back from financial challenges and maintain a stable financial situation?
- Can we withstand the impact of, say, inflation or a setback with financial implications?

Our behaviors will impact our financial resilience and therefore our financial well-being. If our situation is precarious, at some level we'll know that and we won't feel in control and at peace with our money situation.

Social and economic factors

There are a number of social and economic factors that directly or indirectly impact our financial well-being, as they determine to what extent we have access to opportunities, our quality of life, and our well-being overall.

Growing up in poverty as well as facing debt and unemployment are linked to poor mental health and physical health. Being in situations of financial stress and anxiety leads to poor financial decisions: US, FINRA (an Investor Education Foundation established by the US Financial Industry Regulatory Authority) found that financially anxious and stressed adults are more likely to engage in costly financial behaviors, such as high-cost borrowing and withdrawing from their retirement account and are less likely to plan for retirement.[12] So these socioeconomic factors impact both the choices we make around money and how happy and in control we feel about our financial situation.

But again, we are not talking about finances as numbers, we are talking about financial well-being, which is different. Growing up in scarcity won't necessarily condemn us to poor financial well-being nor pave the way for one particular money attitude. Similarly growing up in wealth doesn't guarantee freedom from money-related concerns. It is simply a different and equally complex emotional constellation.

If you grew up in scarcity, impacted by money anxieties that your parents struggled to manage, you might be an adult who is very anxious with money, who never feels they have enough to relax and feel safe and confident in their financial situation. You might hoard money, rather than enjoy it, just in case something happens, feeling trapped by catastrophic fantasies that don't allow you to enjoy it. Conversely, if your parents could manage their anxieties, you might have found ways to be content overall with your financial situation, making the most of what you have, setting realistic objectives, not too concerned with what others are achieving.

Similarly, the wealthy might, on the whole, have fewer anxieties about finding themselves in a financially precarious situation, but their financial well-being could still be impacted by a plethora of negative emotions: insecurities about their abilities to manage the money they have, if it has been inherited and not earned; shame about having more than others, if they are making more than their friends and family ever did; fears of it vanishing, if they saw their parents go through a bankruptcy or big loss growing up. So it's not that scarcity = poor financial well-being and wealth = good financial well-being, but it's your experience of it that might be getting in the way of your financial well-being.

Social class is an interesting one. While the economic status and level of education that come with class has (traditionally) anchored us to a certain potential for earnings and opportunities, what I find most interesting to reflect on is how our experience of class has shaped our attitude to and behavior with money. Was there resentment of the money/power that those of a higher social class wielded, and shame in our inferior status that has left us feeling stuck and powerless? If that's the case, our financial well-being will be colored by a narrative of others will always have more, and maybe feelings of resignation and little agency over our situation. Similarly, growing up in a family contemptuous of wealth and the "greedy rich" might leave us very conflicted if one day we find ourselves having moved up the social ladder, where instead of being able to enjoy our money (and have a strong sense of financial well-being) we are tortured by feelings of guilt and shame.

Other factors that might guide how we feel and behave with money are the state of the economy and of financial markets: We might feel more confident and take on more risk in a growing economy and feel and act very differently in the middle of a recession.

Our age, life stage, and relationship status too might color our money choices and confidence in our financial resilience (we might be more prone to taking risks at a young age and more risk-averse as we grow older; we might be more focused on saving in our early years of employment, and on spending as we approach midlife). But again, the individual experience and circumstances will have the biggest influence on our financial well-being and these socio-economic factors can inform our understanding of our relationship with money, but won't explain it.

Financial literacy

Financial literacy matters because it's key to how confident we feel about the financial choices we make. It also drives sound financial behavior. Making choices that go against our best financial interest, might not be rooted in deep emotional issues but could be down to plain financial illiteracy.

The global statistics on financial literacy are disappointing.

- In the European Union only about half of adults are financially literate.[13]
- There is a gap in literacy between men and women in every country: When S&P Global conducted a large survey across 93 countries, they found that the gap in correct answers between men and women was more than five percentage points.
- In the US, one in three teens don't know the difference between a credit card and a debit card.[14]
- In an OECD study across 33 countries, a quarter of adults cannot work out how much change they should receive from a store (this increasing to around a third of individuals in countries like Spain, England, and Italy).[15]
- 44 percent of UK adults say they would be in much better shape financially if they had been taught basic money management skills, such as budgeting.[16]
- Both in the US[17] and in the UK,[18] three out of four teens would have liked to receive more financial management education.
- 13 percent of parents in the US said their own parents didn't speak to them about money at all,[19] and in the UK even today less than half of parents talk openly to their children about money (this statistic does not vary according to household income).[20]
- In the UK, only 67 percent of adults are financially literate.[21]

On a global level (but in well-developed financial countries too), people who are financially literate and capable of establishing what really is in their financial best interest are a minority. The numbers are jaw-dropping and point us to the urgent need for better financial education. The consequences are huge. Financial literacy has an impact on the economy and our own financial outcomes. It influences our ability to generate wealth and recover from financial shocks. It is linked to having greater savings and wealth, retirement plans, better debt management, and makes one less likely to engage in costly credit card behavior.[22] And of course, it impacts our financial well-being and mental health because the lack of financial literacy creates insecurities, uncertainties, and anxieties related to financial decisions. Studying financial stress, researchers found that the higher the level of financial literacy, the lower the financial anxiety.[23] Knowledge breeds confidence and contributes to a sense of control and choice. It also, in practice, breeds better choices.

Psychological factors

Building Financial Emotional Awareness

Feeling confident and in control of our finances is impacted by a variety of psychological factors, some of which I will cover in depth in this book. A complex web of emotional factors (longings, fears, defenses, inner conflicts, beliefs), past experiences (learned lessons about what money stands for, inherited beliefs, and experiences like financial trauma and social mobility), as well as our personality and mental processes (how we experience the world around us), all determine the money choices we make and how we feel about them.

My goal in this book is to enhance what I call your "Financial Emotional Awareness": your awareness of the psychological elements that drive and shape how you feel and how you behave with money. Many of these you will find might be rooted in past experience, some even in childhood experiences and in many cases in experiences completely unrelated to money. You might discover that your difficulty with finding an agreement on compensation with your business partner is actually about old sibling dynamics that are being ignited by this relationship. Or that your desire to keep funding your children's vacations is rooted in your fear of separating from them, which you struggled to do with your own parents. Or that your habit of dividing expenses to the last penny is about a deep-seated fear of exploitation.

It is not my purpose to strip emotions out of financial decision-making. Could one sign mortgage papers without feeling some apprehension or even fear? Could we invest in our first entrepreneurial venture without trepidation and excitement? Could we bail out our child/partner for the fifth time without feeling some degree of anger? The answer to all of these is probably not, as many money decisions are emotional. Having Financial Emotional Awareness is about your ability to be more mindful, conscious, and aware of the feelings that drive your financial choices so you can make financial decisions you feel more confident about. By developing this kind of insight, you can use feelings to *inform* your choices rather than to blindly drive them. This will inevitably contribute to greater financial well-being.

Sometimes negative feelings are a natural response to a difficult financial choice, not a sign that you are making a bad choice. We might feel the following.

- Shame if we decide to contribute less than everyone else to a gift collection
- Guilt if we treat ourselves to a massage, or a more expensive restaurant than usual
- Frustration if we stop ourselves from making a desired purchase in order to save for a bigger financial goal
- Anxiety if we are taking out a loan to start a business

The negative emotions don't always make these bad choices. Take the gift collection: Giving less than others might evoke shame but giving more than we can afford can trigger regret or even resentment. Therefore, there is no right choice that will rid us of all negative feelings. It's about being clear on the reasons for our choice (rather than acting impulsively, under pressure, without evaluating its consequences) and then managing the downsides of the choice we ultimately make. Problems arise when emotions get in the way of understanding what is best for us, when they cloud our judgment.

Take, for example, Jonathan who gets a promotion and spends his entire bonus on a luxury vacation. Is it a poor choice? Well, the answer is "it depends." The key determinant is whether Jonathan had thought through the reasons behind his choice, rather than acted impulsively, from an emotional place. In scenario one, he is so excited that he finally received a substantial bonus that he, without a second thought, books a luxury vacation. When he returns from his vacation, however, he starts experiencing guilt. If only he hadn't blown the bonus on the vacation, he would be a step closer to getting the down payment for the condo he had his eyes on . . . guilt, regret, and sadness take over.

In scenario two, Jonathan takes time to evaluate the pros and cons of his decision: Yes, taking a luxury vacation will set him back on the down payment for the condo. He might either have to wait longer to have enough money for it or ask for financial help from his family. However, this luxury vacation is something he has wanted to do since he was young. Raised in a working-class family, Jonathan looked at the children in his school who went on trips abroad with great envy. He longed to be able to afford it one day and worked hard at his first job with this reward in mind: finally going on his dream vacation. He can now fulfill his objective thanks to his hard work. Conscious of what he needs to give up, he is able to see the trade-off and make a choice about what feels more important to him. He enjoys the vacation with no guilt or regret.

Same choice, but very different decision-making processes. More importantly, very different emotional outcomes: The latter enhances his financial well-being because even if he is in the same financial position at the end of it, he has allowed himself to enjoy the money he has and make a choice he is at peace with.

Any choice involves giving something up and being conscious of that helps us let it go, in the context of what we are gaining. If we have given ourselves the chance to think through our choices and mourn the inevitable losses, we are in a better place to enjoy what we have picked. It's also an opportunity to think of ways to minimize the downsides of our choice—what alternatives to postponing buying a condo does Jonathan have? In the impulsive scenario, Jonathan probably enjoyed the vacation while trying to avoid feelings of guilt lurking in the background from a semi-conscious awareness that this money could have gone toward the condo. Back from the vacation, the reality of his choice hit him in an overwhelming way. Making choices with Financial Emotional Awareness gives us a sense of clarity about what influences them, greater visibility of the resulting emotional impact (we are less likely to be caught off guard by our feelings after we've made the decision if we have thought about them in advance), and a greater sense of control over them.

Financial well-being cannot be measured with a stick. There are no metrics that determine when our spending tips over into overspending, when a few fun poker nights with friends turn into a gambling addiction, or when being careful with money tips over into pettiness.

However, there are clues, and some are emotional. Tapping into our emotions can alert us that a line has been crossed: A soaring sense of guilt, for example, tells us that something about our behavior just doesn't feel right. What seemed like a habit we could control now feels out of control. Now, of course, the opposite is not always true: If we are convinced there is nothing wrong with a seemingly self-destructive behavior, we might just be in denial.

Facts can speak louder than words, and large or repeated credit card debt or gambling losses can be wake-up calls that something needs attending to. Behaviors too can indicate there might be an issue: Avoidance of money conversation altogether, lies and secrets kept from loved ones, and arbitrary inconsistencies can all alert us that we are not at ease with our finances.

Signs that there might be a difficulty worth exploring could be within reach, close to the surface: You might have received feedback directly or indirectly from others ("Why are you getting so hung up on a few dollars"; "Why do you walk out of every discussion about money?"; "Can't you see where your behavior with money is going to lead?"). You know what secrets you keep (maybe you cut off the tags of new purchases before your partner/ friend/parent notices you've been shopping, or you put off telling your partner about the inheritance from the distant relative that you received); you know what you wish you had censored last time money came up in a conversation ("Why did I have to blurt out my bonus amount to my friend who just told me they didn't get a bonus?"). You might have observed that you are substantially more careful/excessive/risk-averse than most people you know. The point here is not to pathologize differences but to help you be more self-aware and to wonder: What's that about?

* * *

Without Financial Emotional Awareness, we might feel trapped in behaviors and feelings that feel unchangeable. "No matter how much money I make in my career, I find myself still unsatisfied and wishing for more"; "I can't stop arguing with my partner/sibling/ parents about money"; "I keep feeling anxious about money." In all these very common statements there is a desire for something to change on the one hand, but emotionally a counterforce presents a challenge: Something needs to be understood, or a conflict resolved, or a feeling allowed room to be felt. We can identify and overcome these emotional hurdles, but sometimes we need help doing so.

My purpose in this book is to help you think about how you express your longings, fears, and internal conflicts via money, and how your early experiences, even experiences unrelated to money, might have influenced your behavior and feelings related to money.

I will cover a variety of money behaviors in this book, but not all. Gambling or financial risk-taking, for example, I won't cover in depth because many books (both academic and non-academic) have been written on this topic, so I will focus on the aspects of our relationship with money that have received less analytic thought and attention. Having said that, a lot of the themes covered in this book can help inform our understanding of gambling (e.g., masochism, desire of a magical transformation, rebelliousness, or a search for justice and restitution).

CHAPTER 1

How past experiences influence our relationship with money

Money as a symbol

Money is a powerful symbol. A symbol is something out there, in the concrete world, that stands for something in our minds. We use symbols all the time to convey a shared meaning—wedding rings symbolize a commitment between two people, a heart symbol may represent love, a white flag symbolizes surrender, a cross symbolizes Christianity. But aside from the shared meaning of symbols there is also the emotional significance that is affixed to them. It is this element that makes it so upsetting when a wedding ring is lost, a flag is burned, etc. We haven't just lost or damaged an object, but it is *felt* upsetting or threatening because of what it represents.

The symbolic meaning of an object could be shared by many but the emotional significance of it can be very personal. If we asked a group of people what a flag stands for, they might all agree that it represents a country. However, the flag may have a different emotional and psychological resonance for each person. Asking passersby, "What does the American flag mean to you?" reveals a wide array of answers: freedom, power, opportunity, but there are also those who (because of the country's history or their own experiences) will associate it with imperialism or racism.[1] It may bring up anxious memories for a war veteran and evoke comfort and nostalgia to an American living abroad.

Anything can be a symbol if it's a medium that conveys meaning. Psychoanalyst Donald Winnicott pointed out that one of the first symbols we use is the security blanket (or "transitional object" in psychoanalytic terms) because it unites a personal meaning with an object out there in the world.[2] The blanket/stuffed animal/pacifier represents comfort, and it fills a space that is slowly being created between the mother and the child, in the child's developmental challenge of separation. The security blanket therefore takes on a meaning assigned to it by the child, a meaning that is psychological and emotional.

Money oozes with meaning. While its shared meaning (as a medium of exchange) is universally accepted, its psychological and emotional meaning is diverse and unique to each of us. What money comes to stand for in our minds (and inevitably influences how we use it), is a consequence of our life experiences. I won't be going into the history of currency and money, but I will invite you to go into your own personal history to uncover clues of what this object represents in your own mind. What does money mean to you?

The variety of money meanings reflects the diversity of our human experience and of our inner worlds. Our upbringing, our past experiences, and how we feel about ourselves will all influence our treatment of it. Money stands for different things to different people and we might use it (and misuse it) to express unconscious feelings about ourselves or others. Money may represent the following.

- Security that we feel we have or that we wish to attain
- Power that we exert on others or that is used as a weapon to control us or limit our freedom
- Freedom to pursue opportunities, to live life to its fullest, to leave an abusive relationship
- Self-worth, when for those who rely on net worth to make them feel worthy of attention, respect, or love
- Fairness, when we seek through pay, or inheritance, or how bills are split with our roommates, confirmation that we won't be exploited
- But many others too, like moral corruption, masculinity, prestige, love

Take, for example, Francesca and Isabel, who both struggled with negotiating a higher salary, but for very different reasons. Francesca was in the middle of a successful career in marketing. She could recognize her achievements and even experience some pride in looking at her career progression. She'd known for some time now that she was underpaid compared to others within the same pay grade and company, but also compared to what the role could get in other companies. Despite this knowledge, Francesca couldn't bring herself to ask for more. The thought of facing her boss and initiating a conversation about salary filled her with anxiety and dread. Reading tips and strategies for salary negotiation hadn't helped. We needed to understand what made it so hard for Francesca to ask for what she knew she deserved.

Francesca had grown up with a mother who was very hot-tempered and critical of her. The mother harbored great resentment for having given up her career to raise the children, and the father had been mostly absent, traveling frequently for work. As a result of this upbringing, although at one level Francesca could recognize her achievements, there was a part of her that had always felt undeserving or not good enough, but also too needy. In therapy, we were going to have to understand this part of her in depth, working through the anger and disappointment of not having had more supportive parents and helping her reality check and replace her narrative of "I am not good enough." Looking at the criticized little girl within her helped her understand and better manage it, so when she had the salary conversation she could approach it with the adult part of her, aware of the reality that she was a qualified and well-performing employee who deserved better pay, rather than a needy little girl. Asking for a raise was hard for Isabel too. She also struggled to ask for what she felt was a fair salary, but her paralysis turned out to be about a narrative in her family that greed is bad and that money is dirty. Having been raised in a family that prided itself on its modesty and hard work, Isabel had taken away messages from her childhood that one should be content and grateful for what one has, rather than unsatisfied and thus too greedy. At one level, Isabel respected the family values and genuinely wanted to live according to them. However, as an adult, she needed help articulating her own version of them, making her own choices about what is ambition versus greed, what is fair versus ungrateful. Verbalizing this dilemma and working through these nuances helped her move from a general sense of anxiety and guilt to a more confident stance from which she felt that she was asking for a salary that seemed deserved and reasonable.

Mismanagement of finances or emotional difficulties with money can therefore be better understood if we access the deep emotional issues that are hidden behind them. Financial Emotional Awareness is about having insight into the desires, longings, or fears that get expressed through money, and being conscious of the feelings that drive our financial choices.

As I seek to enhance your Financial Emotional Awareness by guiding you through a psychological investigation of money, we will inevitably go back to early experiences. This is not because our desire for money starts in childhood, but it's because some of the longings we attach to its symbolic meaning are early longings. Psychoanalyst Lesley Murdin writes, "wishing for money is not infantile. The infant may wish for power, for control [. . .], for love but he does not wish for money. The adult with all his complexity begins to understand that money symbolizes much of what he wants or thinks he wants."[3] We might find the roots of our present money behaviors in our past experiences, because many of us hope money will satisfy longings that were there even before we ever knew what money was. Often, money becomes a proxy for our emotional wants and by understanding what money means to us, we can make more informed decisions.

Because of the emotional baggage that money sometimes carries, it can also get in the way of our relationships. It may be a loaded topic in our minds, but it might also feel like a minefield in relationships because we have allowed money to become a symbol (or a language) for more than just the financial. In other words, we may be using money to express unconscious feelings about others or about the relationship. But the message, transmitted this way, is unclear and can get people trapped in endless unresolvable conflict. Why let money do the talking? Wouldn't it be better to understand what we are acting out through money?

People hold such different views of what money stands for and how it's supposed to be used: What seems excessive to one may seem conservative to the other; what is fair and reasonable to one seems unequal and thus unreasonable to the other. If you have recently been on a date, I suspect a lot of thinking might have gone into trying to guess what the other person might be expecting when the bill arrived. Would they value equality and wish to share? Or would they value or even expect being treated to the meal? An offer to pay may be perceived as chivalry, generosity, a power play, controlling, or kind. An expectation of being treated may be perceived as submissive or entitled. We just don't know.

Trying to guess what the other's view of money is and how our action will be interpreted may feel like a minefield. The bill is left on the table: It's awkward. There is often a sense of shame and vulnerability that comes up for people in these situations; possibly because there is no easy way to avoid giving away (at least in part) some of our views on how this should be addressed.

"Should we split this?" suggests we have no intention to pay for the whole thing. Waiting too long for the other to say something first may be interpreted as a reluctance to pay any part of the bill. With the bill, like with everything else that follows a first date, the two people will find themselves in a dynamic of slowly unveiling their values and views while discovering the other's, hoping not to offend them or lose interest in them as a result of what they find out. Will they be able to understand and accept their differences? Will these be reconcilable? Money is just one of many areas in which couples face this struggle.

Paola (who I will present in more detail in chapter 8) grew up with two very controlling parents. Their control also manifested itself in the realm of money, and while growing up Paola, unlike her peers, was never given an allowance, so couldn't afford to leave the house and join in social plans. Years later, in her initial dates with her future husband, she couldn't allow him to pay for her movie ticket. "We'll go to the movies when I can afford it," she would tell him. For her it was a better option than letting him pay. Why? In her case, achieving financial independence and autonomy had become so crucial and linked to her sense of freedom that allowing him to pay would have evoked the painful and distressing sense of someone else holding the key to her enjoyment. So for Paola, what felt acceptable in relation to an ordinary and generous act was tied to traumatic past events. She wasn't going to let the controlling dynamics that were acted out through money in her past be a feature in her future relationship with this man.

For most people, the dynamics at play through money tend to be subtle and often out of consciousness. We might be unaware that we are acting out interpersonal dynamics of dependency, cooperation, and equality through money, especially if these are healthy dynamics at play that are not causing distress and therefore aren't calling for our attention.

What seems undeniable, in my experience, is that what we do with money, how we interpret it, talk about it, seek it, deny it, avoid it, or condemn it are influenced by our past and not just money-related experiences. A lot goes into and shapes what money means to us.

The emotional imprint of past relationships

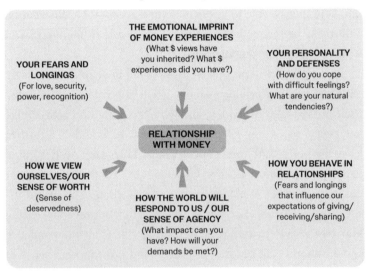

When we think about our relationship with money it is too narrow and limiting to just think about what we learned about money from our parents, how our pocket money was handled, and whether or not we grew up in abundance or poverty (so the emotional imprint of our experiences). From big life events like trauma and loss to the small interactions from crib to the present, our experiences will have had an impact on what we expect of ourselves and of others, on what we long for and are afraid of.

We are the result of our past experiences: These helped shape us, especially if they were emotionally charged. What we did with our feelings (back then) and how the people around us helped us manage them, leaves an emotional imprint on how we deal with similar problems in the present. Our early relationships have a big impact on who we become, how we feel about ourselves, how we build future relationships, and how we experience the world around us.

When a psychotherapist thinks about your relationship with money, they might start with what the problem seems to be in the present, but they will have an investigative tool kit that will attempt to reach for the unconscious feelings and thoughts that might sit behind this behavior, trying to unpack what might be yearned for or defended against.

- A difficulty with overspending could actually be about a desire to fit in.
- A difficulty with spending money could be about our low feelings of self-worth.
- A pattern of keeping money secrets could be about an inner sense of shame.
- A gambling addiction could actually be about punishing our parents for being neglectful.

Let me give you an example from a therapy session:

Michael: "I never *plan* on spending so much money when I am out with my friends, it just happens."

Therapist: "It just happens . . ."

Michael: "Yeah, I mean . . . we are all finishing up a round and suddenly I am blurting out, 'Next one's on me!'"

Therapist: "And how do you feel then?"

Michael: "It's a mix . . . there's like 5 percent regret, the moment

I say it . . . but mostly I am feeling excited . . . and relieved."
Therapist: "Relieved?"
Michael: "Yes, like something in me has calmed down."
Therapist: "As if . . . ?"
Michael: "As if now, for a bit at least, I don't have to worry about them liking me."

Michael was the middle of three siblings and, because of his father's career as a diplomat, had spent much of his school years moving countries and changing schools. His position, in relation to others, often felt uncertain. Even in his family, being the middle sibling and feeling his sister had a strong relationship with his father and his brother with his mother, he often feared feeling excluded and carried insecurities about being liked for who he is. No matter how much budgeting advice he had received from his frustrated wife, this was not a rational struggle, it was an emotional one. There were experiences in the past that had set him up for fearing exclusion and rejection and which needed to be thought about and worked through. Meanwhile, in the here and now he needed to reality-test his fears (will his friends really think less of him if he doesn't exceed their generosity?) and hold on to the belief that the future doesn't have to be like the past, and in the unlikely event that he got the cold shoulder once his generosity decreased, he wouldn't be a schoolboy alone in the playground, but an adult who might decide to look for relationships that feel more mutual.

How we view ourselves and our sense of worth

Past relationships have an impact on who we become and how we experience the world, which is very relevant to what, as adults, we allow ourselves to have, what we long for, and how we behave. A lot of the money problems in this book will find their source in our sense of deservedness, of entitlement, of agency.

Our relationship with our primary caregivers shapes our sense of self: from the initial bonding between mother* and infant, the experiences of being held, fed, and changed, to all later interactions (how they respond to us, how they encourage us, how they express their anger toward us). These are all experiences that influence our sense of how lovable and capable we are. A baby that is responded to with smiles, who is held tenderly, whose needs are adequately interpreted and met by its parents will develop a sense that they are worthy of love, that they have valuable qualities, and develop a sense of trust that the world is a safe place to live in. A neglected baby will grow up with a very different sense of self: They might see themselves as undesirable, unlovable, incapable. The world might be experienced as a threatening, dangerous place in which they feel vulnerable.

Winnicott explains that a baby's personality is shaped by what they see through the mirror that is the mother's face: an uninterested, angry, depressed mother will influence the baby's sense that s/he is good, worthy, interesting. Equally important is attunement, which is how the mother interprets and understands the child's needs. A mother that fails to attune to her child will leave them with a sense of deficiency, of shame. Feelings like confusion and helplessness will overwhelm the baby. The mother (and therefore the world they live in) will seem harsh, cold, and judgmental.

The accumulation of these experiences adds up to a consolidating sense of how we feel about ourselves. Do we feel deserving of good things (like love or money)? Can we allow ourselves to have and enjoy a compliment, a dessert, a loving partner, as well as the good things that money can buy? Money could be hard to have and enjoy because our past experiences have

---

* Please note that in psychoanalytic literature, the primary caregiver is often referred to as the mother and so if I, or the authors I quote, referred to "the mother," this is to be taken to be equivalent to "primary caregiver."

left us feeling that we are not good enough to merit them and so we act in a way that interferes with financial success and with having a balanced approach to money: We might give it away, spend it too quickly, or hoard it in the hope it will boost our self-esteem.

For many people the struggle to have, enjoy, or treasure anything good may be pervasive. They are tormented by shame and feelings of unworthiness. They may momentarily allow themselves to have something good but then can't enjoy it, expect to lose it ("it's too good to be true, it won't last"), or sabotage it somehow. They might feel guilt when they eat, or feel like an imposter when they achieve anything. I will give you examples of people with this kind of predisposition in the underspending and the self-sabotage chapters, where we will meet those who would rather financially self-destruct or become "money anorexic" than allow themselves to have and enjoy money.

The mother-infant dyad (which is pretty much all the baby can register in its early weeks of life) expands to include others. We begin to register interactions with our father, siblings, grandparents, teachers, society. These interactions also have important implications for how we feel about ourselves. Within our family unit, it's interesting to explore which parent you identify with most. If you are struggling to understand why it is that you second-guess yourself in business decisions and feel like an imposter when you accomplish something, it's worth thinking about whether your defeatist attitude is there because you identify with a parent that didn't feel confident in their skill, or who didn't have what it takes to be successful.

But of course we don't fully identify with one parent on all aspects of life: We might identify with one parent in relation to work and money attitude and with the other when it comes to relationships. These are complex, unconscious, multifactor phenomena which we can't study in a scientific way, but we can nonetheless use them to add to our understanding of who we are.

How we feel about ourselves influences how we manage money. Equally important is the ability to recognize, name, and manage our feelings. This too is learned through attunement with our primary caregiver: Their ability to read our emotions and our needs translates, with enough good experiences, into our ability to do that for ourselves. Research[4] of emotionally deprived children has demonstrated that these kids lack self-awareness and the ability to name and think about their feelings (what psychoanalyst Peter Fonagy called "mentalization"), but also their ability to understand the mental state of others. We are much more prone to acting out our feelings in destructive ways if we cannot think about them, let alone manage them. We will see examples of this throughout the book.

How the world will respond to us and our sense of agency

The many experiences that shape who we become also shape our sense of agency and our expectations of how we'll be received and responded to in the world. These are both essential to our ability to succeed financially but also to feeling we have agency in the management of our finances.

From early infant-mother interactions, our early relationships shape our expectations of how the world responds to us. As Jungian analysts Deborah C. Stewart, Lisa Marchiano, and Joseph R. Lee discuss in their episode "The Money Complex" in the *This Jungian Life* podcast, if an infant turns to the breast to find that the breast is offered in return, they will grow up with a sense that when they reach for something, the world responds favorably.[5]

A mother who gives enough experiences to her child of being emotionally present, attuned, and responsive will help the child not only feel worthy, safe, and cared for, but will also instil a sense in them that their needs can be met (they are both acceptable and satisfiable). The accumulation of such experiences plays a fundamental part in perpetuating our sense of agency. In order to build a career, or set out on a business venture, we need a certain amount of faith that the world will respond positively to us.[6] Sitting in front of a client pitching an idea with confidence requires a critical mass of experiences in which whoever the recipient of our message was, responded to it with interest or, at the very least, declined with respect. If this hasn't been the case, we'll either avoid these situations (and be modest in our pursuits) or be overwhelmed by anxiety when faced with them.

Growing up with very critical parents, but also critical teachers/coaches can result in us, as adults, carrying fears that the other (whoever that might be), will be rejecting, critical, or judgmental. So we might avoid interactions, or find it hard to trust others when it comes to money, and we might hear that voice in our heads (the "superego" in psychoanalytic terms) telling us we are ungrateful asking for a raise. Or we might shy away from risk because we expect negative outcomes or criticism, not encouragement or support.

Financial well-being is hard to achieve without trust in our ability to influence and change our situation through our choices. What happens when we go for something? Do we expect criticism and shaming? Do we expect our requests to generally be granted or denied? If we don't feel we can influence others we can't feel the needed sense of agency that is essential for financial well-being.

How we behave in relationships

Our upbringing will also influence how we are in relationships and what we expect from others. This is very relevant to our Financial Emotional Awareness because of the following.

1. It can help us identify some of the unconscious expectations we have of others when it comes to relationships, which often get translated into financial expectation.

- Do we expect to give more than we receive (and end up in relationships in which we are financially supporting our partner too)?
- Do we expect equality in every aspect of the relationship (and therefore seek equal division of anything from parental responsibilities to financial contributions)?
- Are we used to, and therefore expect to find, dynamics in which we are controlled (and unconsciously end up relinquishing control easily when it comes to our finances)?

2. It can also help us identify when we are using money to communicate something about our needs, fears, and desires beyond the financial.
   - For example, are we asking for a more generous gift when, really, we want more affection?
   - Are we complaining about our partner's excessive travel expenses when we are really worried about their increasing absence and feel emotional distance?

Money conflicts abound in relationships and trying to resolve them simply by addressing differences in money views and values would be shortsighted: A lot of money conflicts are not about money at all. Understanding what emotions sit behind our money conversations will improve our sense of financial well-being as well as our relationships.

There is no doubt that how we related to our parents and how they related to one another influences how we relate to others. Sometimes we reenact money behaviors and relationship dynamics we experienced in our families without being aware of the repetition we are unconsciously enabling.

I had a client, David, who found it stressful to manage a vacation property he had inherited jointly with his sister Sabrina after their parents had passed away. David and Sabrina argued constantly about the financial management of the house. David felt he was the responsible one, always on top of the bills, renegotiating service provider contracts, shopping around for replacements when any amenities were damaged, and that Sabrina was free-riding, essentially using the house without any effort on her part and even having a negative impact on its finances by making impulsive and thoughtless purchases for the house from the joint account they had set up for it.

The turning point in the relationship between these siblings was when David realized that in many ways he and Sabrina were reenacting the arguments they had witnessed at home for many years between their parents. Their father was always collaborative in his approach, trying to involve his wife in decisions that impacted the family's finances, but ultimately taking on a lot of the financial responsibility (not just as the main earner but also in terms of managing family expenses). Their mother was uninterested and unengaged in financial conversations, deferring to her husband. Their father later discovered that their mother had hidden credit card debts due to reckless spending habits along with debt from a past failed small venture. David was treating Sabrina with the expectation that she would turn out to be like their mother: He was suspicious of her intentions, mistrusting of her ability to manage the finances, and on the lookout for any signs that confirmed this. This means that a lot of the interactions were sabotaged at the start. What chances did Sabrina really have to take more ownership of the finances, and prove to David that she wasn't like her mother?

David and Sabrina ended up re-creating in their relationship the money attitudes of their parents—mistrust, lack of transparency, and suspicion. There might have been some truth in David's accounts of Sabrina (maybe she was less organized and proactive than he), but to what extent was his experience of her distorted by his experience of his parents? When we expect something to turn out one way, it is quite powerful how unconsciously we can maneuver a situation so that it fits our view of the world, so that it fulfills our predictions (it's called a "self-fulfillling prophecy"). David's fear that Sabrina would turn out like their mother led him to make choices that limited her ability to contribute and equally share the workload related to the financial management of the flat. They both had enough reasons to place the blame on the other, but only by reflecting on the roles they had taken on and cast the other person in could they begin to shift the difficult dynamic they were in.

The case of David and Sabrina is also a good example of identification. David identified with his father and saw himself as a trustworthy and organized person, capable of managing the property. But so did Sabrina. She identified enough with her father to be able to have the confidence and financial savviness to start and manage her own business: In their relationship, however, Sabrina wasn't given a chance to show this aspect of herself.

How we are in relationships isn't just a replica of how our parents were, it is influenced by many other factors, including how our parents behaved toward us. Attachment theory studies how we approach and structure relationships with others and it can be helpful in identifying some of the desires and fears we bring to our relationships (and sometimes act out through money). The founders of this theory, John Bowlby and Mary Ainsworth,[7] recognized that for biological and evolutionary reasons the infant needs to be in proximity of their caregiver. Our caregiver becomes our secure base, explains Bowlby, from which we explore the world and to which we go back when we feel unsafe. Their availability (most importantly their emotional availability and capacity to respond to a child's changing mental state), is crucial for our sense of safety in relationships. How we attach to our caregiver sets the foundations for how we behave in relationships for the rest of our lives.

Being securely attached means that we feel safe and that we can trust the other. We can build relationships that feel deep and fulfillling, and we can regulate our emotions and manage conflict. If we are securely attached, we are able to ask for help and communicate our needs and frustrations to others. We feel worthy of love and don't need reassurance of this from our partner.

However, negative parenting experiences may lead to insecure attachments. We may find that we avoid relationships (avoidant attachment style). When we are in relationships, we find ways to keep others at arm's length or even push them away. We'd rather see ourselves as independent and self-reliant. No wonder, then, that with money we might seek to keep separate accounts, have financial autonomy, or avoid joint financial commitments (like buying a house together).

Another response to negative emotional experiences is to develop what is called an "anxious/ambivalent attachment style" which is characterized by a fear of rejection and abandonment. Being in a relationship elevates our anxiety as it exposes us to the risk of painful feelings, but we want relationships and dread being alone, so we cling on to our partner, seeking reassurance. I have heard many money conversations in which partners were using money to address their need to get closer: a desire to invest in something together (a car, a vacation home), offering the reassurance that the relationship is cementing; a rush to merge bank accounts; complete delegation of finances to the partner to establish a dependence that comforts us because it makes us feel that our partner wants to look after us.

The final category, "disorganized attachment style," is essentially a blend of the latter two: swinging between wanting independence and reassurance, fearing and causing rejection at once. With money too, messages are mixed. Attachment theorist Jeremy Holmes wrote, "Money is primarily a means of exchange, and human relatedness is based on exchange."[8] Unsurprisingly, then, our approach to human relatedness might be mirrored in how we use money in relationships.

Even if generalizations and categories is not something I am a fan of, keeping attachment styles in mind can be helpful. Rather than boxes to fit people in, I think of them more as tendencies. As some therapists have suggested,[9] we can think of these attachment patterns as a framework in which people may land in one of four quadrants based on the two dimensions of (1) propensity to avoid closeness and (2) anxiety about abandonment. Both closeness and fear of abandonment can be expressed through money.

We can't think of money in relationships without thinking about ourselves in relationships: What emotional baggage are we bringing to it? How is this likely to influence our behavior in relation to our partner?

Psychological defenses: how we manage difficult feelings

To achieve greater Financial Emotional Awareness, I have started with a broad scope: Understand yourself (your sense of worth, your longings and insecurities) and how you behave in the world and in relationships (your sense of agency and your expectations about how others will treat you). The next step is to better understand what you do with your challenging emotions. You will see in this book many examples of how a problematic money attitude or behavior is actually a manifestation of a psychological defense against difficult feelings.

"Defense" is a useful concept in psychoanalysis, which I will come back to frequently because it can explain a lot of the money misuse I will cover. The concept of defense was first elaborated by Freud, who saw it as a way for the mind to keep its peace when faced with the threat of unmanageable distress because a desire couldn't be met.[10] In other words, rather than face a painful feeling, we defend against it by taking action (for example, by shopping or gambling, but of course drinking and other behaviors follow the same rationale). Psychoanalyst Lance Dodes[11] describes the underlying mechanism that is common to many problematic (and often addictive) behaviors: They feel a sense of overwhelming helplessness before they act. By taking action, they feel empowered and more in control (he calls this "reversal of helplessness"). Dodes emphasizes the importance of understanding the meaning of the situation that produces the sense of helplessness: What feelings are getting evoked that are so difficult to cope with?

Even though it is worth thinking about each of the different money behaviors individually (which I will do in this book), many behavioral addictions often coexist and people also shift between them because ultimately for many, the psychological relief comes from taking *action*, whatever that might be.[12]

Here are some examples of how we might defend against negative feelings by taking an action.

◆ "If I stopped buying expensive clothes, I would have to face my sense of inadequacy." The excessive spending is a defense against facing feelings of not being good enough.

◆ "If I stopped lying about my income, I would have to face the shame of having failed financially." Lying is a defense against the shame (and maybe fear of judgment) related to the financial losses.

◆ "If I started to spend the lottery money, I would have to face my friend's envy." The behavior (not spending) is a defense against a fear of envy.

So our negative financial behavior might be serving a good purpose unconsciously, protecting us against a painful truth or a painful conversation.

The psychological motive behind our irrational behavior may not seem obvious at first. This is where a psychotherapist can help you unpack some of the unconscious processes behind a seemingly common symptom. When I saw a young man, Steve, who came to me for help with what seemingly looked like a shopping addiction, it could have been quite counterproductive to make assumptions and treat it as just a problem staying within budget.

Steve was at the start of his career and was still reliant on a monthly income from his father to make ends meet. He had a supportive father that he was very close to, even more so after his parents had divorced a decade earlier. He contacted me for therapy because he found that at the start of every month, he would quickly spend his allowance on unnecessary expenses. Why was this happening? Was it about a difficulty to control impulses? There seemed to be no pattern or logic behind what the money was spent on: "Last week I bought two sets of headphones," he told me. As we went through it, it became evident that there was an urgency to almost rid himself of the money. The key question that unlocked the real meaning behind this behavior was: "What happens when you run out of money, a week after the month has started?" The answer was that he would call his mother to ask for more money. Aha. So how is the relationship with his mother? It turned out that there was a real longing to have a relationship with his mother but, having grown apart, the only reason they ever spoke was about money. There was a big resistance, unconsciously, to fix this money behavior because it would have meant potentially losing all contact with his mother. The money supplied by his mother served the unconscious purpose of reassuring Steve that his mother still cared or was still available to him and in a way was a defense against the fear that she didn't care. But of course, there could be healthier ways to reconnect with his mother and to build a relationship that served this purpose without being financially destructive.

So money can be used to manage an internal sense of feeling unsettled, dissatisfied, and we can adopt counterproductive money behaviors when money is attached to negative emotions.

The emotional imprint of money experiences

Looking more broadly at your sense of self and expectations of others can help unpack your attitude and behaviors around money. But money-specific memories and experiences matter too.

Our financial emotional experiences encompass the financial reality we grew up in, and our family's experience of it, which will leave an indelible (and not always conscious) mark on our beliefs and feelings about money. Your financial emotional experience is another piece of the puzzle worth considering as you try to unpack and understand what has shaped your present attitude to money.

Imagine, as a simple example, a little girl watching her mother consistently delegating all to do with money to the father. Dad gives Mom money. Dad pays the bill. Mom hands over the white envelopes to Dad and says, "Don't forget to pay this." Dad is on the phone talking about money with someone. Dad hands over cash to Mom. Mom asks for more because of an event she is attending. Dad looks annoyed; he asks her something. They argue. Dad raises his voice and storms off. Mom looks sad.

What patterns, meanings, messages will the little girl internalize (adopt, absorb) from these interactions? Is money something that dads/men deal with? Why is Mom having to ask for it? Is money so important that they argue about it? Interactions like the one observed by this little girl will inform the shaping patterns being recorded in her mind about money. She'd be registering information about her mother's financial abilities or inabilities, her mother's autonomy or dependence, about gender roles, about what happens when we ask for more, about how we manage anger, frustration, and conflict. The accumulation of experiences (at home at first, but outside of the home as we grow up), the piling up of evidence, information, and emotional experiences will mold our minds, our view of ourselves, our view of the world and influence our expectations.

How money is spoken about in the family matters. Ann Turkel writes, "Every child senses the parents' attitudes toward money through their ability to speak about it, their regard for its importance, their ease in dealing with it, how much there appears to be of it, and how they view those with more or less than they themselves have. From these cues, the child develops perceptions about money. A child whose curiosity about parental money is frustrated will mature with an attitude that money is a secret, hence equated with evil and guilt."[13] Watching parents' arguments about money will leave one with the impression that money is something stressful, anxiety-provoking, and difficult to talk about.

Consider these accounts:

"I will never forget the time my mother took my brother and me on a shopping trip. We all bought so many things. We were celebrating my dad having sold the company and we were allowed to pick anything we wanted. My brother and I were ecstatic! But then, when we got back to the hotel, Mom was overwhelmed with guilt. We weren't used to indulging like that. The next day she returned most of her purchases. We were allowed to keep ours. But that story stayed with me . . . despite finally having money, spending it burdened us with guilt." Don, 23, oscillates between overspending and periods of withholding.

"I remember my father taking us out for a restaurant meal, for the first time, a year after he had lost his job. I knew we were struggling to make ends meet . . . I knew it from the arguments my parents had. But he wanted to go out for my birthday. I was turning nine. What stayed with me was that feeling, when he opened his wallet to pay the bill . . . it was a deep sadness in his face, in his heavy sigh. It was painful to part with those notes. He wanted to give me something special, but opening the wallet was putting him in touch with all that was lost, all the experiences he wasn't going to be able to give us. One that I became determined to never experience in my life." Rafael, 42, is anxious about amassing wealth.

"I remember how excited I was when the tooth fairy brought me my first coins. I remember spending hours thinking about my choices: Should I keep it and wait to have more? Or should I ask for a trip to the stationery store to get the eraser I had my eyes on? I decided to keep it so I could buy the full stationery set when I had more, but it felt freeing to have the choice. My mom, who always told me what to do, with money would just say: 'It's yours, hon, so you choose.' I felt so free! I had freedom with money." Cristina, 31, occasionally overspends.

I am not suggesting that any of these experiences could have single-handedly defined one's attitude toward money. However, being conscious of the imprint they left can be an opportunity to discern the contributing factors to a present disposition toward money. As the examples above suggest, a lot is communicated nonverbally. A parent taking a deep sigh at the till. A huff when a bill arrives in the mail.

We learn so much of our behaviors/attitudes toward anything from our parents, and sometimes we do more than that, we absorb parts of them: In psychological terms we internalize them. We grow up to be, at least in part, like them and it's important to acknowledge those parts of them in us. In adolescence a process ideally takes place in which we begin to shape our separate identity, deciding (consciously or unconsciously) which qualities of our parents we want to continue to hold on to and which we want to let go of, or manage differently. Do we want to be miserly, like Mom, or enjoy life (and money) to a fuller extent? Do we want to be more sensible with money than Dad was, or do we accept that there is a reckless part in us too that we'll continue to indulge from time to time?

Everything from habits to feelings can get passed on; hopes and anxieties about money can be unknowingly absorbed by children. Their money-related insecurities may become our own even if our circumstances are substantially different! For example, parents might have been emotionally scarred by growing up in poverty, facing the difficulties and sacrifices that come with real scarcity, but as adults their children (who worked hard to secure a solid financial position) find that no amount of money can make them feel secure. It's irrational, but psychologically viable: We take in feelings that belong to them, think of it as a sort of emotional inheritance. As we reach within us for greater financial emotional insight, it is important to give thought to our behavior and attitude to money and how it would have been shaped and influenced by our parents and their own experience with money.

It is inevitable to be influenced by the money beliefs and attitudes in the family one grew up in, but that doesn't mean these beliefs are swallowed whole. Our experiences outside the family will also influence what our adult relationship with money turns out to be.

As we grow older, we begin to think of money in a wider context, and our parents have the opportunity to help us make sense of it. We might start to notice that others have more or less than we do. Why are some people begging on the street? Why do friends have bigger houses? Why did the tooth fairy bring them $3 and only $2 to us? How parents respond matters. Do they normalize differences (some people have more, others less, that's life)? Do they judge (we are better for having more)? Do they emphasize the importance of the material (we are lucky to have more)? Answers will shape our view of what money represents. Were you only praised and rewarded (with gifts, medals) when you performed well? Or were your efforts celebrated too? Linking giving to performance runs the risk that we'll grow up thinking that we are only loved for our products, for what we have, rather than for who we are.

Society begins to compound messages related to money. Western cultures (which is the view I am writing from) emphasize material wealth as a measure of success and personal achievement. "Money brings happiness" is a common illusion advocated by society, used by advertisers to convince us that possessions can do that too. Social media is now both a display of people's latest acquisitions and a stage on which we set our imaginary contests, an ever-changing benchmark against which we compare. There is always more to be had and more to be spent on, and as we acquire what we thought we wanted, the bar keeps moving.

And of course our growing perception of the social hierarchy of class informs our view of the role of money in society, where money and power are intrinsically linked. It is worth, for example, considering the emotional difficulties that come with class mobility. Such experiences would have a great impact on our behavior and attitude toward money. Moving up the social ladder might feel empowering. If you were already enjoying an internal sense of confidence, then you might find confirmation of this in your external upward move. You might feel that money grants freedom and power.

But a more fragile self-esteem might find that the upward move triggers feelings of inadequacy and money becomes a source of discomfort (if not even resentment). I have met people who began to loathe money, having been catapulted into a new social reality in which they felt they didn't belong. They become consumed by feeling fraudulent and unwanted because of their late arrival to the higher social class (and might pass on this ambivalence to their children, the first-generation inheritors). This sets a rather uncertain stage for our financial well-being, for feeling confident and in control of our financial choices, as internal conflicts and fears abound. We might hold in our hands heaps of powerful lucre but find ourselves dwarfed by those who feel entitled to their wealth. We might want to spend it and enjoy our newfound financial freedom but fear being accused of being show-offs by our long-time friends and of being parvenu by the new ones. We might be financially able to give our children what they ask for but find that it clashes with the values we hold about what is appropriate for children to have. We might feel both pride and guilt about having more than our parents ever did. The emotional impact of social mobility on your relationship with money will depend on many factors, but mainly on what internal beliefs about your worth, your sense of entitlement and your fears of exclusion or criticism it is hooking into.

Families rise from poverty to affluence, but the opposite is also true. Watching parents endure great financial losses and even bankruptcy can leave a powerful emotional imprint on the child and influence profoundly their future relationship with money. There are those who might react to such experiences carrying a great deal of anxiety with regard to financial management and/ or becoming highly risk-averse. The experience of it all vanishing from one day to the other becomes an indelible memory that haunts future choices: Spending might be fraught with guilt, investing contaminated by fear, the only solace found in hoarding money. Many children who grow up with such negative experiences (which some would call "financial trauma") might even pursue economics/business degrees, consciously/unconsciously seeking to avoid the repetition of history, or seek a partner who represents a financial stability they have been left longing for.

What matters more than the actual loss is the family's reaction to it. If all hope was lost along with the money, the children might internalize the message that money is all that gives hope. If the loss could be mourned and moved on from, the children might grow up with a less idealized view of what money will get them.

Generalizations are not helpful in psychotherapy. Psychotherapy is about understanding the nuances, the complexities of each person's approach to money. So even though we can think about some broad common beliefs among people struggling with poverty or basking in abundance, we can't assume that these are homogenous groups with similar experiences.

In fact, within the same family, siblings may have very different experiences of the same parents and very different money behaviors. We are all different and what seems enough to one person might seem little to another, even if you have grown up in the same neighborhood with the same amount of money. This is because we are shaped by so many factors at once: the interactions we had, how we interpreted people's actions and feelings, which defenses we adopted, which parent we identified with, etc.

Fears and longings

I will often come back to the idea that we are unconsciously seeking to fulfill, through money, emotional longings or address fears and insecurities rooted in past experiences.

Love is a big driver behind the pursuit of money, but not the only one. Longings to be taken seriously, to be noticed by a parent, to have an approving nod or pat on the back might be driving our pursuit for more. Painful experiences of loss, deprivation, and abandonment may leave us with a desire to hold on to things tightly, worried they'll be gone or taken away again, and money can give us an outlet for expressing the desire to hold on. We cannot understand money behaviors using purely rational or cognitive tools. Sometimes the answer is not in whatever money lessons we picked up at home or in society, but deeper within us: in our most profound desires and fears.

We are complex beings, and our behaviors are driven by an intricate set of emotional, cognitive factors shaped by our personalities and our history. The way we are with money could be linked to "phantasies" we have been holding on to for years. A "phantasy"* (spelled different from "fantasy" to differentiate it from the ordinary use of the word) refers to, in psychoanalytic literature, imagined scenarios that involve unconscious content (desires, fears, conflicts). For example, we might hold a phantasy and desire that more money will get us more love, or a phantasy and fear that people's envy can actually be destructive, or a phantasy that we are invincible. Accessing phantasies is helpful because it allows us to better understand our inner world and our motivations.

An expression of our wider personality

Our behavior with money could also be a reflection of a more pervasive aspect of our personality.

- Are you overall risk-averse in life? Do you worry and imagine negative outcomes, and are you prone to catastrophizing? No wonder, then, that you are a cautious investor and maybe tend to save excessively rather than spend and enjoy your money. Money is one area in which you manifest some pervasive character traits.
- Are you a "black or white" person, usually engaging in all-or-nothing thinking and acting, swinging from deprivation to excess? No wonder, then, you might find yourself swinging between bouts of overspending and withholding of money.

---

* Please note in psychoanalysis this term has no one, clear definition that all analysts adhere to. While Freud's initial definition of it was limited to the imaginative fulfillment of frustrated wishes, the term's meaning was then expanded to incorporate a broader organization of wishes, fears, and beliefs relating to oneself and others.

◆ Do you struggle with boundaries (maybe you fail to meet deadlines, you overshare, overeat, or drink excessively)? No wonder, then, that you might regularly exceed your credit card limits, pay hefty overdraft fees, and have a poor credit score.

In all these examples, trying to address the money behavior exclusively and specifically might be a struggle in vain. Money, in these examples, is just one manifestation of an aspect of yourself and how you approach your feelings and the world in general. We bring ourselves to every interaction and situation, so understanding yourself more broadly will help you better understand your relationship with money and everything else.

* * *

We walk into any relationship, including the therapeutic one, carrying our emotional baggage, inherited from all our previous experiences. And as a therapist I can assure you that our early experiences are those that most profoundly determine who we become and how we interact with the world. I have had clients in their fifties or sixties so quickly linking their insecurities in the present to events that happened before they were even teenagers. Here we are, 30, 40, 50 years later, and those experiences still have a grip on how they act in the world today.

A therapist aims to walk into a session with pure curiosity and no assumptions (as much as that is possible). The fact that a client has told us they have anxiety about money tells us nothing more than that. We can't know with that statement whether they grew up in wealth or not, whether their parents agreed or disagreed on money issues and it certainly tells us nothing about the quality of the worries. Is it a fear it will be taken away? Or it will run out? Or a sense that it's never enough? I caution you too, as you read the book, not to jump to conclusions and not to look for linear answers.

My more scientific or business-minded clients are often frustrated by the non-linear quality of the journey (and so was I when I first started!). What is the goal? How will we get from A to B? And you might be a reader hoping to get to the chapter titled with your money problem and find a clear answer in it. But the human mind doesn't work that way; it is far more wonderfully complex than that.

There is no way to predict how two people with similar experiences will defend against difficult feelings in the future: Similar situations can lead to different outcomes, and these may be polar opposites. For example, a person may react to an abandonment by becoming overly clingy in future relationships or by avoiding them altogether. Similarly, a person may react to having felt unimportant to his parents by becoming a splashy spender trying to attract admiration from others or might work tirelessly to accumulate wealth, hoping it will enhance their sense of importance. Experience A doesn't always lead to outcome B.

There will also be multiple explanations feeding into someone's behavior in the here and now. So behavior B could be influenced by a multiplicity of thoughts, fears, or desires. Tracing it back to a single reason would be tunnel-visioned and leave out a lot of interesting insight.

However, despite all this, there is still a lot of meaning to be found as we navigate the irrationalities and complexities of the human mind. A lot can still be uncovered and understood, a lot of links made and enlightening moments achieved, but the path will not follow the common rules of logic. Sometimes it takes months or even years of circling a topic, peeling away layers of meaning, chipping away at it bit by bit until something can settle, and a relief can be found in joining two dots together. Emotional insight can be freeing, calming, and empowering at once.

CHAPTER 2

Overspending and its many drivers

I am often asked, "How do I know if I have an overspending problem?" Well, it's all about how you interpret the "over" in "overspending" as there isn't a clear metric to define it. But let's break it down.

Does "over" mean beyond your means? What if we spend within our means but are tortured by guilt and regret? What if our means now allow us to spend more than we could ever dream of growing up and our definition of what is "excessive" needs to adapt? As you can see, defining overspending is not just subjective but even for us, as an individual, the bar might shift because of external circumstances (financial realities) or internal ones (emotional factors that color what we perceive as excessive or not enough).

I recently had a one-off session with a woman named Helen, who started the session by saying, "I have 103 dresses."[1] Without making assumptions, I asked her how she felt about that. She continued, "It's not that I've gotten into any debt or spent money

I don't have on shopping . . . more that I don't feel in control of it. I do a lot of impulse buying and feel guilty about my overflowing wardrobe." Some people might feel that owning 103 dresses is excessive, but what raises a flag in terms of financial well-being is the fact that she didn't feel in control of her spending, alongside the guilt about the overflowing wardrobe.

Is guilt enough to define overspending? Not at all. In fact, there are people who feel guilty even just allowing themselves bare necessities. But guilt along with the uncontrollable urge to spend means that at least in part, we feel we are making money choices from an emotional, rather than a rational place. Helen wishes she could behave differently and is not at peace with her behavior.

So, how do you know if you are overspending? In my experience, if you are wondering about it, the answer is probably yes. Many overspenders at the very least suspect that something in their spending patterns needs attending to. Their thinking and time is taken up by shopping. Feelings of shame and guilt may be close to the surface. Behaviors like lying, hiding shopping bags or bank statements are common ways to dodge judgment from others, when in fact they are already judging themselves.

We don't all need to share the same definition of what's too much to spend (what is an excessive expense to one may be a completely rational and reasonable choice to another), so one person telling us we spend excessively on dining out doesn't make us an overspender. But when we are overspending, friends, family, parents, or partners may express concern and even complain about the impact of our actions on them. Sometimes the habit takes so much time and mental preoccupation that it takes away from relationships, work, and other areas of life. So be it debt, friends, our own lies, guilt, or feeling out of control, it will start adding up until, well, the penny drops.

The spending behavior

Spending is a pernicious habit. It's a part of living an ordinary life and it becomes hard to pinpoint the moment in which we have crossed the abstract line into overspending. Retail therapy has often been used to describe a mostly benign use of money to self-soothe. A bit like with alcohol dependence, metrics can be helpful (so recurrently falling into debt is a sign you are spending too much), but what matters most is how in control you feel about your behavior and what impact it is having on your life and your relationships. We might all, on occasion, buy something we don't really need to treat ourselves. However, when this is a regular habit, leading to an accumulation of stuff we don't need, combined with a difficulty resisting the urges to buy, we have crossed the line into a compulsion or even an addiction.

Lifestyle inflation can be a common form of overspending. Lifestyle inflation describes a situation in which as your income increases, your spending increases too. This may compromise your ability to save, repay debt, or work toward other financial goals. People who move up the financial ladder face a choice. They either increase their spending and use the new financial freedom to indulge in what they always desired and couldn't afford, or continue with the present lifestyle and use the extra income to fulfill any other financial objectives (like save to buy a house, repay loans). People make all sorts of different choices when it comes to this: Some manage to limit the indulgence to a few extra evenings out, or an extra star in their hotel booking for vacations, but lifestyle inflation can for some reach a point in which they end up in a worse financial situation than they started in. They don't just stop saving but compromise their existing savings. These individual judgments are based on personal goals and preferences and on what we grew up valuing, dreaming of, or fearing.

We can regard lifestyle inflation as a form of overspending when either the inflation (the extra money we spend to upgrade our lifestyle as our earnings grow) is deteriorating our financial circumstances or when (even if not financially threatening) it isn't a *conscious* choice that we are at peace with but rather the result of one of many emotional drivers, like a felt pressure to conform, insecurities that have roots in the past, or desires that we haven't fully understood.

An extreme form of lifestyle inflation often happens when people suddenly become rich, like a lottery win or professional athletes who quickly rise to fame and lose their newly acquired fortunes in short amounts of time. Excessive spending is one of the key drivers of ensuing bankruptcy. First of all, they are making spending choices considering their peak earnings, with little consideration of the fact that those are not sustainable and that, in fact, in their choice of career, the years of high earning potential are quite limited. Then, there are emotional reasons, like the allure of joining the club of the envied superstar players and acquiring, like them, shiny possessions (cars, mansions); there is the excitement of being able to afford what one could hardly dream of as a child growing up (often) in poverty. And there is the emotional pressure (external or self-imposed) of sharing their fortunes with family and friends (or even the extended community that supported them). In many cases, it isn't just the overspending that leads to their financial failure but also a combination of poor financial education, poor investment advice, often alongside gambling addictions. A wealth manager to some of the top football players (who wished to remain anonymous) tells me: "There is undoubtedly a sense of financial omnipotence with no long-term thinking, no track-keeping of spending. But the whole world they are absorbed in is encouraging them to spend: peer pressure, family, friends. I end up often having to help them think through outrageous expenses and sometimes they spend it not because they want it, definitely not because they need it, but simply because they can."

According to a *Sports Illustrated* report from 2009, an estimated 78 percent of National Football League (NFL) players are bankrupt or under great financial stress only two years after retiring.[2] Similarly, a study found that lottery winners are more likely to declare bankruptcy within three to five years than the average American.[3] Some attribute this to "mental accounting," which is a distortion in our thinking in which we treat money differently depending on its origins or intended use.[4] In the case of lottery winners, this often means that money won is more easily spent than money earned, which explains the speed and often carelessness with which lottery money is squandered. But it is a combination of factors, akin to those mentioned above: the combination of unthinkable wealth alongside pressures from others to invest, donate, share the money, along with poor advice and lack of adequate financial education that create the perfect storm.

Overspending is therefore hard to define, but a "compulsive buying disorder" (also known as "oniomania") or even a "shopping addiction" (or "spending addiction") are more universally understood. In both, there is a compulsive need to spend, and the focus is on the *act* of buying rather than the *object* of the purchase, which seems almost insignificant. Purchasing becomes the default response to any negative feeling or event. Thoughts about buying (cravings) are frequent and feel intrusive and irresistible.[5] The buying often exceeds needs, financial resources, and even the time intended to be spent on it, interfering with the ability to uphold other commitments (like work or studying). A compulsion tips over into an addiction when one needs to increase the frequency or amount spent to get the equivalent prior "fix," as happens with other addictions (like substance addictions).

Shopping addiction is therefore what psychologists call a behavioral addiction because it is an *action* that becomes addictive (rather than a substance). It is estimated that roughly one in ten people may suffer from a shopping addiction (but estimates vary greatly). It has been shown to go hand in hand with substance abuse disorders, eating disorders, and other impulse control disorders.[6] As Pamela Roberts, addiction program manager at one of the Priory Hospitals in London, says, "People with oniomania feel completely ruled by the compulsion to 'shop and spend'—either for themselves, or by excessive gifting to others. The time, let alone the emotional stress, involved in online searching, social media scrolling, visiting shops, juggling credit card bills, hiding purchases from family, and returning goods can cause severe disruption."[7] The Priory Group estimates that 8–16 percent of the population suffers from shopping addiction.

Despite the number of people struggling with shopping addictions, it still hasn't been included in the *DSM* (the *Diagnostic and Statistical Manual of Mental Disorders* which is a publication used by the American Psychiatric Association) for the classification of mental disorders) or similar manuals used by professionals, where behavioral addictions like gaming and gambling might feature. While the debate on whether it should or shouldn't be included is extensive and beyond the scope of this book, it is worth highlighting that shopping addiction can feel as intractable as a gambling addiction and have a similarly negative impact on someone's financial and emotional lives and should therefore not be dismissed as just a bad habit.

What makes us spend

There is no doubt that the society we live in is one that promotes spending. The advertising industry uses decades of research to tailor messages to consumers in a way that drives further purchases. They know that promising happiness, a better life, or increased desirability will increase the appeal of a product. They use cognitive biases (common distortions in rational thinking) to carefully position their messages, products, or pricing. For example, they know that as humans we tend to value something if we believe it's in scarce supply, so messages like "last chance," "limited edition," and auctions take advantage of our predisposition to be lured by scarcity while simultaneously appealing to our fear of missing out (FOMO). They know that we will register the number five when reading $599, thus distorting our rational view of the price (the "left digit bias"). Or that we are more likely to buy an item if we can see it has been discounted from a higher price (because our perception of its current price is distorted through the comparison with the higher number—the "contrast effect").

There are also physiological reasons why shopping is pleasurable. Studies[8] have shown that the process of looking around and particularly *finding* something we like can stimulate the pleasure center in the brain as does finding a bargain: In both cases we anticipate a reward or a gain and this releases dopamine in the brain. The chemical response to this experience and the feeling it evokes is usually referred to as the "shopper's high." But dopamine release is also linked to addictive behavior because it conditions our body to seek more of that experience in the future.

Retailers know what to do to make us feel like we got a deal. For some people, the same mechanisms that are activated in response to real-life threats are activated in response to the competitive environment generated by sales. This all adds up to a complex picture. The retail industry lures us into purchases, our physiological responses drive us to seek out the experience over and over again, and social media fuels competition and offers opportunities to show it all off. Meanwhile, a mixture of guilt, regret, financial strain, and even environmental and social concerns act as a deterrent to indulge in the temptation, and fuel movements such as slow fashion and decluttering.

The advent of the internet, smartphone, and shopping apps has facilitated the boom in online shopping. Now, we don't need to leave our homes to make purchases and we can spend money 24 hours a day. Even when we leave the house, the pervasiveness of contactless machines and e-wallets has moved transactions further away from an awareness that cash is leaving our pockets. Where there was cash, there then was a card, and now our mobile phone is racking up expenses in one gentle motion. Whereas the pain of paying might have been a deterrent in the past, it is becoming ever more removed from consciousness. Research shows that paying via credit card leads to greater spending because the *decision* to spend and the *actual payment* are separated in time (a phenomenon called payment coupling).[9] The new field of neuroeconomics is finding physiological evidence that suggests that when we are deciding whether or not to make a purchase, the parts of the brain that are activated are those that evaluate the anticipated pleasure from the purchase against the pain of spending money—and the fact that the payment is now increasingly painless could explain, scientists say, why we are more likely to make purchases when buying items with credit cards instead of cash.

A survey of 1,045 consumers found that a fifth of respondents spend out of a fear of missing out. Social media influences what we spend on and allows us the opportunity to share the experiences we've indulged in with our desired audience. We don't just show off possessions—we may overspend on nights out, treatments, experiences, and holidays. Social media enlarges the opportunities for comparisons, envy, and idealization and facilitates spending that in part is driven by a hope to match or keep up with others. Close to a third of respondents don't feel comfortable saying no when a friend suggests an activity they can't afford. Around 40 percent of Millennials (born between

1981 and 1996) overspend to keep up with friends and quoted social anxieties like the fear of being left out in the future, feeling like an outsider, losing friendships, and being judged as key reasons for their overspending.[10]

There are phases of life in which this desire is more accentuated, like adolescence (which stretches into the twenties). In this stage of development, we mold our sense of identity through groups: Adherence and belonging become important and so there are deep emotional pressures to conform and to fit in. We will screen peers and admire others for clues of how to look and behave. We use the group to establish a sense of belonging as we internally negotiate a slow separation from our parents in preparation for adulthood. Some people remain stuck in adolescence, exhibiting traits of this phase of life beyond their teens and twenties. Struggling to resolve the question of identity, they continue to seek a sense of who they are through spending on clothes, for example, changing their look, as if trying on identities. The spending is driven by a need to define themselves, which finds an external expression, when the struggle is actually an internal one.

Thinking about the generations that are growing up now, with the availability of social media, the pressures of adolescence are amplified. As they try to grapple with their changing bodies and establish a sense of self, social media has generated a platform that facilitates the availability of idealized people: The opportunities for comparison and competition are only one click away. And what they are exposed to are carefully selected, Photoshopped, and often unrealistic versions of others, creating unachievable expectations of themselves. Pre–social media, there was the popular girl in school who might have been the subject of our idealizations and envy, but now on social media she doesn't have a bad hair day and is always perfect. She might have more "likes" and be perceived as more likeable, desirable than us. She is only a click away, available to be admired and envied at any time.

As a psychotherapist, although the social context I described is an important backdrop, what I focus on is the individual's unique emotional context for the spending. The reasons are varied, complex, and, in my experience, often rooted in the past. But not always.

I have come across cases in which the answer is quite straightforward. If you grew up in abundance with a sense that money was unlimited and your parents didn't guide you in thinking about choices and trade-offs, you might turn into an adult who spends carelessly. You are then shocked when you realize that money is, in fact, a limited resource. A simple but painful process of realization and readaptation needs to take place to face the realities of money as a limited resource. Disappointment and frustration are inevitable, and some of these (usually young) adults might enlist a third party (be it a coach, therapist, or partner) to act as a temporary parent (or "externalized superego" in psychological terms) to keep them accountable, and help them get through the readjustment. This kind of overspending resolves more easily than the one driven by emotional undercurrents. Those are the difficult ones to untangle and change because that's when we are not just, "oops," accidentally overspending, but we are using money to deal with our feelings, be it to fulfill an unconscious desire or placate a fear.

A desire to fit in

Having explored different forms of overspending, we can now think of the underlying emotional drivers of our desire to buy in an out of control way. Often, when people acknowledge that they overspend, the next question they ask is, "How do I stop?" but to curb the behavior, the more useful question to ask is, "Why do I overspend?" When people come and see me, they have usually tried a few things: getting rid of credit cards, budgeting carefully, enlisting a friend or family member to report back to on their spending. The problem is that tools and strategies can only go so far if we don't tackle the very reason why we do it in the first place. In my experience, there is an intricate web of psychological and emotional reasons that can help understand the overspending and, with time and effort, change it.

Overspending is sometimes rooted in a desire to fit in. In the case of Helen, with her many dresses, the overspending was linked to early memories of not fitting in, both in school and in her neighborhood (where hers was the only foreign family). Past experiences of feeling left out (experiences of exclusion in school, bullying, or even a sense of isolation within your own family) may fuel our anxiety about dressing the part and feeling included in the present. Those old fears of not belonging, the isolation we felt, the awkwardness, inadequacy, and even humiliation we might have experienced, may be sitting in our unconscious when we spend on yet another pair of shoes. Even though the adult part of us knows that work colleagues aren't as brutal, or even simply as critical as the kids in the playground, that adult part isn't quite available to us as we make those choices. Let me explain. In the driving seat is the child, who now has a credit card in hand and can shield themselves from the potential of feeling like an outsider by securing that one new thing. The longing for a sense of belonging alongside the fear of ever feeling again like "I did back then" are powerful drivers of the spending choices we might make today.

There are all sorts of experiences that may leave one feeling like this. Children who didn't feel they belonged in their school or community, either because of a disparity in socio-economic status, physical appearance (racial background, weight, hair color), or even simply an internal sense of difference that can't be attributed to something external ("I always felt like a weirdo"). Even family experiences of exclusion can leave that longing in us. If we grew up in a family in which we felt other siblings were loved and understood more than us, we might spend our adult lives looking for a "family" to which we feel a sense of belonging, and in some cases the desire to be part, feel part of a group (which could be the adult's "work family," or a friendship group) is expressed through money. We invest effort and energy and money to give ourselves the best chances of inclusion, of not feeling like the black sheep ever again. We might often pick up the tab to make sure we are liked. We might contribute to every group collection (even ones we don't agree with), for the sake of being included.

So, the first step toward change is not a budgeting plan but rather an acknowledgment that those 103 dresses are an emotional relic of a time when fitting in and going unnoticed was a defense against the frightening prospect of feeling alone and isolated. But as an adult, Helen can ask herself the questions, "Do I still need that protective armor?" and "Will my present-day friends and colleagues be as punitive as those primary school kids back then?"

This is not to say that every child is permanently affected by such experiences. Sometimes, despite their differences, children fit right in. Sometimes victims of bullying can develop resilience and triumph over these experiences. But other times they are left with an emotional imprint (fears, insecurities) and acknowledging the child left longing to be like everyone else can be liberating and offer opportunity for change.

It is possible for these longings to get passed on from parents to children, instead of being a relic of our own direct experiences of exclusion. If your parents longed to keep up with the Joneses, you might harbor the desire to catch up or keep up. You might have picked it up in bits and pieces: comparisons of how much others have, their envy of others' things, an air of competitiveness or even overemphasis of what we have that others don't. It isn't one comment, but thousands of interactions, responses, remarks, that might have left in the child a real sense of the parents' discomfort and feeling of not belonging. We pick up our parents' emotions and we sometimes swallow them whole. Their longing to fit in, their shame, may become ours.

Vivian, a 42-year-old woman, sought therapy, conflicted about her spending. She described quite literally two parts of her that wrestled. One part felt a great deal of power and satisfaction when she spent on experiences that she could then talk about in her social circles. She liked being able to tell her friends about the recent ski trip, or prestigious tennis camp that the kids were enrolled into, and proudly held her designer bag. Although she was spending within her means, it was clear that she was confused about what was and wasn't reasonable to spend money on. She felt she lacked a compass to help her navigate decisions about spending, yet in some areas of her life she was in fact quite frugal. What helped Vivian find the compass was the realization that many of the things she chose to spend on had the very purpose of allowing her a sense of fitting in with the social circle she was in now.

Vivian had grown up in a lower-middle-class family, but her family had longed to move up socially. The parents stretched their budget to give their children a good private education and the opportunities they never had growing up. This, however, at some level, had always had an impact on Vivian. As she went through school she picked up on differences. Her family took regional vacations when other families went abroad. She remembers declining or finding excuses not to join ski trips in her university years (embarrassed to admit that she didn't know how to ski). She changed the subject or escaped in her mind when friends would start comparing beaches in Thailand to those on the Mediterranean coast. In different ways, Vivian had been experiencing the discomfort of not fitting in throughout her life.

Like her parents, she ensured her kids attended private schools and gave them opportunities she herself didn't have growing up. But unlike her parents, Vivian indulged in luxuries. She bought designer clothes and went on expensive vacations abroad. There is no doubt that a part of her was simply indulging in the comforts she could now afford. In her words, "I feel rich when I spend, and that feels good." Through those expenses, she could finally feel like she could keep up with the Joneses. But there was that other part of her who felt confused and unsure about her choices. And this confusion was a reflection of the fact that her choices were at times rational and at times driven by her longing to fit in and not to feel the envy and discomfort that she had experienced growing up. She had to unpack and understand those motives. In therapy, she worked toward accepting the parts of her that were like her parents (her aspiration to move up the social ladder and join the Joneses) and analyze her desire or even desperation to fit in and evoke the response, validation, and at times even envy of those around her. It was only until she could face these aspects of herself that she could find a compass to use for deciding what felt like a good enough reason to spend and what didn't.

Things are more reliable than people

Spending may, for some people, be rooted in a fear of abandonment or being let down by people. Ultimately, the issue is an ambivalence about relationships. Buying objects becomes, temporarily at least, a triumph of self-reliance, a seemingly perfect defense against an unconscious fear of being let down, or maybe even abandoned by people. The action of buying offers a short-lived experience of self-soothing: "Here is me, giving something good to myself, something that will last." However, as time passes, feelings of emptiness or loneliness reemerge. The object cannot replace the desire for a relationship and although it does provide constancy, it doesn't provide fulfillment of the emotional desire that sits behind it. Along with the longing, we are also left with remorse for having potentially spent beyond our means, or on something unnecessary and ultimately unsatisfying.

It has been revealing to find the breadth of human experiences that may be interpreted as a betrayal and abandonment. It is unsurprising that a parent leaving the family and cutting off ties would be experienced as such, but a parental divorce, or even a death might have been seen as an abandonment. We need to imagine how the child saw it, and how they might have experienced and interpreted the events. A client once told me, "I know it wasn't my dad's fault he had cancer. But it still felt like he abandoned us, like we weren't worth living for." The painful feelings of betrayal, desertion, or even rejection may have fossilized back then and left one hurt and longing for years to come.

Sylvia Plath, who is still remembered as one of the greatest poets of all time, lost her father when she was eight years old, a loss she never quite recovered from. The world changed in her eyes and the magic of childhood disappeared. In her own words, from an interview, she said, "I stopped believing in elves and Santa and all these benevolent powers and became more realistic and depressed."[11] Gone was her faith in religion and her desire to live. In her young mind, her father didn't just die, he abandoned her. She coped in part with her feelings of abandonment through fantasies that she could join him again in death. She sank into a deep depression with which she struggled throughout her life, attempting suicide every decade, until succeeding at age 30. In *The Bell Jar*, she writes, "If you expect nothing from somebody you are never disappointed."[12] And in her incredibly powerful poem "Last Words," she tells us of her desire to be buried alongside things—her desire was for objects to be placed in her tomb (or sarcophagus, to be precise).

I do not trust the spirit. It escapes like steam
In dreams, through mouth-hole or eye-hole. I can't stop it.
One day it won't come back. Things aren't like that.
They stay.[13]

She emphasizes that "[things] stay" and her words so powerfully capture the effect with which some people treasure the possessions they can allow themselves to have because they are no longer just "things," they are "things that stay"—they are emotional objects representing a permanence, a reliability that is being sought emotionally.

These incredibly painful experiences are powerful triggers for the construction of defenses that will prevent us from ever feeling that pain again. A determination to become self-reliant in this defensive way risks shutting us out of relationships altogether and seeking a replacement in things.

The psychoanalyst David Krueger describes working with a client who overspent and who described it as feeling "frantic and frenzied. An urge to get something *more*. I'd get very anxious— just like bingeing—the same feelings. Then I'd go buy some clothes. I felt like I couldn't leave without something. Even if I didn't find what I wanted, I had to leave with something."[14] Krueger interprets it as this person creating an illusion that she could have anything and everything she always wanted. She could give to herself in a way that people hadn't given her emotionally. In this kind of defense, money becomes a medium through which one can buy comfort, a reassurance that if others can't give, at least I can give to myself. Spending then acts as a soothing tool, but it also buys a temporary illusion that something significant will stay and can be held on to.

Watch ME!

A gut-wrenching headline in the Greek news, in June 2022, reported a group of young men ordering 200 bottles of champagne in a beach bar in Greece, only to spray them at each other.[15] "Vaskning," a Swedish term meaning "sinking," is used to describe the ostentatious act of pouring champagne into the sink. When

Swedish bars banned the spraying of champagne, those stuck with the urge to emphasize their excess began buying bottles only to ask the bartender to pour it in the sink. The scale and absurdity of the act is shocking, but money spent for attention-seeking isn't uncommon. The prodigal, the flaunting spender—we might all have seen one in our milieu. You might have called them a show-off, they might have made you cringe or roll your eyes or evoked your envy at some level. These are the people who spend mainly to attract attention and envy. In my experience, they are variably conscious of this desire: Some are oblivious to it, while others might admit that, "Yes, I like attracting positive attention."

And even though just a few years ago the audience was limited to those in our physical proximity, watching us parade our new vehicle or sport our new jacket, we now can broadcast our new possessions to a vast audience on social media and sit back brewing phantasies of the adulation we have rallied. The "likes" begin to pour in, reassuring us that we obtained the response we wanted. Each one validating and reassuring us that we are worthy of love and likes.

To some extent, the desire for positive attention is common to many of us, but when does this become an urge so strong that it starts getting in the way of other things, or even backfires? Going back to the difficulty in defining overspending, I think we need to ask not only "When does this overspending get in the way of other financial goals?" or "Are you feeling guilt and regret about how much money you spent on your new car or watch?" but also "What impact is it having on our relationships?" Using money in this way may not just be detrimental to your feelings and finances but may also get in the way of relationships. Put simply, bragging or showing off could result in admiration, but it usually evokes negative emotions in the witness (turning people off rather than on).

What recent research has found is that people engaging in bragging are oblivious to the impact it has on the other. Firstly, one study found that witnesses were fast to recall instances in which people bragged about making money, having money or material possessions (rather than maybe remembering an instance in which the other was showing off about achievements or accomplishments). Secondly, those who self-promote or show off greatly underestimate the extent of negative emotions evoked in the recipients and overestimate any positive emotion the recipient might have felt.[16]

I suppose it's not news that seeking attention so brazenly is often an overcompensation for a sense of internal lack. Freud used the term "narcissism" to describe a form of psychological functioning in which the person is, apparently, inflated with self-love and admiration to mask an unconscious sense of vulnerability and fragility. It is the lack of an internal, stable self-image that creates a need for external points of reference. As psychoanalyst Laurence Spurling explains, "The hard outer shell gives a form of stability and consistency to his experience, but this rigid structure is really hollow and, if threatened, the narcissistic person will feel at risk of catastrophic collapse."[17] We unconsciously build a persona that we can hold on to and present to the world, and which keeps at bay (and even buried) the self-doubt that lies beneath; it keeps away our feelings of shame.

Money can be a psychologically useful medium for the grandiose narcissist (the narcissist that presents with an inflated, pompous, show-off image) in that it offers an easy way to preserve the desired shiny outer image and block access to the aspects of the self that are at some level felt as lacking. Money can be used to evoke envy, to elicit awe, to help them feel powerful (and even potent), adding to the picture of grandiosity they are trying to paint, filling the hollowness they feel internally.

It is a powerful defense, but it ends up alienating others. With so much shiny armor, the person within is hard to reach, which is the whole point, but a lonely existence indeed. Although empathy is the last emotion that some grandiose narcissist may evoke in the other, I found in my work that once I am allowed in, there is a very hurt child hiding in the background, afraid of being seen. I feel great compassion as we begin to understand that part of them that may feel unlovable, unwanted, unworthy. It is this part that they are protecting.

I had a client who in many ways displayed a grandiose outer shell. He told me, "I think you should increase your fee." In part, this bizarre request reflected the fact that I was being idealized at that point in the therapy. Maybe it was also about showing off that he could afford a lot more than I was charging, to counter the potentially humbling experience of being in therapy. But it was also part of his defense: the inflated part of him that sought prestige, that dressed up his image with expensive things. Having an expensive therapist upheld this image of only having the best of anything.

There is no clear answer to what causes a narcissistic personality to develop, but there are various parental styles that may be linked to the development of it. Narcissistic parents are more likely to breed narcissistic children for complex reasons. In part, it's the fact that we take in bits of our parents, so if our parents were narcissists, we will inevitably develop a narcissistic part of us by mimicking and internalizing their approach to life and others. But it's more than just that. It is also the impact of being parented by narcissistic parents, who generally swing between idealizing and denigrating or criticizing the child, leaving them with an unstable internal sense of themselves.

Furthermore, children of narcissists are seen by the parents as an extension of their own image. The parent may place great expectations and pressures on the child to fit the desired ideal image. There is no space for the child to find out who they are: They are there to serve the emotional needs of the parents, with little room left for their own emotional needs to be expressed, acknowledged or met. The child tries and inevitably fails to be all they are asked to be (attending to the needy parents, fulfillling their ideals, realizing their dreams). And the only way for the child to get love, attention, and recognition is to attend to parental needs, so they conclude that their own ideas, wishes or negative feelings are uninteresting or unacceptable.

Children grow up without enough positive responses, thus expecting their needs to be left unmet. This can happen too with overly critical, abusive, or neglecting parents. It can result in a similar emotional wound and inner narrative that goes something like: "My needs don't matter, I don't matter." The child learns to bury those unacceptable parts of themselves and starts defending against them.

Following this very mechanism, having parents who were overly praising or pampering may have the same impact. The child feels there is no room for their "bad parts" or for feelings that deviate from the idealized image the parents are painting and these parts of them get hidden away and experienced as unacceptable.

The hope for the magical transformation of self

Overspending may also be masking a wish to achieve a desired transformation of oneself. However, even though the spending might be focused on an external transformation, the desired transformation is in fact internal. Spending is a way in which we may be acting out an unconscious phantasy that we will like ourselves or that others will like us more if we dress more fashionably or get one more aesthetic surgery—the magic promise of a changing room.

A journalist writing of her own struggle with shopping addiction confessed, "My endless spending was an attempt to 'fix' the things I didn't like about myself [. . .]. Yet it didn't feel relaxing. I was in a constant state of agitation, waiting for my next outfit to come. Then the clothes arrived and let me down. I was always hoping to find the dress that fixed everything. I'd keep spending money until I liked my reflection in the mirror. But that moment never came."[18] It so poignantly lays out the emotional process. The desire and hope at the moment of purchase that a magical transformation would result from these purchases. The anticipation and anxiety as she waited for the items, followed by the disappointment when they failed to accomplish their impossible task of fixing everything.

The phantasies that suffuse all sorts of magical qualities to the desired items (or surgeries or makeovers) in the hope for an internal transformation are often rooted in experiences that have shaped a sense of self that isn't good enough. A parent that seemed uninterested or was mainly absent, or struggled with depression and was unavailable to respond positively to their child, could all have left the child with a sense of not being lovable or enough. Seeking validation externally is then a defense mechanism to reassure the person that they are indeed worthy.

In some cases, the desire for an internal transformation, expressed via spending lavishly, isn't so much rooted in past experiences but rather a struggle with emotions in the present. I have seen this occur often during midlife (the so-called midlife crisis) when people sometimes decide to buy the fancy sports car, the trophy mansion. In the *This Jungian Life* podcast episode on midlife crisis, the three analysts explain that psychoanalyst Carl Jung was one of the first to focus on the second half of life, which starts at the tipping point (midlife), being a time full of possibility for personal growth.[19] At this time, for many people, a search for meaning in life emerges and becomes a prevalent preoccupation. Having reached career objectives, having had children, a mortgage, questions like "Is this it?" begin to trouble us. Even failure to achieve those objectives might leave us wondering what we really value, what we are really looking for from life. Our mind fills up with questions, anxieties, longings from parts of ourselves that we never gave enough expression to and if we don't allow ourselves to consider these thoughts and feelings in a real and thoughtful way, we might end up acting them out, changing the external (buying a Lamborghini, quitting your job, as they mention as examples in the podcast) when what we are really longing for are internal changes. Rather than attending to the inner call we act on these troubling and discomforting feelings instead.

Money to self-soothe

So far we have looked at some specific emotional drivers behind our spending. Sometimes, however, money fulfills a simple purpose: It allows us to act (to spend) as a way to distract us from any negative feelings we are trying to avoid.

Managing negative feelings is a learned skill. It's one that we pick up from our caregivers mostly unconsciously. Can a parent cope with a distressed infant or toddler, decipher and put into words what the baby is feeling, instead of breaking down into a panic, failing to attune to the baby's needs? These experiences shape how capable we then are to put our feelings into words, expressing them and containing them (rather than acting them out).

Having had parents who struggled to contain their feelings, to manage them, to express them in a healthy way has an impact on children's ability to manage their own. We observe and absorb what a parent does when they are angry, sad, etc.—do they express it? Do they talk about it? Do we get a sense that they can sit with that feeling and manage it? Or do they act out, hit, shout, walk out, reach for a substance, reach for food? We might end up copying their coping strategy: acting instead of sitting with feelings that are uncomfortable. We might not take the same action (we might overspend, whereas our parents smoked/drank/overate), but the psychological mechanism is the same: acting instead of naming and trying to address or talk about difficult feelings.

Unsurprisingly, it has also been proven that compulsive buying disorder runs in families (and that in these families mood, anxiety, and substance use disorders are excessive).[20] The parents' inability to access a sense of resilience, of managing their feelings, becomes the child's inability to do so.

But alongside the repetition of our parents' coping strategies, there is also the reality that a parent suffering with depression or an addiction is less emotionally available to the child, which makes children more likely to suppress emotions rather than having the experience of expressing them and learning to manage them.

When negative feelings begin to overwhelm us, we try to find ways to divert our attention from them. It's sometimes a useful coping mechanism if used occasionally and it doesn't turn into systematically denying or suppressing our feelings. It's a matter of how often we use this as a coping strategy and what do we actually *do* to distract ourselves. As there is a difference between having the occasional comfort food and regular binges, or weekend drinks with friends to an alcohol addiction, there is a difference between buying something as a treat and a shopping addiction.

For many overspenders, the answer to the question "What would happen if you didn't shop when you felt the urge?" is "I'd be left with my thoughts/feelings." And what those are can vary—it can be boredom, sadness, anger. Rather than feeling their feelings, they spend, which makes them feel good initially because it takes their mind away from the disturbing thought or emotion and gets them engaged in a process: They are now scrolling down a website, searching for something to buy. In Claer Barrett's podcast, *Money Clinic*, a self-confessed shopping addict, Brooke, says, "When I am in a store, none of the stressors of the outside world matter. You know, I'm there and I don't have to think about the stress of work. I don't have to think about, you know, the fact that I don't have a whole lot of friends. So sometimes just being able to walk around the store, it's like I can take a deep breath."[21]

Studies have shown that compulsive buyers are experiencing negative feelings (sad/depressed, anxious and bored) right before going shopping.[22] Immediately after the purchase, respondents feel "high," "powerful," "excited," "elated," "more important," and "like someone else."[23] It gives them control at a moment when something brewing under the surface feels unmanageable. We have seen that there are both psychological and physiological reasons for the temporary lift in mood that follows a purchase, but the high is short-lived. Guilt and distress are typical of a shopping spree hangover (and let's not forget that the original negative feelings we were trying to avoid in the first place haven't been dealt with either).

With compulsive buyers, the focus is on the actual need to purchase something, more so than the object itself (which often remains unopened and unused). What seems irresistible is the *action* of purchasing something rather than the object itself. Buying often exceeds both needs and financial resources (often resulting in debt) and even the time intended to be spent on it is excessive, interfering with the ability to uphold other commitments (like work, for example).

An effort to identify and name some of the feelings behind this behavior can be the first step toward achieving greater control over it. Then the question becomes, what to do with them. You can address them, express them, explore them, and sit with them. If it's sadness you are avoiding, what is the sadness about? Can you sit with your sadness without having to act it out? Can you find a healthier way to defend against them? What else can distract you from your loneliness? What can you do instead of online shop when you feel lonely?

Research[24] has demonstrated that it goes hand in hand with other mental health issues (like depression and anxiety). I have heard a young woman say, "What else would I do if I didn't shop? What would I have to look forward to? Nothing."[25]

Frequently, people who suffer from buying addiction also suffer from eating disorders, alcohol addiction, nicotine dependence—other addictive compulsive behaviors. In fact, research found that compulsive buyers are more likely to abuse substances and have a mood or anxiety disorder.[26] In my view, this is testament to the fact that the shopping here is an action, one along with many others that are taken in an attempt to manage depressed and anxious feelings.

In one episode from the TV series *Only Human*, a therapist helps a woman understand what might be behind her excessive spending, which took on many forms, including hosting, partying, and nights out with friends. As she explored the reasons behind her habits with a coach, what surfaced was that she had for years kept hidden painful and strong feelings related to her father moving out of the family home when she was three. Back then she suppressed the negative feelings related to her dad leaving and just focused on the playground moments and fun activities she had with her dad on the weekend. In the present, a lot of the spending seemed to re-create fun times in a careless way, concealing or ignoring the self-destructive side of this (as her debt exceeded her annual salary). She focused on the fun, ignoring the pain and hurt that she both carried from the past and was creating in the present by getting herself in such a precarious financial situation. This was also a feature of her hidden eating disorder: What the world would see was the fun and indulging side of her, but there were difficult feelings she was trying to evacuate through her bulimia. Getting in touch with the "hurt little girl" inside of her helped her unlock a deeper understanding of her overspending. In her own words, before getting in touch with the feelings behind her spending she felt "scared, alone, and frightened."

* * *

While the unconscious drivers of overspending can be as complex as the human mind, I found that the most common phantasies held by overspenders are that the objects money can buy will either make them more desirable, give them a sense of belonging, or provide comfort that they have something good that stays.

For others, who more generally struggle with acknowledging, naming, and sitting with their negative feelings, money becomes just a medium for acting, a tool for their impulsivity: shopping instead of sitting with difficult thoughts, shopping instead of sitting with uncomfortable feelings.

If you find that you are spending more than you would like and are unsure about why you keep accumulating objects, gadgets, and accessories, it's worth wondering, what are you really hoping these things will get you? If you could draw the cloud-shaped vignette that verbalized the semi-conscious phantasy of what the object will get you, what would it say? Trying to explore what could be behind your overspending is not always straightforward (and I will give you suggestions about how to do this in chapter 12, but starting to be more emotionally aware in the various stages of the purchasing process is a good starting point. How does the process that ends in a purchase start? Are you with friends scrolling on your phones? Are you alone when you decide to go to the store? What are you feeling in those moments? Patterns help you unpack what emotions set it off. For one client it was "any time I have to go to an event," pointing us toward her insecurities about how others will see her and her discomfort in social settings. For another it was at bedtime, which pointed us to her feeling of loneliness.

Ask yourself the following.
- What are the feelings and thoughts that come to your mind when you find an item you desire?
- What happens when you purchase it?
- What about when it arrives?
- Do you keep/return it?
- How would you feel if you didn't spend, or when you have maybe tried in the past to restrict your spending?
- What emotions are evoked then?

If the overspending is a behavior you are using as a defense against difficult feelings, remember: Defenses are there for a reason. Defenses protect us from pain. But it's worth reevaluating their usefulness when they fail to give us what we want or have such detrimental consequences that we end up in a worse situation than the one we were trying to avoid in the first place. The financial stress and guilt associated with 103 dresses hanging in our wardrobe might weigh on us so much that facing our fear of being left out might be a scary, yet worthwhile exercise to undertake instead. Or our narcissistic showing off might have isolated us to such an extent that it backfired on our search for followers. We need to wonder whether there might be better places (less damaging, more fulfillling) than stores or spas to find what we feel is missing.

As author and psychotherapist Stephen Grosz once wrote, "At one time or another, we all try to silence painful emotions. But when we succeed in feeling nothing we lose the only means we have of knowing what hurts us, and why."[27]

Chapter 3

Greed: when money is never enough

When money becomes intrinsically valuable, idealized, full of magical powers (like that of fixing everything), we have set ourselves up for a life of dissatisfaction. The classical Greek philosopher Socrates said, "He who is not contented with what he has, would not be contented with what he would like to have," implying that there is an illusion that more will satiate us. This is the tragic truth about the anxious pursuit of wealth—no amount will ever feel enough because the pursuit is symbolic and not about the money.

The trouble with the definitions of greed is that they focus on wanting more than one needs,[1] but who is to say what is beyond need? Is need about meeting our basic necessity of food and shelter? Or is it about maintaining the lifestyle that most people with our salary have? Won't every person have a different view of what a sufficient level of income or savings is? The other problem with defining it as such is that we leave no room for healthy ambition. Is wanting more than we need greedy or just a sign of having big aspirations, or for example wanting to give our children more than we had?

Most people wish they had more money (in fact, according to Gallup over 60 percent of Americans would like to be rich one day),[2] but greed isn't just a longing for more, it is an *insatiable* longing alongside a constant preoccupation with not having enough.[3] The word "greed" comes from the Old English words meaning "voracious, hungry."[4] But, the desire is not gratified. The hunger is not satiated. In the eyes of the greedy they never have enough—and the fact that often this is in no way supported by the financial reality of their situation, begs the question: Enough for what?

To explain the constant preoccupation with not having enough, the term money dysmorphia (not a psychoanalytic term) has been used recently by the media to describe someone's distorted perception of their financial reality. A person might *feel* like they don't have enough, when in reality they are not in such bad financial shape. The term draws on the body dysmorphic disorder, which is a mental health condition in which someone becomes obsessed with perceived flaws in their physical appearance (which are usually imperceptible to others). Similarly, the person with money dysmorphia may have an unrealistic view of their financial situation, feeling a financial lack where in reality (or at least a part of them knows) there isn't. So, like the body dysmorphic working tirelessly to correct the fault in their appearance, the greedy person turns workaholic or obsessively hoards money in the hope of addressing their financial lack.

The other characteristic often attributed to greed is the disregard for others that often accompanies it. Undeniably the negative connotations of greed are related to this aspect of it: Hunger prevails and is prioritized over everyone else. We pursue our desired object (money in this instance), trampling over those who stand in the way.

In a series of studies, Kouchaki and colleagues[5] demonstrated that mere exposure to money can trigger unethical intentions and behavior (like lying, cheating, or acting in one's self-interest with little regard for others), concluding that "money is an insidious corrupting factor."[6] Even simply exposing participants in an experiment to money-related words seemed to influence their subsequent behavior completing a task, making them more likely to take unethical actions (like lying). This isn't the first piece of research to try to link an interest in business to competitive and self-interested behavior.

But wealth too can influence an ideology of self-interest. Several studies have found that wealthier people displayed lower feelings of empathy and compassion (along with a greater sense of entitlement), suggesting a link between greater wealth and the disregard for others.[7] In one study, drivers of more expensive cars were less likely to stop for pedestrians at a crosswalk. While we can't assume that the wealthy are all greedy, these studies demonstrate that the wealthier we are, the more likely we are to moralize the pursuit of wealth and subscribe to an ideology of self-interest. But of course it's hard to study humans in their complexity through experiments and even though this research is compelling, how do we explain the fact that the wealthy are just as generous (when looking at proportion of income donated to charity), as most other people?[8]

In my view, what many definitions of greed leave out is the actual disregard for the self that is often so typical of the people trapped in this anxious pursuit. Their self-care and relationships often suffer the consequences of them working incessantly to amass more and more wealth. As essayist Ralph Waldo Emerson said, "Money often costs too much."[9]

So far, we have insatiable desire for money and persistent worries about not having enough driving behavior that may be self-harming, immoral, or just unempathic.

The Greek word for greed (*philargyros*) literally translates to "money-loving."[10] This captures a crucial aspect of people's pecuniary greed: the money fetishism that often accompanies it. Money is idealized, loved as if intrinsically valuable. It stops being just a means to an end, but becomes a possession, amassed for its own sake. Instead of being seen as a medium for exchange, a tool to enjoy the pleasures of life, money is seen as the thing that will bring happiness and ease all anxieties. Money will heal the depressive feelings. Money will make it all right. That is the phantasy. Yet money doesn't deliver that. And the bar keeps moving.

Because greed is a feeling that we have negative associations with, we are more likely to recognize it in others than in ourselves. This is a phenomenon called "projection." We unconsciously project (place in the other) feelings we find uncomfortable owning. And usually, the more we are irritated by other people's greed, the more likely it is that there is a greedy part of us that we are not acknowledging and trying to unconsciously deny or get rid of. So if you find yourself frequently annoyed by other people's greed, it's worth wondering, what about your greed?

As we dig into the nuances of our money attitudes it is important to distinguish between greed or avariciousness and stinginess or miserliness. There is a world of difference from a psychological perspective, even if in everyday life we might use these terms interchangeably. The miser is someone who displays both an obsession with hoarding money (being greedy) but also a difficulty with spending. But in my experiences these two things, while they often go hand in hand, are different: Wanting to save is not the same as not wanting to spend. And not wanting to spend on oneself is different from not wanting to spend on others (but that's a topic covered in the next chapter). Here, however, when we talk about greed, I am focusing specifically on the desire to amass.

I have met people (often wealthy people) who are capable of spending on a lifestyle many of us would dream of, yet still struggle with their greed (which might be expressed as a workaholism and a consuming need to gain even more, at all costs). Despite having enough money to guarantee their financial safety and that of generations to come, they still sacrifice things they value greatly in its pursuit (like spending time with their family, exercise, making time for eating healthily, or traveling).

Origins and perceptions of greed

Over time, economists and philosophers have held different views on greed. There are those who see it as a drive for self-preservation[11] and as a force of economic growth at a societal level.[12] Michael Douglas's famous monologue in the movie *Wall Street* (1987) (in which he plays the role of the fictional financier Gordon Gekko), captures these views: "Greed, for lack of a better word, is good. Greed is right, greed works. Greed clarifies, cuts through, and captures the essence of the evolutionary spirit. Greed, in all of its forms; greed for life, for money, for love, knowledge has marked the upward surge of mankind." It has also been suggested that political systems designed to eliminate greedy behaviors have led to poverty and chaos.[13]

Greed is innate and present not just in humans but in animals too. The desire to accumulate food or money is a survival strategy in part. Money is linked to our survival and the threat of not having enough evokes primitive anxieties. Evolutionary psychologists believe that greed serves our objective of perpetuating our genetic code because, by pushing us to amass status-signaling possessions, we increase our chances of attracting a mate.[14]

However, many hold the opposing view. Economist and political theorist John Maynard Keynes saw love of money as a kind of madness. He called "money-motive" a way in which we turn something bad into something good. We turn ruthless greed into something morally impressive.[15] Greed can be a destructive force both at a societal and at an individual level. It can turn into a harmful, immoral, and exploitative force. Some say that we live in a social and economic system that promotes and even institutionalizes greed, leading to societal problems such as inequality, corruption, financial crises, and even war.[16]

Otto Fenichel was one of the first psychoanalysts to suggest, in 1938, that capitalism was one of the strong forces promoting the accumulation of wealth: "The capitalist, under penalty of his own destruction, *must strive to accumulate wealth.*" But, he says, we are driven by both internal and external forces in our pursuit of money. Internally, we have narcissistic needs that we seek to satisfy through money. He is referring to the fact that young children feel omnipotent and "that throughout their lives a certain memory of this omnipotence remains with a longing to attain it again." Money becomes symbolic of a potential supply of power and of (self-)esteem because in our society power and respect are based on the possession of money. This internal drive for power and self-esteem is reinforced by a societal perception.[17]

He emphasized that it is the interplay of internal and external forces that shape our drive to amass wealth and that it would be limiting to consider one and not the other. The realities of money in society cannot be ignored. He wrote, "In our society the possessor of money is honored and truly powerful."[18]

Melanie Klein, whose groundbreaking work in child psychotherapy has greatly shaped psychoanalytic thinking, also saw the child as being shaped by a continuous interplay of both internal and external factors.[19] But when speaking of external factors she emphasized the caregivers' response to the infant's greed. Greed is both an innate force but also something moderated or exacerbated by the responses we get from our caregivers when we express our desire for more. How does the world respond to us? Do we get more when we ask for more? Do we get told off or punished for being greedy or needy?

Adding to the external forces that shape our perception of greed is religion. Most religions condemn it. In Christianity, it is a cardinal sin (best demonstrated by Judas's betrayal of Jesus for 30 pieces of silver).[20] In Buddhism, it is one of three causes of human suffering (along with ignorance and anger). Examples abound from many different religions. In Dante's *Inferno*,[21] the avaricious (or hoarders of money) and the prodigal (those who spent it lustfully) appear in the same circle of hell to indicate that both groups were guilty of the same sin—the inability to make use of their fortunes in moderation.

In Greek mythology,[22] the story of Midas ridicules the avid pursuit of wealth. King Midas helped Dionysus (the god of wine and ecstasy) find his father and was rewarded with a wish. King Midas wished for anything he touched to turn to gold. In his hastened choice of wish, he overlooked the fact that even his food would turn to gold and was therefore threatened with the prospect of starvation as a result of his foolish desire. In a later version of the story, even his daughter, whom he touched, turned to gold.[23] Some versions of the mythical story have him reverse the curse of his gift, yet others see him die of starvation. Regardless of the version, it is a tale rich in meaning: Money or gold doesn't result in happiness and its pursuit can turn into a curse and become a destructive force. The god that had granted Midas's wish, Dionysus, was in fact a two-faced god in that he represented happiness but could also deliver brutal rage as a result of overindulgence (echoing the dual nature of wine). With Midas too, excessive greed turned out to have a dark side.

Greed often has very negative connotations and some of the people reading this chapter might recognize themselves in some examples but might be compelled to debate that "mine is not greed, it's fear, it's anxiety, it's . . ." However, only until we can face the fact that there are feelings within us (which could very well be fear, but often greed alongside it), that generate our desire for more, do we stand a chance to understand and change our behaviors. It is only when we can face the fact that we may be incessantly longing for more that we can stop and ask ourselves: Why isn't what I have enough? What do I imagine *more* will actually give me? What am I afraid of?

And then there are those who, despite having accumulated more wealth than they ever imagined, are still feeling empty or unfulfillled. Money was supposed to deliver something, and it failed. For some it's a sense of love, for others a sense of inner worthiness, and yet for others happiness. Imagine working tirelessly for an entire lifetime to end up in the same place where you started. It was all an illusion. Money was idealized, and we attributed all sorts of magical qualities to it, only to find out that what we were hoping to buy wasn't up for sale.

Greedy behaviors

The anxious pursuit of wealth takes on different forms. One of them is hoarding money, like the character Ebenezer Scrooge, protagonist of Charles Dickens's novella *A Christmas Carol*. Scrooge is described as a merciless miser, consumed by his preoccupation with money. I think even more vivid is Disney's depiction of Dickens's character as Scrooge McDuck who was "the richest duck in the world" and was often found swimming in a vault full of money, reveling in the delight of touching his intrinsically valuable possession.[24] Despite his riches, Uncle Scrooge was so obsessed with the accumulation of money that he lost contact with family and friends and focused on making more of it.

Whereas we don't see them swimming in pools of gold, there are many people who take pride in their industriousness and hard work, but what lies behind is an obsession with having more. They might be admired for their shrewd business dealings. They might be accused of being workaholics by partners and friends. I use the term "workaholism" in its broader (not just clinical) sense. Defining workaholism as an addictive, behavioral disorder includes assessing the extent to which one works, one thinks about work and the extent to which one compromises other aspects of one's life (like health and relationships) in favor of work (often without any external expectation that one works so much). A difficulty enjoying activities outside of work, denial of this, and lies are also signs.

It is one thing to enjoy one's work and engage in it out of pleasure, and a healthy sense of motivation and ambition. Engaging in it because of an incomprehensible inner compulsion is very different. Research has shown the former (also known as "work engagement") to be linked with positive feelings (joviality, attentiveness, and self-assurance) and the latter (workaholism) to be linked with guilt, anxiety, anger, and disappointment.[25]

Workaholism can be a feature of a compulsive character, as we saw with overspenders, people who act instead of sitting with their feelings (whatever those may be). It may also be a feature of a masochistic character (who is unconsciously punishing themselves). Other times people work extensively to avoid an unhappy marriage or a difficult family situation. Yet some workaholics, the ones I am focusing on here, do it for the money. They are driven by greed. Those around them watch perplexed wondering at what point they will feel like they have enough. The goalposts keep moving, and the sense of hunger is never satiated. Sometimes they drive themselves to burnout, which the American Psychological Association defines as "physical, emotional, or mental exhaustion accompanied by decreased motivation, lowered performance, and negative attitudes toward oneself and others."[26]

To understand someone trapped in the anxious hoarding of money or exhausting themselves on the hamster wheel to amass more of it, we need to ask: What do they imagine money will give them? What are they longing for (is it a sense of comfort and safety)? What does money mean in their minds (is it a measure of worth)? What are they afraid of (running out of money/annihilation)?

Fears related to experiences of poverty and financial loss

A client summed up her situation as follows: "At 30, I am terrified of running out of money. I live from day to day feeling that one wrong move could end in catastrophe, which is not only illogical, but damaging. I'm hypervigilant. Petrified of saying no to work, I find myself burning out frequently. Now, more than ever, the stress of responsibility to be able to earn enough to live, survive, and thrive has just become an unbearable pressure."[27] This young woman, despite an awareness, at a rational level, that her need for more was illogical and fear-based, couldn't control the compulsion to work more, earn more, have more.

There are many people who struggle to manage their fear of not having enough, and in my experience, these fears are often rooted in real experiences of poverty and financial loss, or in experiences of *emotional* deprivation, leaving them struggling for an internal sense of security that gets acted out through money.

The real experiences of poverty are a simple (yet still painful) explanation for the anxieties of running out of money and the resulting pursuit for more and more. The fears are often not based in the present reality of their situation. Many people who fear poverty work hard to ensure they are not in what is (objectively) a precarious financial situation. However, that's not how it feels to them. Usually, a rational part of them knows that, but knowing it rationally does little to alleviate the anxieties.

The reason for this is that they grew up in an environment that left an emotional imprint of fear and loss. They watched their parents make painful compromises and self-sacrifices but most importantly they *felt* the feelings that parents felt in those circumstances. They also might have themselves been left longing for things or experiences that others could afford, but they couldn't. And while those memories might have, in part, provoked the pledge to never be in that situation again, it also left residues of fear. Greed is held on to to ensure they never end up in the same place as their parents, or that they never again have to long for something they can't afford.

Big financial losses (personal or in the family) can leave an emotional scar too. They can fuel catastrophizing thoughts; what-ifs abound in the person's thinking. These are legitimate responses. After all, the lesson learned is that people can be caught off guard and lose everything from one day to the other. However, there is value in challenging the *degree* to which the fear of suddenly being left with nothing is being defended against. I am not at all saying that one shouldn't save for a rainy day or build some negative scenarios in their financial forecasting (in fact these are healthy financial habits), but there is a world of difference between being cautious and living in fear. When the fear is paralyzing, it starts to get in the way of your financial well-being. Working more, amassing more, saving more, becomes the only way to alleviate the anxieties (albeit temporarily).

Often a consequence of experiences of poverty or financial losses is also an unconscious phantasy that money will resolve all problems. Whereas money-related hardships might have caused great distress in the family growing up, money becomes a catchall for every negative feeling. Therefore, a sense is created in the child that more money could fix everything. Money could heal unhappiness, depression, and the family would argue less if only there was more money. Those holding these beliefs end up living with the hope that enough money/ happiness is within reach, and if they just work a bit more, squeeze in another project, get another promotion, they'll have enough.

What is helpful for those who struggle with the ghosts of financial trauma is firstly to acknowledge the links between their present feelings and past experiences. Being able to give space to those feelings, and allow oneself the opportunity to work through them, understand in greater depth what happened, can be liberating. A lot of people find it hard to recognize how something that happened to their parents deeply impacted them—it is dismissed as "their trauma, not mine." But once room is given to what *they* felt, to the meaning *they* gave to the experience, we can better understand the emotional residue that is behind their greedy behavior in the present.

Reality checking can also be valuable. I am not talking about reassuring yourself that "you have enough money, so don't worry" because that doesn't ease the anxiety. It is about being conscious of when you are catastrophizing (focusing on low probability scenarios). But also being aware of the amount of control you actually have over your circumstances, which can involve putting in place financial measures (like safety nets) to prevent being caught off guard. Sometimes reality checking involves getting in touch with the difference between you and your parents—for example, the fact that they had been negligent with finances set the stage for a very different outcome to you now, so on top of your numbers. As obvious as these factors might be, the person struggling with the anxieties often forgets that they are not their parents and that they have already done plenty to prevent history from repeating itself.

A lump of love (secure base)

Therapists tend to agree that a struggle with greed often has its roots in early experiences of deprivation. The infant that is anxious about being deprived because it has experienced some non-responsiveness to their demands will become greedier. Neglect can fuel anxieties and insecurities about the supply of food/love/money and an insatiable hunger results. Klein described the greedy child evolving into an adult who is likely to become ambitious, but ultimately dissatisfied with their achievements, always longing for more.

As experiences of deprivation differ, so does its impact on each individual. How are we seeking to fill the gap left internally by the lack we experienced back then? In other words, what meaning has money taken on in our minds in relation to the gap we are trying to fill? Is it love, happiness, or a sense of worth that we are trying to achieve through our accumulation of more and more wealth? Unearthing those can help us understand the greedy part of us that is expressed in our money behavior, and inevitably, in other aspects of our lives too.

"I thought money was going to fix everything," a client once said to me. He had moved himself out of poverty and into the millionaires' club. Yet, to his surprise, he wasn't happier. "Maybe some of the anxiety about finances got better, but that's about it." It is often the case that people come to therapy with what they might call existential preoccupations, about the meaning of life and the pursuit of happiness. They acknowledge that the more they work, and the more money they have, the less close they feel to reaching the happiness they were striving for.

Psychoanalyst David Krueger gives the example of the client who came to him for therapy when he ran out of space on his office walls and in his trophy case for his achievements. He says about his client, "[. . .] another award to achieve or more money to make were perpetual spurs to hope. He had simply upped the ante with each achievement, keeping alive the hope of getting what he did not get in his childhood, of filling his emptiness."[28] Clients often talk about an internal sense of *emptiness* that can't be filled. The language is interesting—we picture the empty, starving stomach that metaphorically stands for an emotional lack. Money is often being used in an effort to satiate that hunger, that longing for more.

Where does that insatiable longing originate? One useful lens to use to think about this is that of attachment theory. Decades of research have established that a child's attachment pattern is determined by the "mother"*–infant interaction at home, and that one's attachment pattern in infancy influences how they will build relationships as children, adolescents, and adults.

If our caregivers were available, responsive, attuned to us, and our experiences of them were overwhelmingly positive, we are most likely to adopt a secure attachment style, meaning that we feel safe in relationships and trust others. We are able to manage conflict, regulate our emotions, and communicate our needs and frustrations to the other. We feel worthy of love and don't rely on external reassurance and validation.

But many don't have an overall positive parenting experience. They grow up in an environment where needs are inconsistently met, parental figures are unreliable or unavailable, and where rejection, criticism, or indifference prevail. So the child grows up lacking its secure base.[29] They inherit an emotional script that expects people to be unreliable, so they set up relationships from a place of insecurity and fear. They struggle to connect to others in a meaningful and fulfillling way, and instead, in some cases, they cling on to them seeking validation and reassurance. They become anxiously attached holding on tightly to the other, fearing abandonment. Despite others' efforts to deliver on these requests, what is lacking is internal: the inner secure base, in other words a faith that their needs will be met in a good enough way. The void, however, is unfillable and they end up

---

* I use quotes around "mother" as it refers to any primary caregiver.

frustrated and unsatisfied. Money is held on to anxiously in the same way; it becomes one way in which they express the hunger for security and love, another means of potentially filling that gap, but it doesn't work either. Jeremy Holmes, psychiatrist and renowned attachment theorist, says "The deification of money is a perverse response to [. . .] emptiness. If I cannot have love, then at least I will have money: my unsatisfied greed turns to money-lust."[30] He explains that from a lack of real security and attunement comes a creation of a secure base in money.

Even in Dickens's novella, Ebenezer Scrooge had been emotionally deprived as a child, and as the ghost of the past reminded him, he had been left alone in boarding school, even on Christmas Day. The emotional longing had turned for him into a desire for more money. The unconscious sense is that if we don't hold on to something, if we don't stock up on it while it's there, then we are exposing ourselves to the risk of being left hungry, longing.

For Scrooge, it was the ghosts of present, past, and future that helped him change. It was a confrontation with the early trauma, the awareness of the hurt that his current behavior was causing, and the reality of where the current path he was on was leading him to. We need to confront the part of us that felt deprived. We need to mourn the loss of the parents we wished we had. And we need to take the adult view of what is really missing so we don't look for it in the wrong place.

Money can be counted on—a desire for self-reliance

Like those who buy and treasure possessions because they are more reliable than people, others may seek to accumulate money as it will give them that sense of independence, of not needing anyone else, not having to be reliant on potentially disappointing others to satisfy their needs.

There is a healthy developmental goal in wanting to be financially independent: That's not what we are talking about here. That is very different from wanting to accumulate more and more in order to never be left longing again.

Having personally met Warren Buffett at a turning point in my life, it left me with great curiosity about the driving force behind his extraordinary achievements. The more I dug into his biographies for clues about his early experiences, the more his case study brought to life for me the many contributing factors that shape our future relationship with money. In Warren's history, money lessons learned in the family, identification with a resilient and shrewd father, and emotional deprivation and trauma in his relationship with his mother all influenced the development of what would turn out to be one of the wealthiest men on earth.[31]

Buffett decided he was going to be a millionaire at a young age. He was born in Nebraska in 1930, not even a year after Black Tuesday—the day Wall Street crashed. When he was almost one year old, his father announced that his bank had closed and he had been left without a job.[32] It was a time in which an entire country was anxious about money. Depression and suicide abounded. But Buffett's father, Howard, made the brave decision to start a stock brokerage firm and steadily grew the business. Maybe that was the first valuable lesson Buffett learned about life (and money)—that with a sense of resilience, courage, and determination one can survive even the most unlikely (financial) challenges.

Buffett recognized the great influence his father had on shaping his approach to life. Speaking of his father he says, "He was *really* a maverick. But he wasn't a maverick for the sake of being a maverick. He just didn't care what other people thought. My dad taught me how life should be lived."[33] This concept, which Buffett called "the inner scorecard," played a great role in his financial success. It was the identification with his father that allowed him to have the courage needed to pursue his goal and stick to his convictions, as he did, for example, by not selling his stocks when everyone was panicking in a declining stock market.

His cautious approach, his choice of companies and businesses, his holding on to cash when investments didn't meet his criteria, were all in line with the messages taught to him by his father and grandfather.[34] But I think it would be limiting to look at Buffett's exceptional success only in light of the money lessons taught at home. In my view, what was key to Buffett's obsession with amassing wealth was the difficult relationship with his mother along with the longing for more time with his father, which fueled his greed.

Buffett's mother, Leila, came from a family with a trans-generational history of mental illness.[35] She struggled greatly to manage her anger and both Buffett and his eldest sister tell stories of how small triggers would send her off in endless outpours of furious accusations. During those episodes, she wouldn't stop until the children were reduced to tears, weeping helplessly.[36] Because often these events occurred when his father was not at home, he couldn't protect the children from them and in Buffett's family, feelings were notoriously left unspoken. Buffett was left to manage the anger, shame, and guilt that might have resulted from such events on his own. His wife Susie said about him, "All that confident chatter about stocks [. . .] was wrapped around a fragile, needy core: a boy who was stumbling through his days in a shroud of desolation."[37]

Buffett was obsessed with numbers from a very young age.[38] He would spend hours with his friends filling out notebooks with licence plate numbers of passing cars.[39] It is common in latency years (which roughly spans from the age of five to eleven years) for children to go through an interest in collecting (usually pebbles or marbles and later coins) and to engage in activities that may seem repetitive and monotonous (like counting, listing, ordering). Most children, however, move on to different interests. But young Buffett continued to search for comfort in collecting, hoarding, and immersing himself in numbers.

I wonder if numbers, for Buffett, became a psychological escape from his mother's rage, a place in which things could be counted on, where things were predictable, rational, and easily understood. In a 2017 HBO documentary called *Becoming Warren Buffett*, he stated, "I find it enjoyable to think about business or investment problems. They are easy. It's the human problems that are the tough ones. Sometimes there isn't a good answer with human problems. There is almost always a good answer with money."[40] He coped with the fear of an out-of-control mother by collecting, counting, numbering and gaining a sense of control and predictability from it.

By the time he was eight years old, Buffett spent a lot of time outside the home, "out of his mother's way."[41] But he did crave his father's attention.[42] His father would often retire in his study to read and so Buffett might have been left longing for more. I wonder if his greed, collecting coins, was the physical expression of an emotional longing. He coped with wanting more emotionally by hoarding objects.

The decision to make money came in a visit with his father to the New York Stock Exchange where, age ten, he had lunch with an impressive Dutchman who had a custom-made cigar rolled for him after lunch. As a psychotherapist, I won't overlook the fact that it was this man's cigar that infatuated young Buffett, but I don't think that in his eyes it was a symbol of power and potency but rather one of resourcefulness. This man wasn't ever going to be hungry. The Dutchman could satisfy his own needs and desires and get himself what he wanted. For young Buffett, I imagine that there would have been something deeply appealing about that: the idea of self-reliance and the phantasy of not being left longing for anything.

Buffett wasn't interested in money for its transactional value. In fact, he didn't spend it and was notorious for his unwillingness to buy new clothes, a larger home, etc. There was an emotional desire that he sought to satisfy through it.

His mantra was "be fearful when others are greedy and greedy when others are fearful" referring to the markets, but it makes me wonder whether Buffett's experiences of having weathered the storms at home, of having to find resilience in moments of desolation, had built an internal resource that he found a way to use to his favor. He had to cope with managing both his fear and his greed from a young age. As an investor he was unperturbed by market volatility. When everyone sold, he bought or held on to his stocks and vice versa, showing a confidence that he didn't display in other areas of his life. His message to investors was—don't be swept away by the emotions of others.

Buffett might have developed coping strategies to deal with stressful emotional experiences as a young child which he was able to direct toward a productive pursuit. Money perhaps gave him a sense of control and served his phantasy of self-reliance. Money also represented an emotional currency, his way of feeling richness despite experiences of deprivation.

A measure of worth

Although for some the accumulation of money more directly links to ideas of love and security, or of self-reliance, for others the pursuit of wealth links to an equation in their unconscious where self-worth = financial worth. Money becomes a compensation for a sense of inner lack, and the reverse stands too. When money is lost, it feels as if a part of the self (or one's self-worth) is gone with it too. As we saw earlier, with Fenichel's idea that money could supply self-regard and power, then it follows, as he says, that the "pathological fear of impoverishment" is a fear of losing "self-regard."[43]

The crystallization of this internal equation (financial worth = self-worth) can result from *conditional* love. If love, growing up, was felt as conditional on performing well in school, on being the good girl/boy, on sports medals and obedience, we don't grow up feeling *entitled* to love but feeling that it needs to be earned. We obtain loving responses when we give others what they want from us, when we showcase our strengths. Our weaknesses are unacceptable, undesirable. Succeeding, in phantasy, will get us love. What often happens is that we end up surrounding ourselves with people who value us for our possessions and collude with our view of the world—that we are only worthy for our achievements. Success (financial success) appeases the anxious part of us that worries about losing love if we were to be, heaven forbid, ordinary.

While some might spend money to obtain an external sense of validation, the avaricious are trying to give substance to a part of themselves that feels insubstantial. Something is being inflated (bank account, self-perception) to compensate for a sense of an inner lack. In fact, sometimes the greedy person proudly shows off their wealth, also searching externally to impress and obtain validation. Other times it is a more humble and solitary pursuit for more.

When you speak to someone who might unconsciously carry the inner equation of self-worth = financial worth, you get a real sense of money as important and full of meaning. Most of us would like more money but we might not pay such a high price to obtain it: We don't value it to the same extent they do. We might have anxieties about having less (especially when we are being bombarded by gloomy financial news), but for them the fears are of a different proportion because the stakes feel higher: They wouldn't be losing just money. "What would happen then?"

is what I usually ask. Answers start with, "I would have to give up the lifestyle I have" (the rational answer), but the deeper answers quickly emerge: "What would people think of me?"; "What will it say about me?"; "What will be left then?" The feeling is that they will lose value as a person in their own eyes and in the eyes of others. A deep sense of shame would prevail and feel unmanageable.

Shame, not guilt. You see, guilt is what we feel when we make a mistake (like a poor investment choice). Shame is a sense of *being* bad, an internal sense of something lacking within us. The focus is on us, not our actions, what it says about who we *are*, not about what we *did*. Shame is deep and pervasive, and it takes a long time to resolve. So financial losses, for someone whose sense of self and worthiness was based on the accumulation of money, can feel catastrophic and irreparable.

Losses that put our livelihoods at risk can be deeply distressing for anyone, not just for those struggling with greed. Working for years toward a financial objective and watching it crumble is devastating. However, in my experience, the more intrinsic value we attribute to money, the more difficult it is to mourn its loss. We find ourselves up against the fear that we have lost self-worth, credibility, respect, and love along with it. Andrew (68, married, father of four children and one grandchild) confessed, "I feel like there is nothing left. There is no point in fighting any more. I have lost everything." Look at the ambiguity in his words. Is he talking about money? Or about himself? His life? The loss transcended the financial.

Can we distinguish between "I feel *as if* I lost everything" and "I lost everything?" Can we separate the symbolic loss from the real loss? For Andrew, the financial losses had been large and undeniably disappointing, infuriating, even tragic. But at times he couldn't see that he hadn't actually lost everything—he still had loving children, a supportive wife, and (!) a few million dollars in his bank account—because it felt as if he had.

There are people who lost a lot more than Andrew and who don't lose hope to the same extent. There are families who find themselves tipping into poverty, resorting to food banks, who cannot buy their children Christmas presents. Yet many find the resilience to mourn the losses and focus on what can still give meaning to life outside the material because to them what is lost is money and the things it can buy, not their own sense of value.

Of course nothing is ever black and white for anyone. Financial loss may feel devastating and shameful. It takes time, like any process of grief to get to that point. First the full range of feelings needs to be allowed space to be experienced: anger, fury, regret, sorrow, embarrassment, shame, fear, and a deep, deep sense of loss. The past is replayed in one's mind: What if this, what if that . . . if only. The future is contemplated in terms of what could have been versus what will be. There is a process of making sense of what happened and here a lot of introspection and learning can take place. But then grieving needs to take place: mourning the losses, giving up the hope that the past could be different, and letting go of what is gone.

For those who lost money that stood for self-worth, the loss becomes a powerful reference point in their mind: Life is seen as "before the loss" and "after the loss" as if everything, their entire world, changed at that moment. They often feel alone in their pain. Sometimes there is a real sense of shame, not just about the loss but also about their feelings, their inability to just get on with it. Friends and family reassure them "it's just money" but that gives them no comfort. It wasn't just money for them. For some, like some of the more narcissistic clients I worked with, the financial loss meant a crumbling down of the outer shell that they spent years building. The shell that kept them feeling powerful enough, big enough, strong enough, but now they were left bare and vulnerable, exposed for the wounded little child they were trying to hide all along. It's devastating.

For those who didn't lose it, they might feel stuck in an unwavering resolve to relentlessly stockpile what is seen as vitally important capital.

Desire to be taken seriously

Proving our worth through money and financial achievements can also be linked to a desire to be taken seriously entrenched in early experiences. I have seen this play out especially as a result of sibling dynamics, but of course it may happen to a single child too who felt unseen or unnoticed.

These experiences can result in an often unconscious longing to have a voice, to be heard and to be taken seriously. Their greed is also born out of an emotional deprivation and a sense that as they are, they don't warrant the respect, attention, and love that others do. You can almost get a sense of a money-made pedestal they spend their lives building, hoping it will raise them to the level of their siblings or to a level tall enough for father to take notice. Money, for them, stands for credibility and respect. The phantasy is that once they have squirreled away sufficient wealth they will show them that they are, in fact, deserving of the attention and respect that was longed for.

They might, in phantasy, even become the preferred one, now more able to provide something of value to the parents. There is a desire to be noticed, to be seen, to be praised and admired in a way that was longed for back then and still searched for in the here and now.

Legacy and immortality—a means to transcend death

Irvin Yalom, author and existential psychotherapist, wrote, "For some of us the fear of death manifests only indirectly, either as generalized unrest or masqueraded as another psychological symptom."[44] I found that sometimes an anxiety about hoarding money, particularly if developed later in life, may be one such masquerade.

Entering the third age and beginning to face the reality of our inevitable fate can open up questions about the meaning of life. Have we accomplished enough? What are we leaving behind to mark our existence? How to cope with the unfathomable prospect of no longer being? For some people, something shifts when they begin to grapple with these questions and their anxiety about the future (and regrets about the past), turns into an obsession with both frugality and hoarding. Stashing away wealth may provide a sense of control in the face of something that is so out of our control.

An effort to accumulate all the wealth one can may also be an effort to leave something substantial behind, something that offers an illusion of living on. We may harbor an ever so strong desire to leave a legacy as a means to achieve, in phantasy, a sense of immortality.

Most people only begin to wrestle with the idea of death later in life, yet others have early experiences of death (death in the family, a sibling, a parent) that mark how they go about experiencing life. Even though early experiences of death don't result in greed per se, they might create what psychoanalyst Salman Akhtar calls a "death-defying energy,"[45] in that they spark a "strive for achievements to make them 'immortal.'"[46] These "survivors" work tirelessly to accumulate money because it can offer an illusion of living on through one's inheritance, philanthropic acts, or simply as possessions left behind after the body fades. Things stay.

* * *

From immortality to filling a void that was left from experiences of emotional deprivation, money can fulfill many psychological purposes. As we saw, experiences of lack get internalized and responded to in different ways. Some people hoard money because that's what they learned to do with good resources: stock up on them while they are available and ensure they have enough so that they are never left longing. To them, money stands for love and safety.

Others amass resources because deprivation left them with a sense that *they* are insubstantial, so money helps patch up their deficiencies, helps them feel worthy. To them, money stands for self-worth and value.

Yet others hoard it hoping it will give them a stronger voice. To them, money stands for credibility and respect.

Money is an object and a symbol, so when we spend our lives preoccupied with its accumulation, it begs the question: What does it represent in our minds?

CHAPTER 4

Underspending: when we can't enjoy money

The miser who lives with the bare minimum. The date that doesn't tip the waiter. The friend that disappears to the bathroom when the bill arrives. The one that asks you to order the Uber and then doesn't pay their half of it. What they all have in common is a challenge parting with money for other people's sake, or for theirs.

A difficulty with spending money can take on many forms. It can involve living a miserly life despite having heaps of wealth collecting dust in the bank account, or wrestling with feelings of guilt any time we spend on ourselves, or going well out of our way to save money on small purchases (obsessively collecting coupons and discounts), and many others.

At what point does being thrifty turn into stinginess? Like with overspending, it is hard to define underspending because we all have very different definitions of what is a frivolous versus a necessary expense. It is all relative, but there are clues that help us recognize if we have gravitated toward behaviors that are now different from mere frugality.

Often a part of us has some awareness that our spending is unusual. We might, at some level, wish we could enjoy the money we have more, or maybe feel envious of people who do spend and enjoy their wealth. We might recognize that when we bring ourselves to spend, we feel guilt and regret, which are part of the reason why we avoid it altogether.

We might have been called tightfisted or been told that we need to let go a little and enjoy more. We become defensive when people criticize our frugality and may ourselves have been openly critical of people who overindulge. These are signs that, internally, we are not at peace with our attitude toward our spending.

It is important, when we are trying to understand under-spending, to make a distinction between a difficulty with spending money in general, a difficulty with spending money on ourselves and a struggle to spend money on others. Words like "miserly" and "stingy" don't quite help us make that distinction which, psychologically, is important.

"Parsimony" isn't a good enough term either because people can be self-denying (depriving themselves of the good things that money can buy) while managing to be generous with others, and vice versa. This distinction is important if we are trying to understand what is behind their behavior. To be able to explore these differences, I will call "self-denying" the person who struggles to spend on themselves and "withholding" the person that struggles with being generous.

Self-denying

I have met people who can't allow themselves to have hardly anything but wouldn't hesitate to hand out money to someone in need. Financial anorexia (a term used by the media) has become a popular way to describe those who are self-denying in their attitude toward money. They can't allow themselves the pleasures of spending. Like the person struggling with the mental health disorder of anorexia nervosa, who denies themselves food in an effort to keep their body weight to its lowest, the money anorexic denies themselves the good things that money allows us to have. There isn't a consensus on the definition of financial anorexia. One definition reads "someone who takes inordinate amounts of pride in having few financial needs and is more comfortable living in deprivation."[1] However, in my experience, pride is not universally felt by those who are self-denying with money. There might be, in fact, a great deal of frustration and shame about the fact that spending for them is so difficult. I will come back to this as we explore the different roots of this behavior.

Financial anorexia interferes with our financial well-being, particularly with our ability to enjoy what we have rather than restricting our enjoyment unnecessarily and from an irrational, emotional place. The denial of spending can take such extreme forms that it may interfere with our relationships and our quality of life.

Withholding

There are those who are financially withholding with others, while having no trouble spending money on themselves. They might try to avoid paying for things, not contribute to collections, or find excuses to avoid gift giving. For them *giving* is hard. Sometimes they are perceived as exploitative. They might even brokefish (misrepresent themselves as lacking in financial resources), hoping the other will pay for them and feel a sort of victory if they can get others to spend on their behalf. I will call this group "withholding."

Overall parsimonious

For the parsimonious, spending money in general is hard, be it on themselves or on others. Parting with money is difficult, anxiety-provoking, and avoided at all costs. Their parsimony might be pervasive and not limited to the financial. They might be emotionally withholding too. Giving in general is a challenge—giving a hug, giving time, showing love. Their self-denial too may exceed the financial (in fact co-occurring with anorexia or other forms of abstinence and self-restraint).

* * *

What I focus on is a *difficulty* with spending and enjoying the money we have, which is different from having made a conscious choice not to spend. A new movement, named FIRE (Financial Independence, Retire Early),[2] has been gaining traction. It consists of the adoption of extreme saving techniques (as much as 70 percent of one's income) in order to have financial freedom in the future (to either retire early or have a choice about when to work). We can wonder what the appeal of such a strategy is, but ultimately it is often a choice made consciously rather than a struggle with underspending per se, even though it might give a purpose (or legitimize) underspending for someone who was already struggling with it in the first place.

Social context

It is interesting to think of financial self-denial, at the time of writing in 2023, when the news is dominated by headlines on the cost of living crisis, inflation and a looming recession. Anxieties about spending abound—the threat of financial instability, uncertainty, and even potential financial losses are unsettling for most people. The natural response is to try to restrict spending.

Tight budgeting is praised and advice on saving energy, food, and more helps people slash spending. Whether preemptively or because they have no choice, people are applying restrictions to their spending.

Anti-consumerism movements condemn the extent of buying and consuming. They denounce the actions of corporations seeking to maximize profit by manipulating consumers into buying more while seeking the cheapest ways to offer their products (often at the detriment of their physical and social environment). They encourage recycling, upcycling, living more frugally or minimally rather than spending thoughtlessly, and criticize disposable purchases, the fast fashion culture, the implications of "made in China." Religions too, historically, have praised the frugal and condemned the prodigal.

However, in my experience, parsimony is less a result of external pressures and more a result of internal ones. Environmental and social pressures, but even family money scripts, only go so far in understanding the mind of those who struggle to spend. It is by looking at the structure of their inner world that we find insight into underspenders' behavior: how they feel about themselves, especially the parts of them they don't like; how they cope with feelings of greed, shame, and envy; how they employ control as a defense mechanism.

* * *

There are many psychological reasons why someone may find it difficult to part with money. Some I have covered in the discussion on greed: Money might feel too valuable to give up because of the symbolic meaning it takes on (as a proxy for safety, love, or filling an inner sense of lack). It may also be about a dysmorphic view of our financial situation (feeling poor when in fact we aren't) because of past experiences related to money having been scarce or suddenly lost, or just a general anxious attitude with tendencies to picture worst-case scenarios and catastrophize about the future.

But those are not the only possible explanations. I will explore a range of reasons that stop us from spending: a lack of entitlement, wealth shame, feeling pride in deprivation, and issues of control. Even though the list is non-exhaustive, it begins to shed some light into the many reasons why we hold on to things (and in this case, money). It is only by understanding what lies behind our difficulty letting go of money that we stand any chance of living a life in which money can be enjoyed and shared, used both for pleasure and to connect with others.

Reasons for self-denying

When we don't feel deserving of good things

It may seem paradoxical, but feelings of low self-worth can be acted out as much by overspending as by hoarding and underspending. We can use money to buy things that might help us feel more desirable. We might hoard money hoping that it will compensate for our internal deficiencies. Or we can, despite our hard work and effort to earn money, deny ourselves the good things money can buy because, ultimately, we don't feel entitled to things.

The self-denying spender who doesn't feel deserving of good things may present as someone who prides themselves on their thriftiness, on finding a good bargain. They might not be aware of the reasons behind their self-denial and justify it as mere frugality. They might be tired of beating themselves up over every little expense and wish they could be like others who can relax and spend instead of being tortured by anxieties about not having.

They often have no trouble spending on loved ones or giving to charitable causes. In fact, in their minds, there is a clear distinction between a guilt-provoking expense (spending for one's own pleasure) and a justifiable expense (a business expense, something for the house which other roommates can also benefit from, a gift). The bottom line is: If it is for their own enjoyment, then best to avoid the purchase. People who struggle with this rarely make it to therapy (reflected in the lack of literature on the topic), because investing in one's own wellness and self-improvement feels too indulgent.

When Flavio came to see me, he was already self-denying in our first encounter. "Could we meet every other week?" he asked. Flavio was in his mid-twenties and he came to therapy to cope with his depression and a growing sense that something was wrong with him for not being happy despite having accomplished a lot of his goals. Flavio grew up in a family where money was scarce. Having had a joyless upbringing in a very deprived neighborhood in southern Italy, Flavio often retreated in his room as a child to study. He decided early on that his ticket out of that place would be good grades and a good career. And so he did it. He studied science, earned a PhD from a reputable university in Rome and now had his first job in Milan, working at a big pharmaceutical company where he could apply his skill while earning a high salary. Despite having made it, Flavio couldn't enjoy his new-found financial freedom.

"Milan is a cold and gloomy city. Yet, despite having been there for a whole winter, I cannot bring myself to buy a coat. Which is insane, I know . . . how can I feel bad about buying a coat considering how much money I am making? I don't understand it . . ." The gloominess of Milan very much reflected Flavio's internal state of mind that had been influenced by his upbringing. It wasn't just the coat that Flavio couldn't spend on. He would eat restrictively, spending the bare minimum on food. He would walk miles before taking public transport. The examples of self-denial were multiple. Despite the fact I never meet with clients less than weekly, as this tends to be more beneficial to them, I felt that Flavio was already ambivalent about allowing himself to have therapy and that the very reason why he was seeking help was to work on this self-denying part of himself. So I granted his wish for every-other-week sessions, setting a mutually agreed time limit by which we would revise the situation and see if switching to weekly sessions felt possible.

With Flavio, and like with most people too, there was a complex web of contributing factors to his struggle with spending (and with finding happiness). There was first a history of financial deprivation. Memories of his father not being able to afford the stadium tickets, of his mother having to leave shopping items at the register because of insufficient cash. In Flavio's narrative, there was a real sense of empathy for his depressed mother: As a boy, but still as an adult, he carried a desire to make life better for her. In his recent attempts to share some of his income with her, which she didn't accept, Flavio was left feeling the same helplessness he felt as a little boy, unable to cheer her up. The eldest of four brothers and with a father that seemed uninterested in everyone, including his mother, Flavio felt the responsibility and desire to be the helpful one, the one that would make his mother happy.

It became evident that his father's disinterest, his indifference to Flavio's achievements, his dismissal of any efforts to connect, alongside his mother's sadness, acted as a double whammy for Flavio's self-esteem. As children often do, unable to comprehend his parents' unhappiness, he deduced that maybe he was the problem. Although these thoughts are often unconscious (we don't necessarily *remember* thinking "oh, it must be my fault"), they leave an emotional imprint in our inner world. We might grow up to believe, at some level, that there is something wrong, unlovable, or ultimately faulty about us because we couldn't make our parents happy or interested enough in us. With that emotional setup, it would be difficult then to feel deserving.

If our internal world was threaded with memories of being silly and no one laughing, of trying to help Dad fix the car and being shooed away, of parents that couldn't themselves enjoy what they had, what chance do we stand of feeling worthy of the good things money can buy: the nurture of a meal, the warmth of a coat?

But also, how could we allow ourselves to have more than our parents did? I will come on to this topic in the self-sabotage chapter, but it's worth mentioning here too. Flavio now had more money than they ever did. Could he allow himself to have that? Or would the guilt of having more also get in the way of his enjoyment?

Pride in deprivation

The idea of pride in deprivation is an ancient one, and one that is reflected in various religions. The self-imposed poverty advocated by Buddhism and Hinduism, the austere lifestyle avowed historically by Christianity, are just examples of the idea that there is virtue in the denial of desires and even needs.

Flavio's mother was described by him as the ultimate martyr. What he meant was that his mother lived a life of self-sacrifice for the benefit of others. She consistently put herself last, always seeking recognition and sympathy for all that she had given up. Her life was arduous almost by choice. She preferred the hard way as if that was more admirable. Flavio mimicked this in his own way: Rather than devoting himself to others, he adopted the practice of self-denial as if there was virtue in that.

Like the anorexic who thinks of eating as indulging, the financial anorexic often believes that frugality is a virtue and that waste (rather than fat) is shame-inducing. One person who historically struggled with an eating disorder says, "Now I struggle with spending on things for myself. I need to justify what I eat, what I own. I got into minimalism and purged my belongings multiple times, and it helped, since I owned less and could stop looking at the evidence of waste in my room. When I used to own a Nintendo, it plagued me at night as I knew its cost and how it was a waste on me."[3] In this example, we can see pride and shame sitting alongside the financial anorexia. Having less in her home was admirable and inextricably linked with the idea that what she had spent on was waste and shameful evidence of her undeserving excesses.

For some people, the pride in denial of their needs comes from emotional deprivation. And this too might have been the case for Flavio. Alongside the example set by his mother with her self-sacrificing approach to life, he might also have developed this aspect of his character in response to feeling emotionally deprived. If we have been repeatedly denied the space for our feelings, or even blamed for being needy and attention-seeking in response to what was a healthy and age-appropriate expression of our wants, we carry a sense of guilt for having consumed others with our demands, or may even be ashamed of the bad, needy parts of us. In response to this, we may develop a defense in which we can prove to ourselves and the world how not needy we are: We triumph over need. So as Flavio walked back home, on a cold winter evening, at some level he experienced relief (and pride) in the thought that he could manage without a coat.

In other instances, the seeming pride in deprivation could be a defense called "reaction formation," which addresses a desire that feels inadmissible somehow. I have seen this in people who might have grown up in families with strong negative feelings about the pursuit of wealth. What happens is that if you grew up in such a family, then once you begin to experience a desire for material possessions, you might defend against these unacceptable thoughts by taking on an attitude diametrically opposed to [the] repressed wish.[4] Basically, you adopt a "things don't matter to me" attitude and you act in ways to prove this. The withholding, the not spending, is about convincing yourself and the world that you don't want things, as this would be hard to reconcile with the family lessons and values instilled in you for years.

Generally, the way to spot this defense is to look for signs of insistence and emphasis. This isn't someone who quietly struggles to spend, but rather it's someone who repeatedly and publicly emphasizes how *un*important possessions are to them. They might speak with contempt about those who value things and publicly display their miserliness to disguise the unconscious desire for more. The defense, however, often fails, firstly because by constantly talking about its unimportance, they keep thinking about money and possessions. And secondly, because often the internal conflict is felt. There is a discomfort in living unauthentically that will manifest itself one way or another (usually feelings of anxiety, unease, sadness).

An obsession with control

The person struggling with anorexia nervosa may become obsessive about their weight in the way that the withholding spender may have obsessive thoughts about their spending ("Do I need this? Do I not? Where can I get it cheaper? How can I get out of paying for . . . ?"). They don't count calories but might frequently check their account balance and statements. Both become focused on thinking and acting (as opposed to *feeling*). The only feeling which in fact there seems to be room for in their minds is that of shame.[5]

So the kind of financially self-denying person I am speaking about here is the one that tightly controls their spending as a defense against a fear of being out of control. Tightening the grip on their wallet helps them ensure that they will keep in check a part of them that could go wild. There is a pervasiveness to these qualities. They might be rigid and lacking in creativity and playfulness in more than one area of their lives. They might be strict and structured in their spending, but perhaps also at work, where some of these qualities might play in their favor, depending on their choice of profession.

Early parental experiences influence whether we grow up to be adults that are overly preoccupied with control. It seems that a combination of *emotionally* withholding parents and parents that were particularly controlling themselves—stifling the development of a healthy learning environment in which mistakes were allowed, exploration encouraged, creativity fostered—might result in the development of these tendencies. Things need to be done the right way. The child becomes fearful and avoidant of making a mess. The focus is on following the rules, being the good, obedient child. Structure and rigidity become ingrained and a good defense against being told off or punished. Displays of negative emotions may annoy the parent: There is no tolerance for the child's anger, greed, or sadness. They are told they are acting like a spoiled child, being needy, or even selfish for expressing their feelings. No wonder, then, that they would become focused on performance, detail-oriented and very demanding of themselves. They inherit and apply the high standards that were set for them and internalize them as an inner critic. They punish themselves for having negative feelings that, rather than being allowed, remain unexpressed or worse, suppressed and unrecognized.

Ultimately, however, what they are unable to do is be accepting of their messy parts, be it their negative feelings or their imperfections. They carry around a sense of shame about these aspects of themselves in a way that a child who has had parents that could tolerate errors, negative emotions, and vulnerabilities wouldn't.

So why don't they spend? The self-denying spender may be controlling their desire to spend because they are afraid that by opening the floodgate, getting in touch with their desire will lead into an out of control, insatiable desire for more. The phantasy is that the needy parts of them are bad. They are greedy parts that would make them into the disappointing child that was being selfish. So, to be safe, need is denied. It is better not to eat than to face the shame of eating ravenously. It is better not to spend than to face the shame of one's greed.

According to Freud, many of those who are so preoccupied with frugality and diligence were actually trying to repress and defend against their desire to be the opposite. Their desire to let go and indulge, be messy, reckless, wasteful (the defense called "reaction formation," adopting an attitude opposite to a desire deemed unacceptable).[6] No wonder, then, that many oscillate between self-denying and binging, or in money terms, between overspending and underspending. One person says, "My spending, for the most part, mimics my eating habits. When I'm in a binge eating [. . .] cycle, I'm [. . .] more likely to go online shopping. When I'm restricting, I have to justify every single item on my shopping list, and will not buy something (even kinda essentials) if my brain thinks it's expensive for what it is."[7] Money is just a symbolic object that, like food, gets used to acting out our ambivalence about giving in to our deepest and darkest desires on the one hand, and withholding, controlling, being good on the other. Sometimes it is a real fear of our desires (the "opening the can of worms" fear), but other times we just fail to regulate how much we allow ourselves to have (maybe because of bad examples growing up—with an indulging or overly restrictive parent).

There are a lot of overlaps in the reasons I have given for self-denying. Ultimately, there is a critical part of us that stops us from enjoying what we could have. And in therapy, one can begin to, with time, work on developing a sense of worthiness so that having can feel possible. It's also about recognizing and integrating in our sense of self all parts of us, even the ones we deem least acceptable (like the greedy, needy, envious parts). If we come to accept them as human and ordinary, we are less likely to have to hold on to defenses that make us keep them tightly under control. If we accept them as part of us that can be managed, we don't have to take the moral high ground: "We are the proud frugal and everyone else being indulging, excessive, wasteful beings." As we learn that all parts of us are acceptable and we are lovable despite having occasional negative feelings, the world stops being seen as so black and white and good and bad. It becomes multidimensional, as does our perception of ourselves.

Wealth shame and survivor's guilt

Behind self-denial may also be a shame about the wealth one has. It is hard for some people to enjoy what they have if it is so much more than what their family and friends had/have. It may, unconsciously, feel like a betrayal and this gets in the way of its enjoyment (I will come back to this in the self-sabotage chapter). What we avoid is feeling guilty if we allowed ourselves to bask in the newfound financial freedom: What would *they* say? What would that *make us*?

In the traditional sense, survivor's guilt[8] is a set of symptoms experienced by victims of a trauma in which they survived, but others were harmed. The term was first coined by psychoanalyst William Niederland who, in the 1960s, observed that many Holocaust survivors experienced feelings of guilt for having survived when others didn't. An overwhelming sense of guilt, but also feelings of helplessness, regret, even depression, are among the symptoms of survivor's guilt. The pseudo-survivor's guilt we are discussing here doesn't necessarily link to one traumatic event, or cause headaches and flashbacks. However, the principle is similar: "Why should I have so much, when they couldn't/didn't?" The self-denial is a way of coping with the guilt of having survived the financial hardships that others endured. We now have the money, but we don't allow ourselves to enjoy it because *they* had to go without it (our parents, friends, in the present or the past).

When it comes to people who themselves survived famines, wars, or extreme economic crises, they may retain some of the behaviors and habits from back then, of which one is not spending, holding back, saving every penny and may develop new, obsessional habits as a coping mechanism for the post-traumatic fears of being found, yet again, in a situation outside their control. Plenty of studies have shown the link between trauma and the development of obsessive tendencies. Some of the tendencies that are developed (like withholding money behaviors) may get transmitted across generations either directly (because we often imitate behaviors we see in our parents and this has a ripple effect on future generations) or indirectly (what gets passed on, unconsciously, is the guilt).

Hetty Green was a businesswoman who became one of the richest women in the US during the Gilded Age (an era of rapid economic growth, spanning from 1870 to 1900). She was known to be one of the world's greatest misers. From the age of eight, when she opened her first bank account, until the day she died, seventy-three years later, Hetty Green pinched every dollar of her immense fortune.[9] Hetty's youngest brother (her only sibling) died as an infant, leaving her as the sole heir to a colossal empire based in the whaling business. Maybe for her too there was survivor's guilt. It was his death that allowed her to be heir to such fortune and when her father died, she inherited a large sum of money and became consumed by fear that she would be assassinated for her wealth. As a therapist I wonder if in her young mind she felt a certain sense of culpability for her brother's death and, as an adult, she projected those thoughts on to others who (in her mind) could be potential murderers for the sake of money.

But as we saw in previous sections (with the example of Warren Buffett), the combination of an early trauma, an emotionally withdrawn mother, the trauma of being sent to boarding school at age ten, and a father with an explosive character[10] could all have contributed to the creation of an anxious person, holding on dearly to every penny in the face of emotional deprivation. Mixed into that a Quaker upbringing (valuing humility and equality), and we can see how multiple factors might have contributed to the development of her extreme self-denial.

And to reinforce the point I made earlier: Hetty was actually a philanthropist. It was her own pleasure she couldn't indulge. The struggle with not spending money was mostly limited to her own self and family but it didn't impact her generosity.

Feelings of guilt about money may also be evoked by inherited wealth. We might feel like we didn't earn it and so, rather than enjoy it, we let it sit untouched in a bank account (hoping the money—or the guilt of having it—will go away, or at the very least protect us from feelings of guilt about having it). In families where self-made parents worked hard and took pride in the struggle and determination that resulted in their success, children might feel a combination of guilt and insecurity with regard to inheritance because it came too easily. Alongside the sense that it isn't earned money, they haven't had the confidence-building experiences that the parents had and so not only do they struggle spending it out of guilt, but they are also afraid of managing it. Would they make poor choices? Mismanage it? And if they did, would they ever have the skills and confidence to earn it back? Full of anxieties, they sometimes choose to leave it untouched—neither investing nor enjoying it. Money becomes a symbol of their inadequacy.

Withholding—when we don't give

A fear of closeness

When stinginess is relational it's worth wondering what happens in your internal world when you give something up for the sake of others. Often, there is a sense of vulnerability, of feeling exposed or even left at the mercy of the other. We might fear that giving leaves us open to the possibility that the other will come back and overwhelm us with their needs and demands. We might go as far as worrying that others will be parasitic or exploitative, depending on what experiences we have had in past relationships.

We may defend against these fears by withholding emotionally and withholding with money, trying to preserve a sense of autonomy and independence. If we don't give, we avoid the potential of financial intercourse, of a potential dynamic of giving and receiving. It could be a reflection of a more general tendency to avoid closeness and intimacy with others.

These fears may manifest at various levels of consciousness: Someone who has been quite literally robbed or exploited financially by a former partner will be very aware of their fear as they enter new relationships. Their reluctance to give, to share, may well be based on very real and recent experiences of having been taken advantage of.

Some people raised in wealth approach relationships with a fear that the other will be uninterested in anything more than their money and suspicious of their motives. Suspicion and mistrust are the position from which they approach first encounters. Psychoanalyst Charles Wahl heard from a rich patient, "I have all my life been used to people viewing me as a resource, a symbol, rather than a person. I learned early to pick up the greed and the resentment in their eyes. This always had a great deal to do with my cynical mistrust of everyone."[11]

But we are not always so aware of our fear of exploitation, and there are more obscure and deep-seated reasons why we may be using money to keep a distance from the other. Going back to attachment theory, what often results in avoidantly attached children (those who set up relationships seeking independence are reluctant to trust and rely on others) are experiences of emotional neglect: parents who are either not physically present or emotionally unavailable. This may include parents who are both physically and emotionally withholding (they might not express their love verbally or through affection and physical touch).

A series of dismissals (we are busy, we don't have time to play and engage with the child) may feel like rejections. A parent's anxiety may lead to repeated experiences of misattunement. All of these external interactions will influence the child's ability to connect with others and feel secure in relationships.

But fearing closeness could also be a result of having felt smothered, having had early experiences of relationships feeling claustrophobic, overwhelming. Overprotective parenting can leave the child feeling engulfed and even controlled. We grow up fearing that our future relationships will be like our past ones and so we keep a distance, we make sure that we have enough space to avoid ever feeling like that again.

But what about the person who generally insists on keeping finances very separate, who doesn't like giving gifts to their partner, nor do they treat them to anything even though, financially, they are in a position to do so? We might wonder if the withholding of money isn't being used as a barrier, a defense against enabling a relationship, opening the door to feeling potentially overwhelmed by the other.

Money can be a powerful tool to express the desire to keep a distance. Giving/gifting stands for lowering a barrier to relating, and can leave us feeling exposed. A determination to not merge bank accounts can come from the most rational and logical reasons, but it may also be about avoiding closeness. Not gifting, not giving, withholding financially are ways of building walls, of not engaging.

A power struggle

Sometimes not giving isn't out of the threat of closeness, but rather an expression of resentment or a power struggle.

Someone struggling to give to one person in particular (like a partner), might be expressing, through money, their discontent about the balance of giving/receiving in their relationship. We might feel angry with the other because something we dislike has been imposed on us. It could be that we are suddenly forced to pay rent to our parents, or we discovered infidelity and feel cheated by the other. It could be that our partner hasn't been sexually available and so our reaction might be to be less giving with them financially. So being the opposite of generous with them is our way of protesting, of claiming something back. When the stinginess is targeted to one person in particular it is worth asking: What makes it so hard to give to *them* specifically? What are we trying to tell them by withholding gifts, or refusing to share a bill, or expecting *them* to pay?

These feelings may not belong to the present but be ghosts from the past (it might be how your past relationships have been), and even though the person you are with now is kind, giving and generous, you might still operate with those same dynamics in mind, applying the old rule of "don't give too much or you might end up feeling robbed." If, for example, your family was plagued by power struggles, you might have inherited a reluctance to give too much away if in your mind what you are effectively giving up is power. The fear here is that you might end up feeling vulnerable and powerless as a result. You find comfort when the balance is tipped in your favor as if the only way to feel emotionally safe is to receive more than you give.

* * *

For every person, what happens in their internal stage as a result of withholding is different. Some might have had few experiences of parental or authority figures expressing gratitude so they have learned this behavior; they might have had sadistic parental figures taking pleasure in depriving them so they repeat this with others, enjoying depriving others or becoming exploitative; or parents who were manipulative and exploitative—always focusing on their own gain, with little regard for the other. But the point is that in their past relationships, pleasure in giving wasn't modeled. Instead, parents (or figures in authority) set up relationships that were predatory, or in which one person gained power at the expense of the other.

Yet others might be trying to establish or preserve a sense of superiority by projecting onto the waiter/waitress the feelings of inferiority when leaving a tip (they are unconsciously expelling these feelings and letting the other person feel them instead). It might be what you do in relationships: You leave the other wanting, waiting, longing, because you derive a reassurance of control and power over them. People who see relationships as a zero-sum game, in which there is always a winner and a loser, are prone to be less giving, in my experience. Rather than seeing giving as a mutually enriching experience, they see it as "if you gain, I lose." Ultimately, they are expressing a deep ambivalence about relationships: There is little to be gained from giving. "Every man for himself" is the unspoken mantra in their minds.

* * *

I hope I have convinced you of the big psychological differences between being greedy, being self-denying, or being withholding. If you think you are an underspender then the first step is to understand if your struggle is a general difficulty letting go of money (which could very well be linked to greed and anxiety/fears about not having enough money). If those don't resonate, then ask yourself which things/people/events it feels easier to spend on and which feel more problematic and guilt-inducing. That will already give you a clue about whether you are classifying expenses in your mind and what that might mean. Then think about how you feel when you deprive yourself of things. Is it pride? Is it shame? It's worth unpacking whether there is a part of you that believes that not spending is more noble than allowing yourself to have good things. And then explore other areas in your life in which you might be displaying similar behaviors/thoughts/feelings: Are you in general a person that lives on the bare minimum of everything? You don't allow yourself to have more food, friends, experiences, etc. What fears come up for you if you imagine giving yourself permission to spend more money?

If spending on others is what you find most challenging then try to picture a theater and what goes on in each character's mind when something is withheld (for example, it's Valentine's Day and you didn't get anything for your partner. You know they will show up with a box of chocolates. You still don't get them anything). What would the thinking cloud-like vignette read for each character's minds? It might be revealing to uncover what goes on in your mind (as the withholding one) and what you imagine the other person feels and thinks as a result of the dynamic you have set up. The next question I ask is: Does this dynamic sound familiar?

Chapter 5

Self-sabotage: why we get in our own way

It's hard to watch people who we consider sensible make a mess of their financial situation. Why can't they stop and think about their finances, and make a plan? Why do they fall short of success every time? Why are they still so reliant on others for money? Why do they get into debt? Carl Jung, psychiatrist, psychoanalyst, and the founder of analytical psychology, said that "people will do anything, no matter how absurd, to avoid facing their own souls."[1] When we watch people self-destruct financially or sit passively while their finances deteriorate, it seems absurd indeed. But as Jung points out, there is often a psychological explanation for our bizarre behaviors. Emotions like anger, guilt, and shame that are too difficult to face are stewing in our unconscious, insidiously contaminating our choices.

A traditional definition of self-sabotage is behavior that interferes with our success and well-being. Some definitions use the word "action" but it's important to emphasize that often it is *in*action that could be damaging, and this is particularly relevant when considering financial self-sabotage.

It's rational to want one's financial situation to remain stable, or improve, rather than deteriorate. If we are acting in a way that goes against that, it begs the question: Why are we doing it? And how did we get here?

Is someone who incurs financial losses self-sabotaging? Not necessarily (even though repeated financial failures would invite some investigation). For a behavior to qualify as self-sabotage there needs to be an element of agency about our fate. However baffling it may seem, people enable the sabotage. For example, procrastinating preparation for a job interview; failing to ask for a well-deserved raise; continuing to invest in a failing venture; not opening our bank statements for months—these are all clearly risky/damaging behaviors that we could change, but denial, fear, and other potential feelings get in the way of acting in our self-interest. Our business failing because of an economic crisis whose impact we did everything to avoid is clearly not self-sabotage. So an element of agency is important.

The other important factor to consider is knowledge or financial literacy. As I mentioned in the introduction, there are many people who make financial decisions without understanding basic financial concepts. You might decide to invest all your savings and pension in one stock because you genuinely believe it is a good idea. You might not know of the benefits of investment diversification (not putting all your eggs in one basket), you might not understand much about how macroeconomic and market factors could impact the value of your stock (investor sentiment about the whole industry). If you are unaware of this financial knowledge when it comes to investing, for example, you could be making what you think is the best choice with your money (and thus not self-sabotaging).

It's OK to hold different views on risk (to me it feels like a safe bet) and we might all make different choices when it comes to that. However, when reckless bets are a pattern and are made by someone who understands enough about what they are doing, it might be helpful to investigate what is happening—especially if their choices are repeatedly not paying off.

Finally, as we try to spot self-sabotage, *patterns* are useful to consider. Forgetting to pay our taxes once can be a genuine mistake; we might have been stressed by other commitments, but when it happens twice or three times, it is worth wondering what is getting in the way, unconsciously, of keeping this deadline in mind.

One subset of self-sabotage is when we interfere with our success when it is within reach. Psychoanalyst David Krueger describes the person who is working diligently while success or a completed achievement seems to be at a safe distance, but as the goal is approached, he becomes anxious and sabotages efforts at successfully achieving that goal or, just after achieving success, depreciates the achievement or the enjoyment of it.[2] Ruining the enjoyment of the accomplishment can be an emotional way in which we sabotage our success, and it can be harmful to our well-being even if the financial (or other) objective has been accomplished.

Things are rarely black and white, so self-sabotage is not easy to identify. You might have a sense that you are setting yourself up somehow but not much of an idea as to why you do it, and the reasons may be multiple too. So if an educated investor is clinging stubbornly to one stock, with no back-up plan we might wonder: Is this a part of them that clings anxiously to things? Are they afraid of making financial choices in general so they just make one (pick one stock) and avoid more? Have they idealized the owner of the company for some particular reason (in their minds they represent the confident and fearless boss/father they wish they'd had)? Or are they setting themselves up for failure, hoping to be rescued by someone? In other words, it's worth looking into potential emotional contaminants in their decision-making process.

Opening your mind to the possibility that you might not be doing what's best for you, with also a curiosity as to why that might be, is the only way to begin to unpack what lies beneath.

Self-sabotage behaviors

I think it's useful to consider the breadth of behaviors that could fall under financial self-sabotage. Let's start with actions. Overspending can be a form of self-sabotage; taking on a lot of debt or risk; gambling; investing carelessly; rushing into financial choices without doing much due diligence. At the extreme end there is financial domination.

Why have I split overspending and self-sabotage into separate chapters? Isn't overspending just another form of self-sabotage? Overspending may be detrimental to one's finances, mental health, and relationships, but the psychological *purpose* of the overspending is not necessarily that of seeking harm. It is about fulfilling a need, or attracting admiration, or feeling lovable and desirable or self-sufficient. Overspending is a form of self-sabotage when the unconscious drive behind it is destructive: a part of us sees a psychological benefit in failure.

Sometimes *in*action can be financially self-destructive. We might avoid checking on our finances, leave debts to accumulate, money uninvested, or delegate all finances to our partner without giving ourselves any chance to input and express our desires or objectives. These are all forms of self-sabotage which can interfere with our financial well-being.

People may avoid acting out of fear or as a way to self-sabotage. What is the inertia/delegation/avoidance achieving? If we use financial failure as a defense against our feelings—like our fear of being autonomous, our fear of taking over the family business, our shame about having inherited the money and not earned it—then it's self-sabotage. Consciously or unconsciously, we hope that *failure* will get us what we want (or get us out of what we don't want).

Many of the people I see in therapy are trying to achieve their full potential as human beings, but something gets in the way. They feel stuck. They know what they need to do to improve their finances (start budgeting, stop wasting money, stop playing risky games), but they just don't understand why they can't bring themselves to do it. Something feels difficult to unpack or decipher. Common questions are "Why does this keep happening to me?"; "Why is it so hard to do what I know is best?"; "Why do I get in my own way?"

I found that, broadly speaking, there are three predominant feelings that drive self-sabotage:

- Guilt and shame
- Anger and resentment
- Fear

You might find that there is more than one factor at play in any one example of self-sabotage. But looking at each separately may help unpack what might be going on for the person stuck in these unhelpful and self-harming patterns that interfere with their financial well-being.

Guilt and shame

Money is a dirty pursuit

Entrepreneur Dorothée Loorbach told a TEDx audience about her experience of losing all her money: "I was raised in a way to believe that money is not important. And I inherited this conviction somehow [. . .] that people with money are not nice people. So when I had money, I would spend it as soon as I could."

It was as if ridding herself of money was her way of addressing her inner belief that money corrupts people.[3]

Some people regard money as a dirty pursuit (Freud himself referred to money as "filthy lucre").[4] They may be quite conscious and vocal about these beliefs. Yet others may hold these beliefs unconsciously, as relics of the past that manifest as a sense of guilt associated with financial success. Our feelings are not always easy to decipher, nor are they definite and we might both want and not want something; we feel two opposite feelings at once. Ambivalence is a common human state, but it can lead to internal conflicts that are hard to manage and leave us experiencing anxiety and a sense of stuckness that I have seen all too often in relation to money. Even though a part of us is aware of our need or even desire for money, another may be very conflicted about it because of what money and "the rich" represent in our minds. The more we are aware of the ambivalence that sits beneath the surface, the more choice we have about what we do with it and the less likely we are to act it out by unconsciously orchestrating a sabotage.

I have heard people qualify the desire for money as superficial, bad, and dirty. We know that these associations come from money lessons learned at home, along with other environmental influences.

As we explored in chapter 3, greed is condemned by many religions and political movements. Imagine a child raised in a socialist family that vocally condemned the pursuit of financial success. Core values in the family were humility, generosity, and finding happiness in a modest lifestyle. Now, age 22, they are trying to move up the ladder in a corporate banking job. At one level, they never agreed with the family views. Unconsciously they harbored a desire for wealth, envy of those who could enjoy the pleasures money can buy and wanted that for themselves. It could be difficult, psychologically, to hold these contrasting views in mind. A part of them might enjoy, feel pride, defend their ambition, while another part might harbor guilt or even shame about what their ambition says about them. Have they become the disparaged, greedy capitalist that father used to criticize? I have seen this internal arm-wrestle so often. If you haven't had a chance to really think about the internal conflict that you face, to jettison your family's beliefs and build your own sense of what feels right, you might be stuck with your ambivalence about financial pursuits and employ all sorts of unhelpful behavior to address these feelings.

People might resolve conflict in various ways and some eventually manage to either let go of their parents' beliefs or endorse them fully. Those who let go of the parents' beliefs do so by articulating and accepting their own, different views of money and success and choosing to continue to pursue their goals.

Financial self-sabotage is one way in which guilt gets expressed, unconsciously. They might make a big mistake at work, or invest the fruits of their work carelessly, their ambition might suddenly fade without them understanding why. Others might have been raised with religious views that directly influence how the pursuit of financial success is represented in their mind. The Bible is not short of condemnation of money. St. Paul wrote (in 1 Timothy 6:10): "For the love of money is a root of all kinds of evils. It is through this craving that some have wandered away from the faith and pierced themselves with many pangs" (sorrows). Or "It is easier for a camel to go through the eye of a needle, than for a rich man to enter the kingdom of God" (Matthew 19:21–26)[5] implying that the pursuit of riches is inevitably linked to sinful behavior. How literally these messages are taken, how reinforced these teachings are by the family and the society one is raised in will vary. But they are lessons often taught at a young and impressionable age and if they resonate with similar teachings at home (like family members taking pride in deprivation or criticizing the wealthy), they can have a lasting impact. If condemnation of money and praise for self-sacrifice are being taught but also modeled by those around us, it must follow that its pursuit is an evil affair.

Growing up in a family in which wealthier others were criticized, judged for their choices, where there is a narrative of us versus them can have an impact on our experience of wealth. "Look at how much *they* spend on holidays, it's ridiculous!" "Do they think they are so important with their fancy cars?" "Money just makes them entitled and rude." Contempt for wealth will leave an imprint that is hard to shake when we find ourselves in the position to be able to make those so-criticized choices. Money may have a representation in our minds as something that *spoils* the other, making them less ethical and less moral. You can imagine the shame that joining their club evokes. Of course, parents might simply have been defending against their envy of what others had when they made those statements or even been trying to teach important lessons about finding happiness in life outside the pursuit of material belongings, but what the child might absorb is a denunciation of wealth.

It isn't just childhood experiences that taint our view of money. There are professions that have been traditionally seen as a vocation and where compensation has been an underemphasized element of the work, out of a fear of being perceived as greedy or insufficiently committed to the greater purpose of the role. Having seen artists, sculptors, and writers in my therapy room, I can tell you that money to many creatives is a coin with two sides. On the one hand it offers the validation and credibility the creative longs for (they can finally call themselves a professional artist/writer and be taken seriously by the people who matter to them—be it skeptical family members or the art world audience itself). But money can also be seen to limit the creative person's freedom or even go against the principle that art should be made for art's sake.

Artist Andy Warhol was probably one of the few exceptions. He was controversial in the art world for his love of money and his shameless embracing of his art as a commercial product. He called his art "business art" and his studio a "factory." From a poor family, Warhol seemed to value the power of money and so he pursued it openly, inspiring future artists like Damien Hirst, who said, "Andy Warhol was the first artist who made it OK for artists to earn money."[6]

One of the best examples of artists' ambivalent stance toward money is the anonymous street artist Banksy. At a Sotheby's auction in 2018, once the gavel hit the sound block and his famous work *Girl with Balloon* sold for $1.4 million, he activated a system that shredded* the work of art in front of a shocked audience. The buyer then faced a choice: Would he still purchase it (even if it had been half shredded?). They did, and the shredded work was renamed *Love Is in the Bin*.

It raised a lot of questions about what art is and where its value really lies. It was a provocative act, no doubt, but for us it raises the question, was it sabotage or subterfuge? He destroyed the work (and could have potentially destroyed its financial value) as a way of condemning the commoditization of art. Maybe for him (as the title suggests) art = love and money interferes with the equation by sending any love of art to the trash once a monetary value is attached to it. So maybe money has somehow negated art's value by putting a price on its destruction. To the point, *Love Is in the Bin* sold for over $25 million by Sotheby's a few years later in 2021.

Carl Richards, a financial planner and sketch artist, wrote about his ambivalence about making money from art. He was only able to cope with the mixed feelings by seeing the profit from one project as funding for the next one. It's a healthier coping strategy than self-sabotage, of course, but it begs the question: What's wrong with seeing your work as valuable and worthy of a reward?

---

* Banksy released a video declaring his intention was to shred the work fully, but that it was a fault in the mechanism that only allowed half the work to shred.

Richards says that once he found this new way of looking at profit, "meetings with my accountant and reconciling my books ceased to feel like dirty chores to be done by an unwashed heathen."[7] It highlights how difficult it is for artists sometimes to reconcile their work with the realities of earning a living without feeling polluted somehow by money.

If unconsciously we view money as a corrupting, evil, or a dirty pursuit, what chance do we stand of allowing ourselves to have it?

Success anxiety and imposter syndrome

Sometimes even hard-earned money becomes wrapped up with negative emotions about being wealthy and having more than friends or family have or ever had. The emotional discomfort of having and enjoying the money is dealt with, unconsciously, by mismanaging it, spending it, or even losing it. Although many of us want to make our parents proud and might showcase our achievements in the hope of finding admiration and giving them relief that they succeeded in their parenting, others experience it like a betrayal. Freud had himself already suggested that there could be something unconsciously quite problematic with the idea of success because in the mind it can be interpreted as a symbolic surpassing of our father, and therefore become wrapped up with feelings of guilt or even fear of retaliation. Sabotaging success, in Freud's view, was a way to avoid Father's anger or even punishment. Having himself struggled with guilt after an achievement he wondered why and wrote: "It must be that a sense of guilt was attached to the satisfaction in having gone such a long way: There was something about it that was wrong, that from earliest times had been forbidden. [. . .] It seems as though the essence of success was to have got further than one's father, and as though to excel one's father was still something forbidden."[8]

All these elements can be at play not just when we have experienced a financial windfall but even when we are trying to succeed financially, or maybe are even on the cusp of doing so and are overcome by success anxiety, essentially a fear of how others will respond to our success (which Freud would pinpoint to a fear of parental retribution). Psychiatrist and psychoanalyst Ann Ruth Turkel cites a case study of a man who was terrified of success as it evoked feelings of guilt and unworthiness. He felt particularly guilty at the thought of earning more money than his father. He often dreamed that he was an imposter about to be denounced by a stronger, larger man.[9]

Along with fear, there is the guilt and shame that comes if success is achieved, even if partially. It starts with guilt about having something good. It can quickly turn into a sense of shame. "What does enjoying this money say about me?" But then, people may begin to feel guilty even about their feelings: "Why can't I be happy and grateful for having so much?" or "Why can't I just be happy about it?" They feel guilty about feeling guilty and so on. The key to exiting this negative cycle is to understand and manage the guilt and shame that are associated with having it in the first place. Does it hook into a part of them that always felt unentitled to good things (I feel guilty because I don't deserve it)? Does it hook into memories and attributes they have internalized about what wealthy people are (I feel ashamed because having money now makes me into the greedy and selfish person that I am critical of)?

It is interesting to note that the man in Turkel's case study had a father who always disparaged the rich and this had in part influenced this man's feelings of guilt in relation to now being one of those rich people. But what I wanted to focus on here is the sense that he was an imposter, which is not an unusual phenomenon in people who get in their own way.

Imposter syndrome is essentially a form of self-doubt that is achievement-proof. No matter what they accomplish, people with imposter syndrome cannot own their successes and have very imaginative ideas about what might have resulted in them succeeding (from pure luck to a mistake in the award process or coincidences—anything but their own abilities). People with imposter syndrome are convinced that others have an exaggerated perception of their skills and fear that they will be exposed. In a sense, they harbor an unconscious fear that demands will be made of them that they cannot fulfill. They are afraid of being overvalued, overestimated, of promising more than they can deliver.

What people with imposter syndrome often do is downplay their achievements. It's (financially at least) a relatively innocuous coping strategy ("I will make it seem like an insignificant achievement, so people don't look too closely into it and find out that I am an imposter"). But when the person with imposter syndrome uses self-sabotage as a defense ("I will stop myself short of achieving so I don't have to feel like an imposter or be exposed as one"), it becomes a self-fulfilling prophecy with dire consequences. We might miss out on real opportunities to act in our best interest to confirm our view of the world: that we are incapable.

There are a number of potential causes of imposter syndrome, but it is common to find it in children whose parents overly praised them (especially if this was for their accomplishments), thus leaving little room for the child to be accepting of their bad parts. Instead of having a balanced view of ourselves as ordinary human beings with strengths and weaknesses, with positive feelings and negative feelings, we grow up working tirelessly to preserve our parents' image of us as perfect, amazing. At some level, however, we are conscious of the other side of us (our negative feelings, our faults). Instead of these being an integrated part of our self-image, and as an alternative to the narcissist who denies any imperfections or projects them on to other people, we go through life feeling like an imposter. It's a psychological reconciliation of (or answer to) this dissonance—we are not what the world sees as perfect and amazing because actually we have fooled them all, we are an imposter.

Parents who were overly critical might have a similar impact. David Krueger describes a client, Jack, who started his own computer sales company and experienced debilitating anxiety as he became more successful. In therapy, Jack spoke about having very punitive parents who were frustrated with his "stupidity" and inability to achieve the best grades they demanded. He developed a self-image of someone incapable and lazy. As an increasingly successful entrepreneur he began to feel like an imposter: His business success didn't match with his self-belief.[10] So here again, imposter syndrome becomes a psychological explanation for the dissonance between the image we/others have of us (Jack being useless) and the reality of our achievements, and the only way both can be true is that the achievements were pure luck. As Jack was in therapy, he didn't resort to self-sabotage to confirm his view of himself as useless. In therapy he was able to deal with the fear of surpassing his father and mourn the identity he had built in his mind, in order to develop a true sense of self.

The American psychologist Matina Horner in 1969 suggested an alternative explanation for fear of success specifically in women, which has come to be known as the "Horner effect." In her experiments, she found that when it came to success, women's anxieties were rooted in an often unconscious internal conflict: On the one hand they wanted and pursued success, but at another level they feared the consequences of it. Women felt that displaying ambition was unfeminine. In her view, going against societal expectations of gender roles evoked fears of being criticized and isolated. Horner found that these beliefs were not just held by women but men too. When asked to describe successful women for Horner's research, male law students characterized successful women as unattractive, unpopular, unfeminine, merely a "computer," and overaggressive.[11] The more able and achievement-oriented women were, the higher their fear of succeeding and the worse they performed as a result of this fear. Horner suggested that women sometimes allow their fears of what needs to be given up as a result of success to get in the way and sabotage their efforts.

Horner was writing in the 1960s and in recent years in Western societies, gender stereotypes have been challenged. But the gender gap in leadership roles and pay is still there. In the US, according to a paper published in 2022 by the National Bureau of Economic Research, women in executive roles earn 26 percent less than men. The pay gap falls to 15 percent after accounting for the characteristics of the executive (including experience, education, and age).[12] According to the Office for National Statistics, the median pay gap between men and women has been around 8 to 9 percent over the past five years. Women working in finance earn, on average, 22 percent less than their male colleagues.[13]

The reasons are undoubtedly complex, but one of the many possible contributing factors may be our unconscious stereotypes (which often are passed on from our parents' generation) of what roles a man and a woman should occupy in society. It might sound absurd, in this century, to say out loud that it is unfeminine for a woman to be financially more successful than her husband (especially in a society where couples may be of the same sex), but the reality is that still today, I hear men admitting to feeling emasculated by their wife earning more than them or women associating a perceived lack of virility, potency, power in their male partner because of their financial shortcomings. If a woman at some level holds a view (or imagines others do) that money = power = masculinity, then it might be hard for her to really embrace achievement. And of course, if pursuing financial success also involves practically sacrificing their participation in traditional nurturing and child-caring roles, this can add to the ambivalence. In other words, the anxiety stems from the inner conflict. Can I be feminine (in the way I and society understand femininity), a good mother (in the way I and society define it), and pursue (financial) success?

It would be wrong to assume that there is nothing uncomfortable about being successful and making money. For some people it's what they want (at one level) but what they most fear too. Achieving financial success or a wealthy status could be so fraught with anxieties and can evoke such irrational insecurities that unconsciously orchestrating a way to rid ourselves of it feels like a psychologically safe plan, a good defense. Of course, our rational mind can understand that confronting our fears and anxieties might be a less destructive solution.

Masochism: when we feel we deserve punishment

Self-sabotage can take on perverse forms. When I began to investigate people's relationship with money, I was initially surprised to come across "findom," which is an abbreviation for financial domination. This term refers to a practice of voluntarily engaging in a relationship governed by money in which one is powerless and the other person holds all the power.

Before I started working with people who struggle with findom addiction, I read countless blogs in an effort to get my head around it. Common statements were "I am excited at the idea of someone treating me like their money slave" or "I am turned on when she calls me a money pig and demands I pay her."

The most common form of findom is one in which the dominating partner is a woman and the submissive (in this case financially submissive) is a man. But findom also happens in homosexual dynamics. The dominant party (known as "findomme," "goddess," "money dom," "money mistress," "cash-master") demands money usually in a denigrating and humiliating way. The submissive party (known as "cash piggy," "finsub," "human

ATM," "money slave" or "paypig") complies, obeys, even completely relinquishes control of finances to the dominant party and obtains a sense of psychological release from this dynamic. The very names are indicative of the idealization of the dominant party and the denigration of the submissive. Sexual exchange is not necessarily part of a findom dynamic. What the submissive is essentially buying is an experience of domination and powerlessness. Moneydommes advertise themselves online and the two parties usually don't meet face-to-face but rather online.

What is interesting about findom is that it engages another in the sabotage. It is effectively self-sabotage with an accomplice. Why am I not calling it abuse then? Because the person seeking out findom is voluntarily doing so. But the lines are gray when it comes to the element of choice and control that findom users have. It is not uncommon for people to seek out findom under the influence of drugs, which debilitate their ability to make rational choices. When this is taken advantage of, on the other side, by someone who has essentially been granted consent to quite literally rob them, it is a disastrous combination.

It is probably the most extreme form of self-sabotage: What is being sought out and fetishized is financial destruction. It is destructive, but there is pleasure in the pain of being robbed and humiliated, making it a masochistic behavior. The *Psychodynamic Diagnostic Manual* explains that "'Masochism' is not a unitary construct. The term has been used to refer to a range of phenomena that have different psychological origins and serve different psychological functions, with the common denominator of an apparent (unconscious) investment in suffering."[14] Essentially, suffering and pleasure are inextricably linked. Money is just another medium through which we act out all sorts of unconscious desires—including those of relinquishing total control and power to someone else.

Money in these dynamics represents power. Why do they relinquish it? What is psychologically appealing about giving it (power/money) all up? What does this form of self-destruction accomplish? What early experiences or phantasies may be behind the desire for such a self-destructive dynamic?

In an interview, a financial dominatrix states, "There are two main types of people who enjoy this. One is the guy who craves being abused. He likes to be ridiculed or to feel used. Having someone take your money from you can be humiliating and make you suffer and struggle. The other type is the macho, 'dominating in real life' kind of man. He's stressed out from making business decisions, running a business, and being the one in charge all the time. He really gets off on being vulnerable once in a while and having someone else take charge. It's like a vacation for him."[15] What this findom is picking up on are the differences between someone who is ring-fencing the relinquishment of control to these interactions and otherwise operates from a more empowered place in their day-to-day life, and someone whose submissive attitude permeates all aspects of their life. Although their presentation might be different, ultimately both types of people are finding pleasure engaging in a dynamic in which they are disempowered and humiliated.

Psychoanalyst Emmanuel Ghent wrote: "Masochistic phenomena have often been traced to deprivation, traumata and developmental interferences suffered in the early [. . .] years."[16] Trauma, neglect, and abuse can leave someone full of anger, and even hate. Freud[17] spoke of the internal psychological processes through which we might, in our minds, attack the bad, abandoning object (a proxy for "other"). We might harbor phantasies of retaliating, attacking those who failed us and feel intolerable guilt as a result. Can we bear the reality of our anger or aggressive thoughts? Or do we live life unconsciously believing we deserve punishment? Seeking suffering may alleviate the unbearable guilt we carry around. Findom is one way of seeking punishment, but as we saw in this chapter, there are several ways in which we might self-sabotage because ultimately, that's what we feel we deserve: pain and loss.

In a study of children with a disorganized attachment style[18]—describing children who, as a result of trauma, abuse, or neglect, feel insecure in relationships: They both crave them and are fearful of them—psychologist Jude Cassidy found that they were more likely to describe themselves as intrinsically evil. This is partly because our early relationships are based on identification, so a relationship with a bad other makes us, through identification, bad ourselves. But Ronald Fairbairn[19] added another explanation. He said that it is so intolerable for children to have a relationship with a "bad object" that psychologically they would rather accept a reality in which they themselves are bad and the other is good. It's as if, Fairbairn explains, the child seems to want to purge [the abusive other] of their badness, and, in proportion as he succeeds in doing so, he is rewarded by that sense of security which an environment of good objects so characteristically confers. He tells us: "It is better to be a sinner in a world ruled by God than to live in a world ruled by the Devil,"[20] suggesting that when we have painful traumatic experiences, blaming ourselves for being the bad and culpable one is a psychological defense that protects us from the scarier prospect of living in an unsafe and bad world. We seek suffering to confirm and give expression to our self-loathing. We temporarily alleviate our sense of guilt because we are getting what we deserve.

Suffering may also be familiar, and as humans we are drawn to the familiar, but psychologically we have an opportunity now; instead of feeling like the helpless little child we did back then, we can finally feel in control. A psychological mechanism that Freud called "repetition compulsion" very much consists of re-creating in the present a past traumatic experience unknowingly.

The past experience is not remembered consciously but is acted out in the present. Why? Well, Freud was the first to suggest (and his successors agreed) that by repeating the trauma one was retrospectively trying to master it, or turn a passive behavior into an active one (instead of being a victim of humiliation, now you have control over seeking it and ending it).[21] Essentially, we are relinquishing control in a controlled way (because we have voluntarily engaged with it). Somehow it might feel like we are triumphing over an experience that in the past was distressing and we had no control over. Now there is a safe word that can get us out of it, or we can just shut off the chat and put an end to the suffering and humiliation.

But the relief is short-lived and the guilt comes back "three times worse" as a client once said, because now the guilt that belonged to the past is compounded with the guilt experienced in the present: The hundreds or thousands handed over to the financial dominant. Waking up from the dreamlike trance that possesses them while playing out the findom fantasy in reality, they are overwhelmed by guilt and regret for the damage they have caused themselves: "What have I done?" The financial hole gets deeper and harder to pull themselves out of. Things can quickly spiral into a cycle of destruction, guilt, more destruction, and more guilt.

Anger and resentment

Anger can so often be behind our destructive financial choices. I have seen people quite literally dig themselves into financial holes to spite their parents. Sometimes the connection between the wrecking of their finances and the anger toward the parents takes time to uncover. It might take a lot of introspection (and therapy) to bring to the surface the unconscious desire to rebel against the parents and go against their wishes and desires. I have seen this, for example, in children of parents whose obsession with work would render them unavailable to the kids. The children resented the parents' careers and carried a lot of anger for how neglected they felt. This anger turns into both a desire to define themselves in opposition to the parents ("I will never be like them"; "I don't care about money") but also in a sort of psychological revenge ("I will never give them what they want"). The child that fails to become financially independent, who quits one job after the other, whose career never takes off, who ends up spending their disposable income or even goes into debt to fund an addiction, might at some level be punishing the parents and not giving them what they expect.

Imagine those who grow up with a parent so dedicated to work and building wealth that it had a detrimental impact on their family (maybe it led to divorce, or conflict in the parental couple) and their own health. It would be no surprise if the children grow up determined to live their lives differently. The pursuit of money may be seen as the cause of a lot of unhappiness in the family. Although on the one hand making healthier lifestyle choices is important and therefore that experience might drive some very productive and positive thinking in those children, it is important that they are aware of what is driving them. There is a huge difference between wanting a healthier lifestyle than parents, with more work-life balance, versus defining oneself in opposition to the parent and embracing the anti-pursuit of wealth to spite them. It's OK to search for meaning in life through professions and activities that aren't so focused on the pursuit of money, but when this starts to become an excessively cavalier attitude toward money and eventually results in self-sabotaging behavior, we need to wonder if we are acting in our best interest or whether we are just expressing the anger of how resentful we felt back then that work and money seemed more important than looking after us; or more important than staying healthy and alive for us.

In my first session with Caleb (a man in his late twenties), it would have been easy to assume he was struggling with an overspending addiction. He told me he spent compulsively, going over his budget every month, with no pattern in his purchases, except that broadly it was spent for his enjoyment (be it on purchases of gadgets, clothes, takeout). What was consistent, however, was the amount he would overspend by. I often ask people to explain what they mean by overspending, and most people with a spending addiction struggle to answer this question. There is usually a bit of denial, mixed with shame about their habit, and so the answers usually go, "Um . . . I am not sure . . . It depends . . . I mean last month was different because . . ." Caleb, however, immediately answered, "Roughly $1,000 every month." Even though he said "roughly" his answer was delivered with such speed and confidence that it caught my attention.

I asked Caleb whether he had a sense as to why he overspent. "My father wasn't great with finances," he said right before disclosing that when he was only 18 years old, his father had put down his name against a business loan. When the business became insolvent, Caleb was left starting his working life with a huge debt to repay. Now approaching 30, he was still repaying monthly installments against this debt. Caleb had accepted the reality of this debt and had empathized with how devastated his father had been by the whole matter. I could get a sense that Caleb hadn't really allowed himself to feel and process the anger and betrayal that could have resulted from his father's choices and failure.

It all started to make more sense when I asked Caleb how much those monthly installments were. "About $1,000," he said. Aha! So Caleb overspent by almost exactly the same amount that he was repaying in debt every month. He wasn't conscious of this, but it didn't seem like a coincidence. What seemed more plausible was that this spending was almost a form of restitution—if I have to give away $1,000 because of my father, I will spend $1,000 on myself. It seemed, albeit unconsciously, a way of claiming some justice, asserting his needs, putting his foot down. But of course, a very counterproductive way of doing that.

Not treating himself through the overspending would have left him in touch with how exploited and robbed he had felt by his father and those were very difficult feelings to access, especially because he continued to work for his father's new business.

Why am I citing this example in the self-sabotage chapter? Because there was a destructive element to Caleb's behavior. Caleb seemed to be wasting money away to unconsciously address the anger and resentment that he felt about having to give $1,000 away every month toward this debt. Trying to seek restitution didn't quite work. It gave him little satisfaction, added guilt to his plate, and the original anger remained intact. While on the one hand Caleb wanted to address the spending problem, this would have meant confronting and dealing with the anger that instigated it in the first place—this was something that Caleb wasn't prepared to do (especially when the relationship with his father in the present was good enough, and his job depended on this too). He would have had to face questions like: "Am I really enjoying the money I have or digging a financial hole to compensate for how robbed of financial freedom I have felt by my father?" or "What feelings will I be left with if I didn't spend money on myself and my biggest monthly outgoing was the debt repayment?" Caleb decided not to start ongoing psychotherapy sessions.

When a debt is inherited in an expected way, in a family where the financial reality is discussed and accepted, where parents have expressed their feelings (of regret, guilt), where children have been able to talk and express their own feelings related to this, then the heirs of this debt are less likely to have to defend against their emotions about it by suppressing them and avoiding the subject altogether. In Caleb's case, the debt was the result of his father's financial failure.

I have worked with clients who struggle for a long time to accept the reality of the financial burden left to them, and work through some of the resulting feelings. When the financial burden hooks into an emotional burden (a sense that the parent didn't do their best, weren't present enough, supportive enough), the debt isn't just charged with the emotions linked to it but carries along with it the weight of everything else one is troubled with as a result of the relationship. The debt sits there in their accounts and in their minds as a symbol of what was done to them, the pain they were left with.

It can go both ways. The debt may be left lingering as proof of the parents' deficiencies or we may choose to repay it as quickly as possible as if this could help cut off the emotional ties with our disappointing family. Of course this too doesn't quite work as a defense against the feelings that sit behind the act. Repaying the debt might be helpful financially, but it won't get rid of the anger and pain related to the relationship. So when we are making the choice to either ignore our debt or pay it off prematurely (incurring prepayment penalties), we need to wonder: What's driving the choice? What are we trying to rid ourselves of by paying it off? What has debt come to represent in our minds? What emotions have constellated around it? Separating what belongs to the realities of our financial choices from what we are trying to accomplish emotionally with the debt, is an important decision that enhances our Financial Emotional Awareness and ultimately helps us make better financial decisions.

Fear

Separation anxiety and fear of autonomy

What if self-sabotage is keeping us still financially dependent on others? For many people, achieving financial independence is inhibited by emotions linked to issues of separation.

Achieving a psychological separation from our parents is a long and difficult process. It starts in infancy but is ongoing: The child develops the ability to trust that parents are still alive and keeping us in mind even if they walked off to the next room. The toddler begins to walk and wanders off away from the parent, and eventually, away to school having to trust that they will be picked up at the end of the day. It is still a challenge in adolescence as we begin to create a life more and more present outside the home and prepare to potentially move into a separate home.

Separation becomes ever more difficult if we have had to endure trauma in the process—abrupt disruptions like abandonments, parental loss, being sent to boarding school at a young age will make separation feel emotionally overwhelming if it evokes feelings of loss and abandonment.

Separation is also complicated by parental ambivalence in separating from us: This can add fear and guilt to the emotional challenges of the process of separation. It can become a real emotional pressure acting against any desire to become financially independent (from parents, partners).

I recently heard the interview of a young woman who was addicted to shopping. On the surface it seemed like textbook shopping addiction: irresistible urges, debt, lack of space in her room or time for anything else. This woman, in her early thirties, saw no point in life without shopping. There would be nothing to look forward to. And even though it was clear that depressive thoughts were being avoided through shopping, what I found striking was that despite the journalist's relentless questioning, the only moment in which she became tearful was when she was asked if she ever wanted to move out of her parents' house, get married, and move on with her life. "I can't think of it. I can't think of the day I will leave home." Shopping was a way of continuing to be financially dependent on her parents. This way, she remained the little girl that was cared for and spoiled by her parents, rather than having to grow up and face the responsibilities that come with it. Looking at the family history we see that the parents had waited six years post-marriage for a child. They prayed and hoped, until she came along and, as her father says, she was indulged when she arrived: "I wanted to get her anything she wanted. She was like a little princess."[22] So her resistance to leave might be related to how well her needs and desires were met at home, but we might wonder if it was also linked to a potential reluctance in her parents to let her go, having waited and tried for so long to finally have a child.

Was this an overspending problem or self-sabotage? The answer is probably both, the overspending, however, being a consequence of a deeper emotional driver: the fear of autonomy and leaving the parental home. The overspending is facilitating that goal rather than being the core problem in itself.

Separating from the family is a developmental challenge. We need to trust that we have what it takes to be a functional adult both at a practical level (paying bills and taxes, changing light bulbs, signing a rental contract) but also at an emotional level (addressing our emotional needs, comforting ourselves, coping). Even a healthy separation will evoke a range of feelings from loss and grief to gratitude and empowerment. But the ability to separate successfully (and of course the process is not clear-cut and can sometimes continue throughout life) will depend on many things, like our parents transmitting a sense that *they* can let go of us and be a supportive presence in our transition out of the family home. Otherwise, the parents' tendency to hold on to us anxiously will complicate the separation and we will fear we are unable to survive without them. It might be hard for the growing child to feel able to tolerate the disappointments that come with entering the real world, especially if what we are used to is being treated like a princess.

Freud, in 1926, wrote about the anxiety evoked in the infant at the threat of the mother being absent.[23] This fear is grounded in the mental and physical helplessness that an infant might feel in the absence of their caregiver. The anxiety of separation might be experienced as a fear of survival (or the fear of annihilation as described by Melanie Klein).[24] But it might also fill the mind of the child with destructive thoughts and phantasies (attacking/sadistic thoughts) that result in feelings of guilt and shame. When in the 1990s psychotherapists studied children with a disorganized attachment style (who are most likely to have suffered parental neglect and maltreatment), they found many were prone to see themselves as the helpless victims of catastrophic events.[25] In expressing their phantasies it was clear both how vulnerable and helpless they felt to the outside world, but also how destructive and violent their phantasies could be. A fear of separation, of being abandoned to a state of helplessness, can be very powerful and thus, something we defend against.

If we are anxiously attached, we don't feel secure and safe in relationships. We are full of anxieties about being abandoned or rejected—of facing loss in a damaging and painful way. If this is the case, we could be using financial self-sabotage to prevent what could feel like a traumatic separation. If we are afraid of leaving the parental home because our relationship with them is ridden with anxieties, failing financially to be independent could be preserving a concrete closeness and a sense of being looked after that soothes our anxieties.

Psychiatrist and psychoanalysts David Krueger[26] and Ann Ruth Turkel[27] both saw avoiding dealing with financial responsibilities, remaining dependent on others financially, being a way of expressing a difficulty with separation and individuation. Krueger gives an example I too have encountered in the therapy room of investors who fail to do any due diligence on an opportunity brought to them by a friend. Although many reasons could be behind this failure to do one's own research on whether something is a sensible investment or not, there is in many cases a desire to be taken care of by the other, to relax in their supposedly more experienced embrace and say "please take care of me."[28] Leaving these desires in the unconscious can become a real trap for rational financial behavior and set up blind spots that impair an adult and their realistic decision-making process.

Recurring financial sabotage and the unintentional financial crises from which one might need rescuing may be linked to a fear of autonomy, of separating from parents. The fear is psychological of course, but it manifests in this concrete, material way. We keep seeking reassurance that the other will look after us.

Fear of finding out the truth about money

Self-sabotage could be used as a powerful defense against the fear of finding out that money will not get us what we hoped for. Remember the person, as discussed in chapter 3, who has idealized money and projected all these magical powers onto it (like that of curing one's unhappiness, or resolving conflict in a family)? As they begin to accumulate more riches, they may find that nothing really feels any different, yet they have worked so hard in the hope that money would in fact get them what they wished for. It is hard to give up that hope and so self-sabotaging allows you to go back three spaces, preserving the illusion and denying the reality that money won't fix what is hurting.

* * *

As you try to determine if a behavior is really about self-sabotaging or if financial failure is a mere consequence of something else, you can think of the following questions. For the overspender, for example:

What is money buying you, really? The answer might be love, safety, attention, validation, or something that will stay. *In psychological terms we are seeking to acquire something via the spending.*

What thoughts/feelings are you avoiding by acting/spending? The answer might be boredom, loneliness, depressive thoughts or perhaps self-loathing. *We are using spending as an action that helps us avoid difficult feelings.*

What will financial failure (caused by the overspending) get you? The answer might be that financial failure will address the guilt/shame of having money in the first place or that it will get us revenge, or our parents' care and attention. *What helps us get what we want is not what we buy but what we lose. That's self-sabotage.*

We are often unaware of the fact that we are self-sabotaging. It takes some digging to understand the motives, the feelings, the unconscious phantasies that are behind our behaviors. It is powerful when the light bulb goes on. When we see what we imagine there is to gain through self-sabotage, we acquire a choice to either continue to pay the price of that psychological victory, or find a different way to manage those feelings.

The drivers of self-sabotage are so varied. We saw how being afraid of independence for some has a clear solution: avoidance. Keeping ourselves in a place of financial need, we can avoid what we most fear. We also saw how feeling unentitled to wealth (because it's unearned, or because of deeper reasons, like a pervasive sense of guilt or shame) but also feeling deserving of punishment can all find a solution in financial self-destruction (sometimes as extreme as findom). We saw how anger and resentment too can make us self-destruct to spite others, or lead us to unconsciously set up a more subtle mechanism in which we avoid our anger through the self-destruction (we become the problem and turn anger against ourselves, rather than direct it toward its rightful recipient—in the case of Caleb and his father). We need to identify our self-sabotage and wonder what its purpose is.

Maybe we don't need to feel so guilty about having inherited money, and recognize that the financial destruction we have unconsciously provoked will leave us with even more guilt than we were trying to get rid of in the first place. Maybe we don't need to act out our anger about inheriting debt by digging a deeper financial hole, as that too will only make things worse. There might be a way to manage the anger, maybe even to express it so it loses its power, so we can end up in a healthier place than where we are heading. And maybe facing our fear of autonomy, of growing up, might feel empowering and freeing. Facing the negative side of keeping ourselves dependent on others can help us move on from the financially damaging patterns giving us a sense of safety through dependence.

We could be paying a very high financial price to avoid facing and dealing with difficult emotions. Is it really worth it?

CHAPTER 6

Generosity: from inadequacy to control and why we give

In 1999, I was sitting in Café Rouge, a bar in Philadelphia, with two of my best friends after a long day of attending college classes. We chatted for hours, laughed a lot, and shared a bottle of wine and nibbles. We were the last ones at closing and when we asked for the bill we were told, "A man who was here earlier paid your bill and wishes you all the best." I never found out who that kind stranger was and, given he never made himself known to us, it was clear that he wasn't seeking something in return for his generosity. It left me curious though—why? Did he see something in us that prompted him to do this? Was it his way to share in our happiness? Was he expressing a longing to be with a group of friends? Was he paying it forward, having received an act of random kindness himself? All sorts of options took shape in my imagination.

While generosity is relational (it involves two parties), the act of giving may be used to express feelings about the relationship

(I am grateful to you, I love you) as much as to express feelings about ourselves (I am lacking, I am superior, I have more than I deserve). Human beings are so complex and different that we can't assume that an act of generosity carries the same meaning every time. The message might differ based on the recipient or our state of mind.

Before I explore the potential emotional drivers behind it, what do I mean by generosity? The American Psychological Association *Dictionary of Psychology* defines it as "the quality of freely giving one's support or resources to others in need,"[1] which I don't entirely agree with as generosity isn't always about giving to someone in need. I also take issue with the word "freely," which I can only assume is there to indicate that the giving hasn't been requested but, having seen examples of people feeling trapped by their uncontrollable desire to give generously, "freedom" seems to be an inadequate word. A more open and accurate definition would be "the quality of giving unrequested support or resources to another party" adding, as the *Cambridge Dictionary* does, "especially more than is usual or expected"[2] to capture the fact that generosity often exceeds expectations, in its frequency or abundance.

Behaviors

We can be generous in many kinds of ways. We can be generous with our time, with our emotional availability, with our financial resources, and even by donating blood and organs. Even in the relationship with their therapist, people might express their generosity in either obvious or more disguised ways. There are clients who might bring a Christmas card or a gift, others who express it by bringing funny anecdotes or compliments with the same intention of a gift to evoke pleasure in the therapist, to be liked, or maybe even to complement their presence, which they fear might be in some way disappointing, or not enough.

We might give spontaneously (like handing money to someone asking for help, or giving a gift to a friend with no occasion attached) or regularly (like our contributions to charitable causes, or routine cash transfers to a family member). We might give begrudgingly or with heartfelt joy, in moderation or in an excessive manner. Some people repeatedly go overboard with it, not just giving more (and more often) than is expected by the other but, more importantly, giving more than they feel comfortable with themselves.

Going back to the definition of financial well-being, it is important to feel in control of the choices we make with our money. If you are the kind of person who gives more than you feel comfortable giving, or you give to an extent that makes others feel uncomfortable, it's worth asking yourself these questions to better understand and unpack your giving behavior: What are you trying to achieve through your generosity? What unconscious feelings can we trace this behavior back to and would there be a better way to deal with it? What does the money/gift stand for?

As I explain and discuss the emotional drivers behind giving in the next pages, keep these questions in mind, and be curious about past experiences that might have influenced your desire to give generously.

Pathological generosity or compulsive giving is a condition characterized by an uncontrollable desire to give to others. Giving becomes a compulsion and takes on various forms. It is excessive to the point of even having serious financial and social consequences, and attempts to withhold giving evoke unmanageable guilt and anxiety. It has been linked to psychiatric conditions such as obsessive–compulsive disorder, a manic episode, brain injury, and diseases that affect the functioning of the brain.[3]

Pathological generosity is rare, however a more subtle tendency to give more than we feel comfortable with, or without really understanding what drove our choice to be so generous, is more common. Statements like "I always go overboard with presents, and I am not sure why I do that. I know it's not expected, but it's something I feel I can't help" suggest that you may be driven by an internal psychological need that inhibits your sense of control over how much you are choosing to spend on gifts.

In most cases, when generosity is expressed in a way that is sincere and moderate, it leaves both the giver and the recipient feeling comfortable and happy. Receiving from a compulsively generous person, however, may leave you feeling quite the opposite: uncomfortable, trapped, even intruded upon. This is often not the intention of the compulsive giver, just a consequence of it.

There are various kinds of generous giving that might, unconsciously, have a different agenda than just the other person's pleasure and happiness. These inevitably might not be experienced with the same joy as a gift given purely to solicit positive feelings. Gifts given expressing expectations of a quid pro quo or leaving us with a sense that we owe something, may feel constraining or controlling. Some gifts come wrapped with negative emotions: Consciously or unconsciously we end up conveying our negative feelings through the gift, leaving the recipient feeling hurt. For example, we might have an inattentive friend who has forgotten our birthday, or never asked us about our new job, who is always eager to tell us about their life but hardly ever asks about ours, and we give them an inconsiderate gift that leaves them feeling as unseen as we have felt lately. We might be trying to convey something emotional to them through the gift. When we think about generosity we think of its more benign forms and in some ways these latter ways of giving are better defined as false generosity because of the malicious intent in them.

But the lines get blurred. The feelings that guide our giving may be unclear or even unconscious. Think of a mother who has been trying to hold back comments about her daughter's revealing outfits but then gives her a rather conservative blouse as a birthday present. The daughter opens it, is upset, "This is so NOT ME. Why would you choose this for me?" and storms out. "I thought it would look lovely on you," the mother claims (and believes). We might wonder whether she is trying to impose something on the daughter, knowing (at some level) that it's a gift purchased to fulfill her own agenda of what she hopes the daughter will wear. Or is it a gift picked in the hope it will be liked? Even though it is unlikely that the mother's intention is to leave the daughter feeling hurt and misunderstood, the desire to please that we associate with generosity may be questioned.

We all differ in how and when or who we give to and I argue that this isn't random, but there's meaning to be found in how we make these choices. Why are we compelled to give a tower of presents to our children but then wouldn't necessarily be excessively generous in other areas of life? Why is there one group of friends with which we always go overboard in our generosity? Why were we so stingy with our ex-wife but find it so easy to be generous with our new partner?

Psychoanalytically, generosity hasn't been a focus of much investigation but fields like sociobiology have done a lot of research into the matter of altruism (which encapsulates a broader range of self-sacrificing behaviors) as well as generosity. Many different studies confirmed that there is a natural tendency for humans to be altruistic and that being generous makes us happier.[4]

It's a phenomenon that transcends culture. A survey of over 200,000 people across 136 countries found that, in most places, people feel happier after spending money on others.[5] Having said that, I must flag that as I write about generosity, I do so from my own experience and that of working with my clients who, despite being a very diverse group of people, are largely from Western cultures. Tipping, gift giving, and other forms of financial giving are not homogenous across cultures. For example, expectations of tips and customs around gift giving vary. Depending on the setting, in some cultures gifts may be highly valued while in others seen as inappropriate; refusing a gift may be expected in some cultures and rude in others; in some countries tips in a restaurant are expected yet in others they are simply welcome. I won't attempt to account for a cross-cultural view as, for the purposes of our discussion, it isn't what's most important. No matter which culture you are from, and whatever the parameters and protocols around generosity are, the question I invite you to ask yourself is why might you be exceeding the confines of usual giving practices? Or why do you end up giving more than you are comfortable with? And what are you trying to communicate to others through your giving?

There is no doubt that generosity is seen as a virtue and that religious teachings celebrate acts of kindness and generosity. In Christianity, the Bible teaches that it is more blessed to give than to receive (Acts 20:35). In Buddhism, "dana," meaning generosity or giving, is one of the three central practices along with morality and meditation. "Zakat" is the practice of charitable giving and for those whose wealth passes a certain threshold is one of the five pillars of Islam, and it is seen as both a way to purify one's wealth and a way to help others in need.

We have embedded generosity in different traditions. Birthdays, Christmas, Valentine's Day, and weddings are a time in which it is customary to give gifts. There are also societal norms about giving to people we don't know; tipping is a good example.

Philosophers, social psychologists, evolutionary psychologists, and neuroscientists have all suggested different views on why, as humans, we value and benefit from generosity. There have been debates about whether there is such a thing as pure generosity or whether we always get something from it (making it therefore always about self-gain, like reputation enhancement or self-preservation). Explanations range from the fact that being altruistic has evolutionary advantages (either because it is based on reciprocation or because it promotes the welfare of kin), to altruism being a societal expectation attempting to counterbalance our egoism and greed.

Neurologically speaking, researchers have found that when we donate money, reward centers in the brain are activated. The so-called helper's high is that feel-good sensation that is associated with generosity, which is now evidenced to have a physiological basis and economists call it the "warm glow," alluding to the emotional upside of giving. Several studies have shown that altruistic behaviors have profound positive effects on the current and future physical and psychological well-being of the person performing the behavior,[6] including living longer. Even when giving is compared to acting in one's own self-interest, giving prevails: Some research suggests that spending money on other people has a more positive impact on happiness than spending money on oneself.[7]

The desire to be generous is present from a very young age, suggesting that it is an innate, rather than a learned, behavior. Children actually show more positive emotion when they give rather than receive gifts.[8] Proof of this is in the face of a toddler lighting up with excitement as they wait for you to open the drawing they made for you, containing their proudest scribble.

Not only do we feel good when we give, the reverse is also true. We are more generous when we feel good. It's what psychologists call the "feel-good do-good phenomenon."[9] Generosity can be born out of feeling a certain sense of inner goodness and abundance.

But as I have said before, this book isn't about why most people give or don't give, spend or don't spend. I want to invite you to think about your own internal, emotional drivers. What feelings, fears, or desires might you in one instance be expressing through a gift, or paying for your date, or leaving a generous tip? And if your generosity is more pervasive, what about your internal world and how it's constructed makes you more prone to generosity?

Without our mother's (or primary caregiver's) generosity we couldn't survive our first months of life. As psychoanalyst Salman Akhtar writes: "It is the mother's care that sets the baby on the path to becoming human," and "generosity toward and from others remains a lifelong partner of psychic development and stability."[10] Generosity is a developmental milestone. We move from being the infant that is the recipient of our parents' care and nurture to feeling like a psychologically separate entity able to offer something in a two-person dynamic: a smile, for example, that is (hopefully) received by our parent and delights them.

Psychoanalyst Melanie Klein described how we internalize a sense of inner wealth from our experiences of positive parenting, of having our needs met. We have essentially taken in an experience of a mother that is bountiful and generous and this enrichment of our inner world allows us to feel we have a lot to give. She goes on to explain that with people in whom this feeling of inner wealth and strength is not sufficiently established, bouts of generosity are often followed by an exaggerated need for appreciation and gratitude, and consequently by persecutory anxieties of having been impoverished and robbed.[11] In other words, to be able to give in a generous and rewarding way we need to both feel an inner sense of abundance but also trust that our offer will be well received (without needing reassurance of it).

So when we try to unpack and understand generosity, particularly if it's a pervasive aspect of our character, we need to go beyond the societal, neurological, or learned behaviors around giving and explore the emotional and psychological needs, fears, and desires that we are trying to express through it. Understanding what our giving means is worthwhile because, if decoded, it can reveal feelings and emotions that we might have had no conscious knowledge of, or that are hard to acknowledge or dare say out loud.

Giving to express happiness, love, gratitude, or to ask for forgiveness

Usually, generosity is intended to evoke a positive response from the other person and to symbolically express a positive effect within us, which can typically be love or gratitude. Money and objects are just one of many ways in which we express these feelings through an act of giving. Hopefully gifts complement the many other forms in which we express our love to others. Unfortunately, this isn't always the case. In some families, gifts are the language of love because love isn't expressed in other ways. There are families that don't hug, don't kiss, and don't utter the words, yet love might be there despite how withheld it is in its physical expression. Therefore, gifts might be used as a safer way to express love, or the only way an individual knows how to.

If we feel we haven't been able to give emotionally in the way it was expected, this might be a very difficult confession to verbalize. We might not even be fully conscious of it but have a vague sense of our insufficiency, which we try to make up for materially rather than emotionally. We may use gifts to apologize or atone for past neglect or even mistakes. For example, we sometimes see divorcing parents becoming more generous in their gifting trying to redress the pain they feel they might be inflicting on their children or trying to fill in the gap of an absent parent. Another example is when flowers are brought to a partner after an argument, or to a partner you are betraying, as another way to say "I am sorry" because words seem insufficient, or maybe even impossible to pronounce.

Happiness by proxy

Giving symbolically through money or gifts can be a powerful way to communicate feelings to another individual. We give to induce positive emotions or repair negative ones, but we may also give as a way of experiencing happiness by proxy. Psychoanalysts Beth Seelig and Lisa Rosof write: "We all have strivings that we are physically or mentally incapable of fulfillling for reasons of endowment, opportunity, or life choice [. . .]. If we can gratify such desires through a proxy, our lives are enriched."[12] Watching others, such as your children, experience happiness through your gifts is a way of evoking joy in yourself. This may be a longing grounded in the present (you want to experience joy through them in the here and now), or a residual emotional longing from the past: Maybe you always longed for your parents to gift you a surprise trip to Disneyland, but now, you can at least experience that joy by proxy, taking your children and watching their excitement.

Anna Freud, psychoanalyst and daughter of Sigmund Freud, wrote about generosity that may seem to be altruistic but is really a psychological defense, which she called altruistic surrender.[13] Instead of acknowledging our own desires (which we could never allow ourselves to express or even fulfill because we don't feel worthy), we become generous and help others achieve the fulfillment of their desire instead. Rather than being happy through others, you allow others to be happy instead of you, having given up on the idea that you can have the thing you desire. She gives the example of a patient who had scruples of conscience about getting married, so she did all she could to encourage her sister's engagement or an employee who can't face asking for a raise for themselves but will fight for a fellow co-worker to achieve it. The unconscious thought goes something like "I surrender to the idea of having it, but I will help you get it." We facilitate other people's happiness not so much because we are invested in their joy, but because we give up fighting for what we want (maybe because we feel we don't have what it takes to achieve, or we feel we live in a world in which we don't get what we reach out for).

Being generous because we feel (or fear) the other person's pain

The actress and comedian Amy Schumer was asked what prompts her to leave such generous tips (she has been known to leave tips of 1,000 percent of the bill amount) to waiters and bartenders. She replied that before her big break, she spent years waiting on tables.[14] It is common to feel more compelled to give to someone when we identify with them, or their struggle. We might really feel their pain because we have experienced it ourselves, or because it represents one of our own dreaded fears. Schumer saw her younger self in the bartenders and waiters she was generous toward. A mother might be moved by the appeal of a struggling mother and someone who might have experienced homelessness might find themselves more likely to give to a homeless person.

Our generosity can be rooted in firsthand experience and empathy: "I know how it feels because I have been there," or it may be expressing a fear: "I hope this never happens to me," or hope for reciprocity: "If it did ever happen to me, I would want someone to give, like I am giving." When it's rooted in our own experience it can be full of affect. We might shower our children with big parties and birthday presents if our own birthdays were not celebrated growing up. We want to give them a different experience from the one we had, because we can experience in a very real way how painful it is to feel disappointed or forgotten on our birthday. Or we might be moved by every appeal from a vulnerable person because it resonates with the part of us that feels helpless or fragile.

Giving because it's congruent with our values or to defend against our "neediness"

For some people, giving is a matter of principle. Some people might give because they feel that that is what money is for: to be shared. They are proud of their philosophy, especially because they feel it is at odds with the greedy and competitive world they see around them. They enjoy giving to others, sharing what they have. They usually describe themselves as non-materialistic and express getting more joy out of giving than buying something unnecessary for themselves. Giving, for them, is an expression of their true belief in altruism and desire to live in a world in which self-interest isn't the number one priority on everyone's minds.

In my experience, there are often additional, deeply rooted, emotional experiences that have shaped a view of people (or ourselves) as excessively greedy, and which makes it important to become the one who is generous. I am not saying there is anything wrong with having these beliefs, but rather than just declaring this is what I think is right/moral/ethical, it's worth wondering, what has shaped this moral code?

Could it be that we are trying to disown a needy part of ourselves? For some people, these beliefs take on a rather rigid form. Their way of life is the right way, a better way (rather than simply a different way) from that chosen by others. When it takes on this more unyielding form it becomes what psychoanalyst André Green calls moral narcissism, a longing to be pure, above ordinary human needs.[15] Essentially, holding on to this higher moral code gives us a sense of pride about our superiority, but masks a sense of shame about our own neediness. Freud himself first suggested that generosity could too be a form of the defense called "reaction formation" against owning our greed: Essentially you are so eager to deny your greed that you adopt the diametrically opposite attitude: "Look how generous I am."[16]

Take, for example, Todd, raised by parents who seemed only interested in pursuing their careers. They worked late, traveled a lot, and left Todd in the care of a rotating army of nannies. When the parents were around, they were often entertaining guests and either ignoring him or praising him for being a good and high-achieving child. When Todd did ask for attention, or implored his parents to stay at home this weekend, or simply to allow him to sit next to them while they worked, he would be handed over to a nanny and made to feel guilty for being disruptive or too needy. Rather than feeling the pain of the neglect and the longings his parents would leave him with, Todd learned to deprioritize (or even deny) his needs and focus on other people's. He would bring his mother an endless stream of drawings and creations, which were the rare instances in which she would stop what she was doing to praise his work. He grew up to become someone who presents himself as independent and overtly generous, a defense that allows him to disown this needy and seemingly unacceptable part of himself, and instead he can tell himself and the world, "I am not greedy, I am the very opposite of it; I am giving and generous."

But we might also be using generosity to compensate for our greed (rather than to deny it). As we have seen before, there are people who at some level have negative associations with financial success (greed = bad) and psychologically deal with them by self-sabotaging. Well, another way to deal with the internal conflict (of one part desiring money and the other part seeing this desire as negative) is to take with one hand and give with the other, as the expression goes. Our giving is a balancing act—it helps us address our guilt about our wealth. Amy Schumer, in the same interview about her generosity, was asked by Howard Stern if she felt "rich guilt," to which she responded, "I feel fine about having money [...] I take care of my family, my friends. I think I might feel guilty about having money if I wasn't giving." As I read this, I hear her saying that it is by giving money to family and friends that she can avoid feeling rich guilt.

To compensate for our lacks

In previous chapters, I have spoken about people who grow up with a low sense of self and little sense of entitlement and who feel undeserving. Gifts or financial giving of any sort can be a symbol of a lack we experience in ourselves—a sense of shame. This is different from guilt (it's not about atoning for past mistakes), because it addresses an internal sense of insufficiency. We might unconsciously feel that if we arrived at our book club's meeting bringing just ourselves we'd be disappointing (we are not as smart as everyone else, our insights might be deficient in some way), so we come bearing fruits and pastries. Giving becomes a compensatory response to these feelings.

The gift alleviates our discomfort (it reassures us that me + gift = enough). Although people often recognize that the other (their friend/family/colleague) is unlikely to actually think that we are not good enough, it still feels too risky to show up at book club with just ourselves. It feels risky because we are not comfortable with ourselves, with our own sense of what we have to offer to an encounter. This kind of generosity stems from the self-deprecating part of us, the critical part that doesn't value ourselves enough and harbors feelings of low self-worth.

I worked with a woman who kept injecting money from her personal savings to rescue a failing catering venture she had started with four other friends. The youngest of five siblings, she had always been treated like the little one at home and never been taken seriously. She also grew up feeling dwarfed by her siblings' achievements. In therapy, she came to realize that her generous rescuing of the business financially was rooted both in her desire to be taken seriously, but also in her insecurities about not having as much as others to contribute to the venture. In her eyes, these business partners were perceived as the more skilful older siblings, and so money stood for what she felt she lacked.

Psychoanalyst Hilde Lewinsky speaks of a woman who was born to parents who were hoping for a boy. She would never visit any of her friends without taking them some present. She felt that she would not otherwise be welcome, just as she herself had not been welcome to her parents.[17] Lewinsky called this "propitiatory gifting." This behavior of giving was aimed at compensating for her lack, but also as Lewinsky suggests, a way to prove to herself that she in fact was good (generous = good), despite not being the desired boy.

I will invite you to wonder "Why do I do this?" throughout this book. Even with generosity, which can be a positive and rewarding behavior, my goal is not to discourage you from being giving, but to help you understand and have greater emotional insight into your choice so that you can make a more informed decision about whether or not to spend on a gift, how much to spend on it, and why you are compelled to do so. Is it because you think it's expected? Are you expressing your joy and excitement in meeting them through this gesture? Or is it coming from a compensatory place or out of a fear of rejection (I am not enough, therefore I come with something that might buffer any potential disappointment)? Exploring the question in our minds gives us a choice. We might decide that we'll bring the flowers anyway, to alleviate our anxieties about not being enough, or we might try to address our feelings of inadequacy internally and take the risk of finding out that actually "just us" was enough after all.

A form of masochism

As we have explored in previous chapters, when we feel undeserving we might deny ourselves things, or go further and punish ourselves through self-denial. Generosity can turn into a form of self-denial too. This kind of giving is masochistic, meaning that there is little or no pleasure in giving: The pleasure is in our self-denial and martyrdom. The generous masochist gives and gives to an extent where they can feel the impact of their deprivation, and this impact serves a purpose, psychologically. Suffering fits well with either what we are used to or what we think we deserve, and we might even hold on to an illusion that something good will come of it. It isn't easy to discern whether an act of generosity comes from a masochistic place or not, but think of the difference between Anna and Esther's statements.

Anna: "I would LOVE for my friend Jinny to have my mom's wedding dress. I am not going to be using it anytime soon, and watching her wear it would at least mean it's not going to waste! Plus, she's my best friend and it would make me feel even closer to her on the big day."

Esther: "I am never going to get married, nobody wants to be with me, so I might as well give Jinny my mom's wedding dress. I mean, there is no point in me having it."

In the first statement, there might be a painful sense in Anna that marriage is not on the horizon yet for her, but she doesn't sound completely defeated about it and she is certainly not using the generous act as a way to beat herself up with self-loathing. Anna is happy about giving this gift to her friend, but Esther is more focused on what she doesn't have. The generous act is pseudoaltruistic[18] because its focus is not on the pleasure of giving or of Jinny having but rather it's a masochistic act that says, "I am depriving myself of this wedding dress as a reminder of how hopeless my situation is."

Material generosity may be just one way in which the person is self-sacrificing. They might find that in life they take on the role of the carer, of looking after others, volunteering for heroic tasks, and are notoriously bad at looking after themselves and allowing themselves to have good things. Ultimately, they believe that being generous is the price they need to pay to feel loved, and only if they give more than they receive can they feel they stand a chance of feeling and being perceived as acceptable.

To placate our fears of being abandoned

Having discussed some of the emotional drivers of generosity that are very much rooted in our self-perception, I will move on to exploring some more relational aspects of generosity. Whereas the previous examples have been about an expression of how we feel about ourselves, there are forms of generosity that are influenced by how we set up relationships with others.

Giving can strengthen relationships—it is a symbolic way of connecting, of bonding with the other. There is something wonderful about experiencing exchange in a secure relationship, where we trust that there will be more love than hate, where we know we will feel pleasure in giving and receiving from the other.

But, of course, that is not how many people experience relationships. There are people who are insecurely attached, live in fear that others will disappoint them, or even leave them. Those who are ambivalently attached have not had an experience of important others as reliably available. With these relational imprints, they become preoccupied with drawing the other closer to them, out of a fear of being left or abandoned.

Generosity may then become a psychologically useful way to experience the reassuring connection that comes with gift giving as well as a good way to elicit a reassuring positive response from the other. There could be a secret hope for reciprocity, a hope that with all we have given, surely the other feels indebted and won't ever leave us. It is a form of relational masochism, explains psychoanalyst Nancy McWilliams, which describes the use of self-sacrifice in the interest of maintaining an attachment to the other.[19]

Psychotherapists are trained to help clients understand the meaning of their actions, and so money behaviors related to the therapy fee are thought about and interpreted. Wanting to pay in advance has meaning: one client revealed (half-jokingly) that "this way, I know you'll show up." It might not be surprising, then, to discover that they had been sent off to boarding school at the age of seven.

Psychoanalysts Shelley Orgel and Leonard Shengold describe the case of A, whose mother had always tied the girl to her by continuous, often unsolicited, maternal attentions and gifts.[20] The mother is described as desiring a symbiotic bond with her daughter and using extravagant and thoughtful presents, providing food and clothing to the daughter even after she moved out of the house. In therapy, A successfully decreased her dependence on her mother and for the first time bought herself a coat. The mother, seeing this, was upset and silent. She responded by sending in the mail a new, more expensive coat to her daughter. Was this coat an act of generosity? Or, rather, a desperate attempt to keep the daughter close to her, terrified of separation? Orgel and Shengold write: "A true gift should involve a renunciation of claims for permanent fusion with the [other]." This is a good example of a narcissistic mother whose emotional agenda supersedes the needs of the daughter. A mother who could not help but make the daughter the center of her world as if an extension of herself and whose anxiety about letting her go made her use money/gifts in the hope she wouldn't be left or abandoned.

Generosity as a weapon of control

The mother in the example above was defending against a fear of being abandoned and was anxiously clinging on to her daughter with these material offerings being almost like a physical bond between them. It is also an example of how we might use a gift in a controlling way. Sending that second coat to her daughter could also be seen as a forceful imposition: "You will wear what I give you."

Control can be a big feature of how parents relate to one another, or toward us. There are many ways of being controlling in a relationship, and financial giving can be one of them. If we agree that generosity is about giving something that we hope will evoke pleasure in the other, then generosity that is addressing our personal agenda with a view to control another is a kind of pseudo-generosity. Yes, it involves giving, and sometimes giving quite generously, but it comes with the expectation of being able to exert power over the other: The recipient will either give us what we want in return or do as we say. People who use generosity in this way use money as a weapon of control.

Hope for reciprocity, as we discussed before, can be a feature of generous giving. But it is one thing to give to a disaster-relief charity or to a homeless person because, unconsciously, we hope that if we ever were to find ourselves in that same situation, someone would do the same for us. It is quite different to *expect* reciprocity. Not dissimilar to a bribe, if we give expecting to influence the other person's behavior, it is controlling.

We might want to invite our adult children on a lavish vacation. If the relationship with them isn't harmonious, we might be luring them by offering to pay for them. But is that controlling generosity? I suppose the difference, again, is about hope versus expectation. We might hope they will be tempted to come and, despite the troubled relationships, that being in a nice hotel will compensate for some of the difficulties of getting together. This is different from an attitude of "I am paying for you, so I expect you to spend every day of the vacation with us."

Controlling generosity is much more common than we might imagine it to be. Think of the parents that offer to pay for the wedding, but then demand involvement in the decision-making process. Or those who offer to pay for college tuition, but only if the child attends medical school. Or the mother-in-law whose extravagant gift giving seems to give her carte blanche to dictate what the grandchild should/shouldn't be doing. Are these generous gifts or forms of coercion?

People are not always Machiavellian in their controlling generosity. Sometimes the desire to control may be quite unconscious. We might tell ourselves that we are using our daughter's extra keys to water her plants, or to drop off lasagna, but at some level we might also be struggling to let them have their space with no oversight. Other times we are more consciously trying to impose an identity on the other: the wife who keeps buying her T-shirt-wearing husband collared shirts, or the mother that keeps cooking the pork casserole for her visiting son who declared himself vegetarian years ago.[21]

The desire to control may be about relationship dynamics that are internalized and we repeat, or it may be circumstantial. Take, for example, inheritance. As much as we might want our children, say, to be the heirs of our money, it might be difficult to give up the fruits of our hard labor relinquishing with it control over its fate. Will our money be valued and carefully spent, or squandered mindlessly? We don't need to have been a controlling parent all along to feel this way. One survey found nearly two thirds of parents and grandparents want some form of control over how financial gifts and inheritances are spent by children and grandchildren.[22] A desire to place limits on how the inheritance will be spent may be rooted in realities of having seen the children be irresponsible with their own money or in a desire to continue parenting past our death.

Desiring immortality or fearing death

If existential fears preoccupy us, then donations that immortalize our legacy might address, albeit in part, our questions about the significance of our life. As discussed in chapter 2, a search for immortality can be a powerful force driving our money behavior. Amassing wealth that will be inherited by future generations could be a way of trying to establish a sense of continuity past death, like spending it through generous charitable donations, both addressing our phantasy of living on through our acts. As if a part of us will continue to stay alive through the Vicky Reynal library/bench/plaque, or that we are remembered as giving and generous.

Express anger or establish a boundary

I started exploring why we are generous by introducing some of the positive feelings we might be expressing through our gifts and our giving (love, gratitude, happiness). But giving, as we have seen throughout this chapter, can be used to express negative feelings too. Gifts can be chosen maliciously and can be a passive-aggressive act. The gifting may intentionally fall short of expectations, making it a kind of pseudo-generosity.

A friend of mine (who is a dedicated mother to her three children) told me that for Mother's Day her husband bought her a book called *The Good Wife Guide*. The message was clear: In his view, she was neglecting her role as a wife in service of being a mother. Gifts can send powerful messages and they are not always positive ones.

If we take it a step further, sometimes rather than communicate our negative feeling, in an unconscious attempt to rid ourselves of it, we give the other an experience of it. If we have felt ignored by our partner, we might hand them an impersonal gift for their birthday, so they end up feeling unthought of and unseen.

Money can also be used as a barrier, to keep people at arm's length and to communicate to the other that we have no intention of deepening a relationship. "When he told me I didn't have to pay him for the website design he kindly offered to do for me, I insisted on paying him," Lisa tells me. "I just didn't want to give him the wrong impression." I asked what that would have been, and she expanded, "Well, to be honest, I didn't want him to think I wanted to date him or even feel that I owed him a friendship . . . I just wanted it to be a business relationship." Lisa's insistence on paying (generous in that it exceeded expectations) was a way of imposing a boundary.

* * *

As you do your self-exploration into the possible reasons for your (at times or always) excessive giving, ask yourself whether you are especially generous with certain individuals (children, particular friends, a sibling, groups). To what extent is your gift giving something you actually enjoy or to what extent does it become a sort of irresistible urge that you wish you could rid yourself of? Could you put into words what your giving action is expressing? These questions help us investigate what the true nature of our giving attitude is and possibly understand what internal place it is coming from.

Having worked with people suffering from relentless generosity I find that there is never just one reason for their desire to please and give to others. However, being more conscious of what phantasies, fears, and desires drive our giving certainly helps us feel less imprisoned. It takes time (and often therapy) to change a way of thinking that has been ingrained in us for years.

If your generosity is rooted in a self-critical part of you, and a part that needs to deny and disown your neediness, you might have to acknowledge and change how you view yourself by trying to have a more positive inner dialogue and being more empathic with yourself. You might, with time, take the small risk of showing up to a dinner party with a smaller gift, or resist the temptation to buy a round of drinks (yet again) for everyone. You might give yourself a chance to find out that your presence is enough or that the giving will not prevent people's negative feelings toward you.

Chapter 7

Stealing: reclaiming, rebelling, or redemption?

In 2012, 60-year-old celebrity chef Antony Worrall Thompson was caught stealing grocery items including onions, butter, and discounted coleslaw on five different occasions from a supermarket. A successful chef, with no shortage of access to onions, was stealing from a supermarket. In an interview, he disclosed that he was as baffled as everyone else about the reasons for shoplifting but believed that a series of childhood traumas might be behind his actions.[1]

I have explored all sorts of different actions we can take with money: spend it, hoard it, gift it, squander it, and now I turn to the idea of taking it, even when it's not ours to take. Why do some people feel compelled to take money or items that don't belong to them? Why would a chef, who can afford to buy food, steal from a supermarket?

For some people, stealing is a way of expressing a sense of entitlement ("I deserve more than I have"), for others it's a way of rebelling against authority ("I won't comply with what is expected of me"), yet for others it could be a way of addressing feelings of guilt and seeking punishment (those who steal secretly hoping to get caught). These are only some of the many, often unconscious, motivations behind stealing and some that are worth unpacking one by one, even if at times multiple reasons may coexist in the mind of the person that steals.

Definition and behaviors

For our purposes, we can simply define stealing as taking what isn't ours to take. This can manifest itself as a one-off event or a compulsive tendency to steal. Someone might steal in particular settings (like from their employer, partner, or parents) or might find that they steal any chance they get, irrespective of who it is they are stealing from or what it is they are taking.

Like with other money behaviors, there are extreme manifestations of the behavior. In this case, it's called "kleptomania," from the Greek word *kleptes*, which means thief or cheater, and *mania*, meaning madness or frenzy. Kleptomania is classified in the *Diagnostic and Statistical Manual of Mental Disorders (DSM-5)* as an impulse control disorder, which describes a failure to resist the impulse to steal.[2] Like other impulse disorders there is the characteristic anxiety-driven urge to act, followed by a high during and shortly after, until guilt and regret set in. So kleptomania, like a failure to control impulses such as compulsive gambling and compulsive spending, might be more about a failure to resist an impulse rather than an unconscious way of expressing a feeling/desire or for practical reasons like to fund an addiction. They steal because they can't resist the urge to act. Kleptomania as such is uncommon, and according to statistics from the American Psychiatric Association, in the US it affects 0.3 to 0.6 percent of the population.[3] According to the *DSM-5*, kleptomania occurs in 4 to 24 percent of identified shoplifters.

It is also worth saying that, in some cases, repeated theft can be a symptom of antisocial personality disorder. People who suffer from this disorder seem to have no regard for what is right or wrong and wouldn't experience any feelings of guilt or remorse for their actions. Unlike the person suffering from kleptomania or many of the people who steal to express unconscious feelings, they are not interested in trying to stop their behavior. Lying, stealing and behaving impulsively are typical of someone with antisocial personality disorder. In the vast majority of cases, antisocial behaviors are evident at a young age.

In my experience, people who have stolen either pre-adulthood or as adults are keeping this secret with a great deal of shame. Whether you have done it once or a handful of times, you might experience such discomfort. You might feel guilt and shame alongside confusion about how a person like you, who is generally a good person, could do such a thing. You might have tried to rationalize it ("I was struggling financially") or justify it ("my friends made me"), but you never quite understood it. In this chapter, I will help you reflect on some of the unconscious drivers that sometimes explain what compelled us to do it. Having spoken to clients who have admitted to stealing, when we begin to unpack and explore the reasons behind their behavior, an encrypted emotional message begins to emerge. It may turn out to be a way in which they were expressing something about themselves ("I have been wronged"), about their desires ("I want justice in the world") or feelings about others ("I envy you for having more than me").

Whether you are putting your hand into someone's purse, evading taxes, or shoplifting, these are all different ways in which you are essentially doing the same thing: making yours something that isn't. According to a 2020 study by YouGov, one in twenty people have shoplifted as adults. Even though it seemed that there is no gender difference in terms of prevalence of stealing, research suggests that men tend to do it more for the fun and thrill while women cite more often being unable to afford the item as a key reason.[4]

As this is a book about money, I will try to focus on stealing money, even though some of the examples I will give might involve stealing possessions because I think that the underlying reasons driving the behaviors would often apply (and overlap). Often *what* is being stolen is irrelevant. What matters is the act of stealing, and that is where meaning can be found.

Thou shalt not steal[5]

In practically every modern society, stealing is condemned and punished with laws specifically prohibiting the behavior. It is seen both as a form of dishonesty and as a violation of property rights. Historically it might have been viewed as permissible to steal from enemies or from others within a group if it addressed imbalances in wealth or power or as a means of survival but was generally not viewed as a positive or desirable behavior. Even today there are some caveats to our condemnation of stealing: In a YouGov study, although the majority of people said it is never acceptable to steal (73 percent), one fifth said it may be acceptable under certain circumstances like starvation or poverty. Younger respondents are more lenient on stealing from stores: Two fifths of 18-to-24-year-olds find it OK, as opposed to 12 percent of those ages 55 or over. And overall, people find stealing from a large business more acceptable (16 percent) than theft from a small or independent business (1 percent).[6]

It is often the case that countries with higher corruption tend to also have higher rates of stealing and property theft, but we can't conclude that this is a result of the bad example set at the higher levels of government, because the situation is much more complex. Countries with higher corruption often also suffer from economic inequality, poverty, and poor law enforcement which all influence how common stealing is. Similarly influential may be the level of economic development in the country, levels of education, and employment opportunities.[7]

Even if we go down the route of claiming that the increasingly materialistic and consumption-focused world we live in fosters a culture of never having enough money, we don't all go around filling our pockets with what doesn't belong to us. But some of us do, and the behavior may be as straightforward as pocketing the coins lying around at a friend's place all the way to committing fraud. So I invite you to wonder, what does this appropriation represent in your mind? Who are you really stealing from? What psychological objective is the stealing accomplishing?

Reasons

Let's start with the obvious reasons: Many people steal because of economic hardship or to fund addictions. Although research into why people shoplift, for example, hasn't proven a correlation between economic hardship and shoplifting, it is undeniable that in certain cases, people steal because they see no other option to obtain basic goods. Researchers at the University of Washington who interviewed shoplifters found this to be a central part of their narrative. From interviews of self-confessed thieves, stories abound of mothers without enough money to buy formula for their babies and people who faced a choice to either go hungry or to steal—they all concluded that they had no other option.[8] Even in developed countries like the US and UK, roughly 20 percent of the population lives in poverty[9] and we can't dismiss the distress that comes with real need as one reason for stealing. Lack of money evokes an almost primal fear of survival, which we'll try and defend against whichever way we can. But what about those people who have money, no addictions, and yet still choose to steal? I will explore ways in which stealing becomes a defense we use to deal with difficult feelings and emotions—we use it to avoid our feelings, to deal with guilt, with powerlessness, with anger, and more.

The other common reason is thrill-seeking. Writer Victoria Elizabeth Schwab once wrote: "Some people steal to stay alive, and some steal to feel alive."[10] Some people steal trying to address an inner sense of deadness. The thrill might be in doing something that is against the rules but also in getting away with it. Psychoanalyst Manfred F. R. Kets de Vries discussing the motives behind fraud said, "Generally speaking, however, it is executives with impaired self-control, thrill-seekers who look for instant gratification, who are more likely to resort to risky or reckless behavior and engage in white-collar crime."[11] This could be psychologically rewarding for someone who is hungry to prove to themselves (and others) how shrewd and clever they are. It might feel like a victory to have outsmarted and deceived others. Imagine having felt belittled by a parent your entire life and how psychologically important it might feel to outsmart them. Stealing from their wallet could be a way to prove them wrong, and even prevail over them. There might be real pride in their ability to fool others and get away with things.

If you have ever struggled to make sense of your behavior, start by gathering details, such as who do you steal from? What do you steal? When are you most likely to do it? What are you feeling right before taking action?

These are all important clues that can help you begin to unpack and understand your behavior. Someone who consistently steals from parents or a sibling, but never from someone else, might want to examine those relationships in greater depth. Stealing when we are feeling rejected or powerless may also be indicative of why we do it.

Emotional regulation

Like with shopping/spending, we may use an *action* as a way of dealing with *feelings* that are hard to name and/or manage. We steal because we are bursting with difficult, maybe even incomprehensible feelings, which we don't know how to manage and so we act out. This offers only temporary and superficial relief. Giving us a fleeting sense of control over something, when really, the problem is that we don't know how to tame the negative emotions that are troubling us.

The fact that in the family history of people suffering from kleptomania we find high rates of mood disorders and alcohol addiction suggests that individuals who feel compelled to steal might be doing so because they haven't developed the psychological resources to cope with their feelings successfully.

Triumphing over trauma

Great psychological relief can come from finding a way to have agency and control in a situation that reminds us of a past experience in which we felt powerless. We have seen in other chapters how our present behavior can be a defense against painful feelings in the present that remind us of or evoke emotions linked to past experiences. This time around, rather than continuing to feel immobilized by our lack of control, we try to do something different; we search for a way to triumph over our past trauma.

In the TV show *The Split*,[12] one of the characters, Nina Defoe, is a successful lawyer. Nina is the middle of three sisters, two of whom work in a law firm along with their mother. Her father had left their mother when Nina was very young and she hadn't seen him from the age of eight until now, in her thirties. As the TV series unfolds, we get a sense that a lot of the feelings that

Nina had about her father's abandonment hadn't been dealt with and could be behind her relationship difficulties in the present.

Annabel Scholey, the actress that plays Nina Defoe, says in an interview: "It's been drilled into the sisters by their mother from an early age that they don't need a man. Letting her guard down with a man then possibly being left is the biggest fear in Nina's life."[13] That early abandonment could also be behind other dysfunctional behaviors: Despite a successful career, it emerges that Nina has been struggling with heavy drinking and a compulsion to steal (she is seen in the show stealing food from a café, or found with bags full of stolen clothes with tags still on them). In one scene, Nina explains to her boyfriend her feelings during shoplifting. "I take stuff because I can. Because there is this moment when I am waiting for someone to stop me, and they never do. And then I am out of the door. And it's mine and no one can take it from me." In this succinct and honest revelation, there is a sense of profound sadness as she waits for someone to stop her, alongside a triumphant exit.

It leaves me wondering if, for this character, shoplifting represented a victory over disappointment. It's as if she is saying: "I want someone to notice, yet no one does, no one sees me. But at least I walk away with something." Emotionally it's as if she goes from feeling that there is no one there to having a possession she can hold on to and no one will take away. Nina could have been turning the painful feelings of loss (from her father leaving), of no one there (with her mother potentially emotionally unavailable due to her own mourning), into an action (stealing) that made her feel like she could walk away with something. At least through stealing, she was left with something (clearly symbolic) that she could hold on to and triumph over the trauma.

Sometimes negative emotional experiences don't amount to trauma, but leave us full of fears: like the fear that it will happen again, a fear that history will repeat itself. I have seen this happen with people whose families suffered substantial financial losses that have changed their quality of life and they live in fear thereafter that it could all crumble again. They become so preoccupied with securing a solid financial standing (and maybe also carry a bitterness about what was taken away from them), that they would do anything to prevent history from repeating itself.

One such example was the infamous Bernie Madoff (who ran the biggest Ponzi scheme in history, worth over $64 billion). When asked why he did it, he first named his experience watching his father go bankrupt while he was a teen (and the impact on the family's lifestyle). Later, he married a woman whose father was very successful and who Madoff was very keen to impress. There was a determination in him to be successful (unlike his father) and to impress men like his father-in-law. He longed to be part of "the club" of Wall Street men. In his words: "I watched my father go bankrupt. I was very driven. But I was always outside the club, the club being the New York Stock Exchange and white shoe firms. They fought me every step of the way." He managed to legitimately build a successful business but when he incurred sudden financial losses he faced a choice: to either admit failure or to lie. For Madoff, with the emotional scar of the family's financial trauma and his determination to not be confirmed in his fear that he would end up like his father, lying was the more palatable alternative to admitting failure. As his legitimate businesses flourished, he still chose to continue lying. When questioned about this, he says: "Ego. Put yourself in my place. Your whole career you are outside the club but then suddenly you have all the big banks—Deutsche Bank, Credit Suisse—all their chairmen, knocking on your door and asking, 'Can you do this for me?'"[14] While it is possible that Madoff suffered from antisocial personality disorder and that he was the financial sociopath that many have described him as because of his lack of empathy or remorse, I suppose we cannot discard those emotional experiences as important psychological elements that fed into his choices: not justifying them of course, but shaping his choices. It was better to steal than to face his fears of failure.

Reclaiming

Grievance: "the world owes me"

Experiences of neglect and emotional deprivation leave us full of anger and with a sense that we have been robbed of something. Stealing can be an expression of this grievance; of the injustice we have suffered and it offers (in phantasy) a way of getting something back. You steal because you feel "the world owes me."

Studies have shown that when people feel wronged, even in small ways, they are more likely to feel entitled and behave in a selfish way. In one experiment, for example, participants played a computer game. At the end of the game, they had the opportunity to claim part of a shared prize. Those who lost because of a glitch in the program (an *unfair* reason) selfishly demanded a greater share of the prize than those who lost for a fair reason: Being wronged instills a sense of entitlement that in turn leads to selfish action.[15] Imagine what happens when we have felt wronged at a vulnerable age and in a deeply impactful way: not a video game loss but robbed of a parent by death or illness; robbed of our childhood by a parental separation that means we had to step up into a parenting role for our siblings.

Psychoanalyst Donald Winnicott worked with delinquent children. In particular, he worked with children who were separated from their parents for their protection from air raids in London during World War II. He was left with no doubts that there was a link between the emotional deprivation caused by this premature separation and their stealing. In fact, what seemed particularly significant for him was the loss. He made a point that this wasn't privation (never having obtained something psychologically important) but deprivation, indicating that something of great value was there but had been taken away from these children. In his words, "When there is an antisocial tendency there has been a true deprivation (not a simple privation); that is to say, there has been a loss of something good that was positive in the child's experience up to a certain point, and that has been withdrawn; the withdrawal has extended over a period of time longer than that over which the child can keep alive the memory of the experience."[16] In Winnicott's view, there would have been an early period in which the environment enabled the child to make a good start in personal development[17] but then an environmental lapse of some kind or other that leads to a block in the maturational process of the child.

Stealing therefore becomes an unconscious expression of the desire to claim back what you feel you have been robbed of. In the present, stealing might give you the illusion of having power to repossess what was lost in childhood, rather than feel like the helpless and powerless victim of deprivation. You might even feel like you are filling the gap left by the deprivation through the stolen objects. This, I think, provides the backdrop for understanding the many cases in which the onset of stealing follows the death of a parent. Something vitally important is gone, and a part of us is attempting, albeit symbolically, to get it back. You stand hopeless in trying to stop your behavior if you haven't processed and worked through the pain associated with that early trauma. If the stealing is so embedded in a process of mourning a loss, it is only by accepting and working through the feelings of this loss that you can diffuse the need to act it out through stealing.

Redemption

A desire to be caught, punished, and relieved of guilt

Freud was the first to notice that criminals feel guilty *before* they commit a crime, and it could be that very guilt that is driving them and for which they are unconsciously seeking punishment. He wrote: "It was a surprise to find that an increase in this unconscious sense of guilt can turn people into criminals. But it is undoubtedly a fact. In many criminals, especially youthful ones, it is possible to detect a very powerful sense of guilt which existed before the crime, and is therefore not its result but its motive. It is as if it was a relief to be able to fasten this unconscious sense of guilt on to something real and immediate."[18] Freud refers to the mental relief that comes from committing a misdeed because it relieves the doer from an oppressive feeling of guilt.[19]

When we face a loss, self-blame and guilt often abound: guilt about the things we could have done to prevent the loss, guilt related to our angry thoughts and feelings about being abandoned, guilt about every negative thought and action we took in their regard. These feelings may flood our minds and, without knowing how to deal with them, we might seek a way to obtain the punishment we feel we deserve for them. If we are caught and are punished, locked up, or just reprimanded, we imagine (or might actually feel) some relief from our guilt.

Psychoanalyst Deborah Hindle described the case of two teenagers from different families (Chris and Cathy) who lost their same-sex parent in tragic circumstances when they were 14 years old, the former by suicide and the latter to illness. Both adolescents became involved in delinquent activities, which led to their sentencing to prison. Working with these young people she found a great sense of guilt in both of them. Cathy felt guilty about not saying goodbye to her mother and that not more had been done to save her and had nightmares in which her mother came back to get her for all the bad things she had done. Chris's guilt was more unconscious, but in therapy he revealed that there was guilt about the possibility of having been able to save his father (being the last person to speak to him before the suicide). Hindle saw their repeated offenses as a way to seek punishment and address their guilt.

Chris had a very difficult relationship with his father. Hindle went on to explain that Chris's father had been a heavy drinker, violent to his wife, and abusive toward Chris. He had in fact taken his own life in the family home, following an argument. So alongside feelings of guilt related to his father's death, Chris also carried guilt about the aggressive phantasies he held toward his father in response to the abuse he had suffered. As Hindle writes: "In both cases, prison provided some relief—it was a punishment for both actual and phantasized offenses,"[20] meaning that prison was punishment for both Chris's stealing and the aggressive acts he imagined inflicting on his father.

This case study so vividly describes the impact of such a conflicted relationship with an abusive parent. On top of the anger and guilt that may have been a motive for the repeated offenses, Chris might also have identified with his father. At some level he might have believed that he was like his father, and therefore not deserving of good things, and deserving punishment. Chris had very low self-esteem and his self-loathing was expressed as not being worthy and not deserving anything. The delinquency was therefore both a way of being destructive like his father, and a way of getting the punishment he felt both he and his father deserved. The delinquency, then, addressed guilt that resided at various levels of his psyche, both directly related to losing his father, and because of his identification with a parent that deserved punishment.

Cathy's mother also had a self-destructive element that Cathy might have identified with and was acting out through her delinquency: The mother had died as a result of severe obesity, so both these young people, explains Hindle, had witnessed their parents' self-destructiveness and might have in some way been repeating it.[21] Stealing was not only addressing guilt, but also a repetition of self-destructive behavior Cathy had seen modeled in her mother.

Rebellion

Against authority and to restore a sense of justice/balance

It may be difficult to watch others have something we desire (as we saw above, it may simply feel unjust) and in some cases, when we can't contain the feeling and manage it internally, we might take action that at some level helps us address it. Stealing from the person we envy or are jealous of is one way of depleting them and addressing our inner discomfort about them having more than we do.

We may envy their material belongings (like their wealth) but also non-material wealth (like more love, better relationships, being more attractive). Stealing is of course not about what money/object we are taking from them, but it is a symbolic act. In our minds all that matters is that we are taking something from them; we are diminishing their symbolic wealth.

Envy and jealousy are human emotions that everyone will experience at some point. For some, they are harder to manage. Psychoanalysts have traced these emotions back to very early experiences. We envy our mother for her ability to gratify our needs, and if she successfully and consistently does meet our needs we can integrate envy with our experience of love and gratitude.[22] However, if our experiences of good-enough mothering are sporadic, then envy gets mixed up with our feelings of greed and, as psychoanalyst Hanna Segal explains, results in a desire to rob the other of its goodness but also to deplete [the other] purposefully so that it no longer contains anything enviable.[23]

If envy can be summed up as "I want what you have," jealousy can be summed up as "I want what you have *with them*." Envy requires two participants while jealousy requires three, two of whom in a sense are in competition for the third. Stealing from someone we see as our competitor for the attention of the person we desire is one way to address a jealousy that feels unmanageable. The student sizzling in jealousy watching the teacher's favorite getting all the praise and attention might steal from that other student as a way of addressing their jealousy.

When siblings complain (as they often do) that something is not fair, they are essentially expressing their envy in relation to the other sibling (who seems to have a privilege of some sort) and asking for the perceived imbalance to be addressed. So the desire to even things out and to be equal stems from the thought, as Freud puts it, that "if one cannot be the favorite oneself, at all events nobody else shall be the favorite."[24] We might demand of our authority figures that they establish fairness, but if the injustice is left unaddressed, we might take it in our hands to redistribute resources. We might steal to find some inner peace that finally things feel fairer because we have depleted the other who we felt unfairly had more than us.

I have heard stories of siblings in which financial theft is one way of acting out feelings of envy and jealousy. What might start with a joint business venture in good faith may end up with siblings acting out deep-seated feelings of envy. Struggling for years to manage the (often unconscious) feelings about the extra love and attention that our brother received from our parents, we may find ourselves cheating and stealing from them. I have seen it in couple dynamics too: where one partner is so envious of the resources of the other (in some cases these were non-financial, like psychological strength, confidence, or even a more normal family) that they end up using money to express these feelings: running off with their partner's money or leaving them with a huge debt to repay on their own. Their experience of the partner as being so bountiful may be reality-based and/or inflated by a past experience of a sibling, or a parent having more than them. With that emotional scar in our minds, we might be hypersensitive to envy, often comparing and contrasting what we have versus what others have and find any imbalance quite triggering.

A study of 153 delinquents looked also at the siblings of these children, for comparison. They found that the delinquent child is the one who is frustrated, who feels he is not loved, while the non-delinquent child in the same environment is the one who finds a positive affectionate relationship with the parent or parents or suitable parent substitute.[25]

Carl E. Pickhardt, psychologist and parenting expert, explains that already by age three or four, most children can distinguish between what is mine and what is yours and that boundary cannot be crossed without consent. "By the onset of adolescence, around ages 9 to 13, most young people have this concept of personal ownership firmly installed. And yet, with the awakening desire to break boundaries for more freedom and independence, there is interest in testing old rules and restraints to see if the prohibitions of childhood still hold. [. . .] Out of this motivation, stealing can begin, casually at first."[26]

Stealing can be a way to test limits. Boundary testing, to some extent, is a natural part of development, explains Donald Winnicott. It's a way for the child to find out whether or not the parents can handle them and it's also a way of internalizing a certain sense of stability—it gives one a sense that they can predict the outcome of their actions and that they have some control over their fate. If these developmental needs are not met at home, then the child may seek to test boundaries socially (through delinquent behavior, like stealing) and so the child who does this is merely looking a little bit farther afield, looking to society instead of his own family or school to provide the stability he needs if he is to pass through the early and quite essential stages of his emotional growth.[27]

I suppose it's unsurprising, then, that in the YouGov study cited previously, 23 percent of people admitted to having shoplifted as children (a much higher percentage than adults). A combination of less established moral codes, boundary testing, and peer pressure create the conditions for this behavior pre-adulthood. Adolescence, in particular, is a complex time in life where alongside boundary testing, we are trying on different identities, trying to decide which parts of our identifications with our parents we are going to jettison and which we are going to take on board. As we saw with Chris and Cathy, stealing can be a way in which we are expressing an identification with, say, a father who didn't respect boundaries (as we saw in the case of Chris) or with a mother who was self-destructive through her disordered eating (as with Cathy).

Adolescence is also a time in which we care a lot about what people think of us. Chef Antony Worrall Thompson in his autobiography writes: "Getting in trouble always raised your status with the other boys."[28] So mischief may have appeal as it places us in the cool gang and helps us gain admiration of a group we are keen to join.

Stealing as mischief is also a way to attract parental attention: an important and effective strategy for those who are in families where they do not feel seen. Testing boundaries may be the only way to get the parents to notice us and in some cases, negative attention might feel better than no attention at all.

But it's one thing to be testing boundaries with the occasional disobedience, and another to be declaring a fully fledged rebellion against authority. In those instances, you are not just stealing to see if authority will notice, punish, or reestablish the boundary, but to communicate a more fundamental disgruntlement and assert a challenging stance: "I won't comply with your rules."

I was listening to a podcast called *Armchair Anonymous*[29] in which a young man admitted to stealing increasing amounts of money out of the cash register of the fast food chain that had employed him. His reason? He was angry because of a rule that meant that minors (like him) were paid a lower hourly rate than older employees, and this meant that despite his hard work (and promotion to a managerial position) he was still earning less than some of the new older employees he was training and who reported to him. It was his fury at the absurdity of this setup that he claims drove the stealing. He admitted to even calculating what a fair salary would be in his mind and often his theft would equal that amount as it would help him justify his actions. You see, anger is an ordinary and even healthy emotion, and it indicates a certain level of self-esteem, of knowing what we deserve: It is unfortunate when we can't find a healthy way to address our frustration and are compelled to rebel and act out instead. This will ultimately only temporarily give us relief but is destructive and comes, often, at a high cost.

At one level, then, we might justify what we are doing as restoring a sense of justice, yet often at another level, we are aware that our actions are immoral and often feel guilt and regret after the action. Sometimes we are quite conscious of our envy and the feeling of injustice, but in other cases we might carry an overall sense of having been dealt the proverbial bad hand and so stealing, even if not directed to these others who we envy, may still be about right-sizing the scale. I think of clients whose occasional pilfering occurred in the context of being "the scholarship kid" in private school (surrounded by wealthy classmates who had so much more material possessions) or "the only single-parent child" among classmates with traditional two-parent families. Taking something in that context at some level feels like restoring a balance in which everyone has the same.

When actress Winona Ryder's shoplifting hit the news in 2001, I was intrigued to read about her past. I find it interesting that Winona, whose family had lost many relatives in the Holocaust, grew up in fear that the same would happen to her. She would sleep on the floor outside her parents' room out of fear of being taken. It suggests a real struggle to cope with transgenerational trauma and a sense of vulnerability that unfair atrocities suffered by her family could happen again. Her fears were exacerbated by experiences of bullying in school that ended with her, rather than those who had been bullying her, being kicked out of school. She suffered from depression and anxiety starting in her twenties. I suppose having grown up in a world where unfair persecution is possible might have left her with a sense that the world isn't a fair place and an unconscious desire to take justice into her own hands. I am speculating of course when I wonder if carrying a transgenerational sense of injustice, compiled with her own experiences of it, might have left her eager to even the balance by symbolically taking back what was stolen from her and her family. What these examples have in common is the sense of injustice that these people experience, and which might help explain their actions as a way of restoring justice.

The anger resulting from past experiences of having felt wronged may therefore be the predominant emotion that gets expressed or acted out through stealing. Sometimes the stealing is not just an expression of anger, but an attempt to rid ourselves of it, to place it into another (to project it) and make them feel how we feel. Rather than me, the disgruntled one sitting with it, I take an action that inevitably makes the other feel angry and gives me some form of temporary relief from it. Continuing with Winona

Ryder's example, maybe stealing was an unconscious process that allowed her to project the feeling of being wronged onto the people she stole from rather than having to own it herself: It orchestrates a situation in which now it's another person who will have to carry the feelings that are too painful to manage in ourselves. Psychotherapist Susan Dyke writes about the children that Winnicott studied: "Such children [. . .] are evacuating their anger, humiliation and pain into those around them, erecting ever greater barriers between themselves and any relationships that would reactivate those feelings of vulnerability and hurt that have to be ruthlessly denied."[30] We place the anger in the other and use it as a protective barrier to ensure we won't be close and vulnerable to pain ever again.

Projection is often an unconscious psychological process, but revenge isn't, and stealing may simply be a way to voluntarily inflict pain/worry/distress to those who have caused us suffering. We might have decided that we don't want to give our parents what they wanted from us, to be the good boy/girl and delinquency may be a self-destructive way of getting back at them in our minds.

Search for assertion of power

Since I alluded to fraud in this chapter, which is essentially a form of stealing, it's worth adding one explanation of stealing that applies to white-collar crime more often than to the occasional pilfering: power-related motivators.

In the journal article "The Psychology of Fraud," Grace Duffield (a psychologist with the Australian Security Intelligence Organization) and Dr. Peter Grabosky (Deputy Director of the Australian Institute of Criminology) write "Highflying entrepreneurs tend to be extremely ambitious [. . .] and obsessed with enhancing power and control. Senior managers also usually have a favorable impression of themselves, sometimes unrealistically so. Whether it is conditioned by the successes they have attained during their rise to the top, or whether it is a necessary prerequisite to get to the top in the first place, some develop a sense of superiority bordering on narcissism."[31] Other researchers, including Kets de Vries,[32] add to this picture suggesting that narcissistic personality traits (such as the illusion of omnipotence, alongside the desire to maintain a grandiose image of themselves, along with the often accompanying sense of entitlement), make them likely candidates for fraudulent activities. Since fraud usually involves a great deal of deception, trying to outsmart or make a fool of the other may be an important (and psychologically rewarding) element of their behavior.

Entitlement, alongside maybe a sense of feeling immune to reprimand, can be the reason why some adolescents from families with wealth and power might engage in theft: It isn't just the thrill, but maybe also that broader sense of feeling above the law that they might have picked up from attitudes in their family of origin or by the clues of their social environment.

* * *

It seems that stealing, in any of its many forms, can be explained by a number of different psychological motives, only some of which I have covered in this chapter. Stealing may be just another way in which we self-sabotage, and so some of the explanation for a desire to self-destruct somehow may help us understand one's stealing. It may also be just another way in which we seek thrills or punishment because we believe that that is what we deserve.

As discussed before, one way to cope with feelings of fear is to try and prove to yourself and the world how fearless you are (and stealing is one way to do this). If you are struggling with your dependency on others, one way to address these feelings is to try and establish your self-sufficiency, and stealing, again, can be a way to defend against a reliance you are trying to deny.

Part of the work of therapy and of developing greater emotional awareness is to understand what it is that you are trying to express through the stealing. But it's also about acknowledging that stealing doesn't make you more powerful, more clever: It only compromises your freedom. If you want to curb your behavior you only stand a chance of doing so by facing the longings and fears that are driving your hand into someone else's possessions. Instead of taking Mom's money out of her purse and perpetuating a cycle of negative interactions, it might be more constructive to try and find a different way to say: "I am angry because you weren't there for me." Instead of stealing out of your employer's cash register it might be more helpful to have conversations about how to make the reward arrangement feel fairer.

I have seen people apply their view of the world as one inhabited by rapacious and cunning individuals to their business dealings. If everyone is out there to con you, to trick you, and you believe the world isn't a fair and just place, then what are the chances you will experience the government as a sort of good parent who will fairly use your money in a way that is beneficial to you and therefore pay rather than evade taxes? If your experience is that parents favor the other sibling over you, or that teachers unfairly accused you of cheating for example, then complying with the requests of an authority might be an emotionally charged challenge for you.

Coming back to Antony Worrall Thompson's story, what about his past might have influenced this 60-year-old chef's decision to steal some onions around Christmastime that year? If we look at his history (in an autobiography that predates him being caught stealing), we can recognize a lot of the themes covered in this chapter.

Antony's parents worked as actors in the 1950s. In the first 18 months of his life, Antony's mother was on tour playing a lead role in a play: "I was dragged from pillar to post, with hundreds of landladies at digs all around the country acting as surrogate aunts." His parents divorced when Antony was three years old and his father cut off all ties until Antony was 25 years old. Following the divorce, his mother sent him off to boarding school (yes, at age three). So two traumatic losses in one year: "My overriding memory is of feeling incredibly unwanted," writes Antony. He writes about the painful longing and waiting for his mother to come and pick him up on Sundays, only to be left waiting longer as she would often show up hours late. While other children greeted parents, Antony's mother often robbed him of the few and precious hours they could spend together (until he decided to start walking home on his own, age four, in the hope of having more time with her). Even when they were together, their relationship was far from harmonious: Accounts abound of Antony being made to feel responsible for his mother's unhappiness. "I was often reminded I was the reason my mother was lonely, unhappy and unloved."[33]

As if these traumas were not hard enough to overcome, Antony had more than one experience of sexual abuse from adults who were meant to be looking after him. The first by one of his mother's partners, a staff member at the school he attended from age eight, then a childminder and even a teacher. Violent and inhumane punishments from school principals for his mischiefs fueled the rage and helplessness that abuse victims are often left with. So first loss, then trauma. When it came to anger, he struggled with it throughout his life. In fact, even after training as a chef, jobs often ended up with him violently attacking his boss and leaving.

No wonder Antony rebelled against authority: His boundaries violated, his punishments extraordinarily disproportionate to his crimes, in some ways his rebellions were maybe the only way to triumph over how vulnerable he had felt throughout his childhood; it could also have been a protest against all the injustices he suffered and also possibly an unconscious effort to address the guilt that he had been made to feel by the adults in his life (first and foremost, his mother). He recognizes that he needed paternal discipline, which he never got, and maybe, as Winnicott suggests, he found ways to elicit it from his environment outside the family home with his relentless testing of boundaries and provocations. "I was fatherless and completely undisciplined," he writes.

I don't know what might have spurred him, age 60, to steal basic food at the supermarket. Christmas seems to be a meaningful time for the onset of that behavior: What might have been triggering about that time of the year? Antony spoke of stealing $5 worth of things after buying hundreds of dollars' worth of champagne for a charity dinner. Was it an internal conflict about giving, when a part of him had spent a lifetime feeling robbed? I am speculating of course, but the point is that there is meaning in our actions, even the seemingly inexplicable ones and sometimes, with some help, the meaning might become apparent, and we might understand the psychological drivers that influenced our actions.

Control: a quest for power or closeness?

Parents are expected to provide for their child's basic needs (at the very least), including food, shelter, clothing, education, and medical care, but there are no set rules about the expected level of giving. Similarly, many couples that choose to build a life together start with an often unspoken agreement that "what's mine is yours and what's yours is mine." Whether they both earn an income or not, there is a trust that an agreement can be reached about how to manage finances so that both parties feel a certain degree of financial freedom and autonomy. Some couples choose to reach the arrangement informally while others sign prenuptial agreements outlining each spouse's financial responsibilities. Ideally parents are generous enough and spouses can share in a good enough way.

There are exceptions, however. There are examples of dyads in which money is used in a manipulative and controlling way: It can be subtle and stay so. It might be that controlling behaviors slowly creep in and then escalate to dynamics of coercive and abusive control.

In this book we have come across money behaviors that permeate many aspects of life (we always struggle with boundaries, and so we struggle to keep within budget too; or we are always withholding in life and so we withhold money as well as other things). With control too, we might find that it is a behavior that might be embedded in how we set up relationships or it might be situational (we are controlling with some people and not with others).

I remember vividly the case of a man who was controlling with money with his first wife, who was depressed and emotionally withholding, but not with his next partner. Money was a great cause of arguments in his first marriage. Despite financial abundance, he would manage carefully how much he gave to his wife and what it would be spent on: He would frequently ask where she had been, and what she had spent the money on. He would often check her bank statements and be critical of how much she had spent on her friend's birthday present. It emerged that he had been harboring feelings of anger and resentment about the fact that his wife had become so emotionally inaccessible and unavailable to him. In response to this, he was reluctant to give to her, and money was one way in which he could express a desire to withhold from her because he had felt deprived by her. His controlling behavior with money was also an expression of the lack of trust in the relationship: Where had she been spending the money was often a cryptic way of asking where she had been and with whom. And why were others (like the friend) receiving generously from her, when he had felt so deprived of her love and attention? Money, in his mind, became partly a tool through which to monitor his wife (who are you investing in, if it isn't me?) because of the mistrust and a tool for retaliation (I don't give you money because you don't give me love) in view of the unexpressed anger.

He was, however, quite the opposite with his second wife. In this relationship that felt more intimate, more connected and mutual, the same man found it easier to share his wealth. He spent on joint vacations, was generous with gifts and didn't feel a need to monitor her every expense on the joint account. His lack of restraint and controlling behavior was a reflection of how he felt in the relationship: more hopeful that there could be mutuality of love and affection. When we behave in an unusual way with one particular person, it invites the question: What about that relationship dynamic evokes the need for this response?

One can be controlling with money in many different ways. Think of a family in which the husband is employed but the wife has given up her job to look after young children. They agreed that the husband will transfer money to his wife's account every month. In principle, there is nothing wrong with this arrangement. However, if the husband only transfers an amount that covers the most basic needs and any other expense his wife incurs is scrutinized, criticized, or denied, the wife might feel little financial freedom and autonomy.

Like with many money behaviors, it's all about context, frequency, and scale. It's not a one-off comment that should alarm us, but it's a pattern of behaviors and, most importantly, the growing sense in the other's mind that their freedom is restrained. Context matters because imagine if the wife, for example, struggles to spend in a reasonable way. We can look at the husband's reluctance to be abundant as an expression of his fear that she will overdo it with the spending again, or his way of protecting his wife from falling back into old spending habits, not a malicious intent to control her. Even though being controlling is not the best way to help her regain healthy spending habits, this context provides a basis for the couple to have a conversation in which she might say, "You are being too controlling with the spending and it feels uncomfortable," and he can express his fears about her relapsing until they can find a solution that works best for both.

Continuing with this example, what if the wife starts feeling that she doesn't have much of a say in the couple's big financial decisions? The husband might be (consciously or unconsciously) feeling entitled to more power in the decision-making because he is the one bringing home the money. But is that fair? Or is he stripping her of powers she is entitled to have, since the couple decided jointly that she would sacrifice her income for the sake of the family?

The husband at the start of the chapter is an example of control aimed at expressing anger and mistrust (and maybe also a retaliatory tool) and the couple just discussed is an example of control stemming from a power (and income) imbalance, but there are a myriad of ways and reasons why a dynamic of financial control can manifest in a relationship. In a controlling dynamic there is often emotional manipulation. Any behavior that is aimed at making the other feel dominated or dependent (belittling, threatening, humiliating, or isolating the other) may be a precursor or a tactic leading to financial control or even financial abuse. Think of these examples.

- Making your girlfriend feel guilty for not granting your every financial wish or desire
- Prohibiting your 19-year-old child from finding employment, keeping them financially dependent
- Delivering veiled threats to your partner about cutting them off financially unless they do as you say
- Demanding your name on a relative's will in return for visits/support
- Becoming angry/aggressive when your wife spends money
- Belittling your partner so you can claim decision-making power on financial matters

All of these are examples in which one tries to exert control and strip the autonomy from someone's finances. It is, however, important not to confuse vigilance with control: They are very different. Someone being careful with money is not the same as them being controlling. When there are different views on how money should be spent, a dyad's task is to find ways to negotiate those differences without either party taking an autocratic stance. In a romantic relationship, both people in the couple should feel a certain sense of financial freedom and autonomy. Take this example: "My husband often does not know what is in our bank account, flies off on work, spends a large amount of money on dinner and drinks, and then leaves me scrimping on grocery bills. Does it make me a bully if I check our balance and warn him if his spending is going over the budget?"[1] It sounds like this person feels their partner is spending excessively and they are probably rightfully wary: checking the account, trying to have a conversation with their partner about budget. These are sensible moves, spurred by what sounds like reasonable concerns.

Financial and economic abuse

Although the two terms are used interchangeably, financial abuse is a subcategory of economic abuse and it refers to restricting an individual's ability to acquire, use, and maintain financial resources. An abuser might limit the victim's access to a bank account, steal money from them, accumulate debt in their name (damaging their credit rating), gamble their savings, or even coerce them into changing their will. What is being controlled specifically are one's financial resources.

Economic abuse is a broader term that encompasses behavior that limits the victim's economic situation overall and any opportunity to improve it.[2] It goes beyond financial control in that what is being restricted isn't just money but also the freedom to access basic goods or services. An abusive partner might limit access to essential items like food, clothing, and hygiene products and even control access to transport (taking away their driving license or passport) and technology (mobile phone) that allows the victim contact with the outside world. The victim might be denied opportunities to improve their financial situation through education, training, or employment, for example.

In both financial and economic abuse, the behavior of the abuser tends to be coercive and deceptive as well as unreasonably controlling, ultimately limiting their autonomy.

Research, conducted in 2020 by the Co-operative Bank and Refuge (a domestic abuse charity), found that 16 percent of adults identify as having experienced economic abuse in a relationship. Yet only a third of adults have ever heard of economic abuse.[3] Evidence suggests that during the COVID-19 pandemic, the number of people suffering economic or financial abuse increased, with a staggering 1.6 million people having first experienced economic abuse during this period. In a separate study (conducted by Women's Aid, a domestic violence charity, in 2020), more than half of the 202 victims surveyed either started to experience economic abuse during the pandemic or their abuse worsened during this time.[4] Lockdown restrictions created an opportunity for abusers to exert greater control over their victims (by moving back in with them, for example, or through increased oversight of their activities in view of the lockdown). The economic impact of COVID-19, with income decreasing in many households due to lay-offs and wage decreases, created additional stressors that exacerbated financial abuse.

These types of abuse are almost always accompanied by other forms of abuse such as psychological, physical, and/or sexual abuse. Research by Adams et al. found that 99 percent of domestic abuse survivors also experienced some form of economic abuse in the relationship.[5] Research by Women's Aid confirms that economic abuse might be a precursor to other forms of abuse.[6] The controlling behavior may start with limiting the other's access to bank accounts and escalate to more violent or pervasive forms of control. It is just one way in which the perpetrator is looking to restrain the freedom and independence of the other. Money is often the main barrier to women leaving an abusive and controlling partner as victims might feel that the choice they face is between poverty and abuse. Women's Aid found in their research that 52 percent of abuse victims could not leave their abuser because they had no money. They add: "The manipulation of money and other economic resources is one of the most prominent forms of coercive control, depriving women of the material means needed for independence, resistance, and escape."[7]

While some kind of power imbalance in couples when it comes to money is common (there might be one partner that earns most of the couple's income and tends to have a stronger voice when it comes to the couple's financial decisions), with economic or financial abuse the power imbalance is massively skewed. One person has most of the control and the other has almost none. And let's not forget that there is a difference between power (as a form of influence) and control (which is an effort to direct someone's behavior, limiting their freedom): Abuse restricts freedom and therefore is often the result of an abuse of power.

Some of the strategies most commonly used to exert psychological control over someone include minimizing or denying the abuse, trying to put the blame on the victim, using isolation to prevent any external influences, controlling all aspects of the person's life (whom they talk to, where they go), emotional abuse (like belittling, humiliating, and criticizing), or using intimidation, threats, and coercion.[8]

Like any form of abuse, it leaves the victim feeling completely helpless and powerless. The victim quite often is left to believe that they are to blame for their situation (and this is often part of the abuser's narrative), carrying a great sense of shame and guilt. In healthy relationships, conversations are two-way and respectful. Sarcasm, insults, and disparaging comments are signs that the relationship is abusive. Not only does the victim have no autonomy with regard to obtaining access to resources, but any ask they make is rejected and leaves them feeling insecure, attacked, blameworthy, and even afraid. The abusive partner responds with indifference, a lack of empathy, or aggression. Lies and manipulation are often used to fuel the guilt. "If it wasn't for you, we wouldn't be in this situation."

The reason why financial abuse can lead to a downward spiral of abuse is that it traps the victim, limiting their ability to leave. Without resources they can't go far: The link between money and survival is vividly felt. Even when they find a practical way out, they might feel afraid to do so (having the many threats made to them in their mind) and are left in a psychological prison that is as hard to leave as the physical prison-like situation they might be struggling to escape. A third of people experiencing economic abuse never confide in someone about their experience.[9] This is why often the only way out is with the emotional as well as practical support of someone who can physically extrapolate them from the abusive relationship. It is also a form of abuse that doesn't necessarily stop once the victim manages to physically escape from the abuser as it might take time to settle legal disputes related to the financial abuse or disentangle assets that are jointly held.

Reasons

I have seen clients, who turned out to be quite controlling in interpersonal relationships, manifest this unconsciously in our relationship in small, inconspicuous ways: They might control the space (moving around chairs in the consulting room or leaving little room for my interventions); they might control the sessions by asking for frequent changes to our meeting time or ending the session early (so they are in charge of when it's over); and of course may try to be controlling with money too (reminding me how much they pay for the sessions as a way to assert superiority or make demands).

It is easy to demonize and stereotype someone who is overly controlling. It's not always men, and they are not always malicious in their intent. A person may be acting in a controlling way without being consciously aware of it. They might not recognize their behavior as controlling or be unaware of the manipulative aspect of it. They might justify their behavior as being cautious, as protecting the other or doing what is best for everyone. It's important, therefore, not to make assumptions of someone's intentions when it comes to control: It might not be a plot to disempower the other, but a psychological defense against their own fears.

Control to prevent rejection or even abandonment

Although being the victim of a controlling dynamic is awful, the person who is controlling might have developed this in response to their own emotional disappointments. A history of unmet emotional needs that leave us feeling so frightened of being let down might lead us to adopt a defensive strategy in which controlling the other minimizes the risk of being hurt again. Shouting "I will kill myself if you leave me" is a form of emotional blackmail, but in this threat there might be more than just a malicious intent to control: There might be a real terror at the thought of being left again.

So controlling their partner and overpowering them financially to an extent that limits their autonomy could be appeasing the fear that the other will leave us. We might not be aware of how manipulative we are being, and we might be blind to the detrimental and even counterproductive aspect of our controlling defense, but it comes from a desperate place, where the fear of ever feeling that alone and scared again overpowers anything we might know rationally about what good communication is or what is right or wrong to say and do in a relationship.

Control as a power play to avoid feeling powerless

The fear is different for someone who has suffered from abuse. If we have felt overpowered, taken advantage of, or betrayed, then setting up relationships ensuring we are on top, might offer some psychological relief from the fear that we will ever feel helpless and hopeless again. It is why it's common for abusers (of any sort) to have been victims of abuse themselves: Having suffered at the hands of a dominating abuser, they identify with them in an effort to manage the emotional pain and feel some form of control over it. They take on the abusive role in future relationships to ensure never being dominated again. It's a phenomenon that psychoanalyst Anna Freud called identification with the aggressor.[10] Controlling a partner financially, disempowering them, creates a sense of safety in our minds, that this time we can't be stripped of what belongs to us because now we are in charge.

The opposite, however, is also true. Unable to move on from experiences in the past, victims of abuse might find themselves compelled to repeat them unconsciously, hoping for a different resolution this time around. The victims of abuse might be unconsciously falling into one abusive relationship after another, repeating those familiar childhood dynamics (which I have explained is a psychological defense that Freud called "repetition compulsion" but also known as "trauma reenactment").[11] It is also the case in my experience that people tend to choose what is familiar over the unknown, so when they find a partner who is caring and respectful of their boundaries and autonomy, they begin to feel uneasy and begin to think, "It's too good to be true," or "It feels weird," or "It won't last." It is disorienting and anxiety-provoking to be treated in a way that is the opposite of what we are used to, and therefore of what we expect. Unfortunately, expecting abuse means that it often turns into a reality through a self-fulfillling prophecy.

Control as a form of retaliatory withholding

We saw an example of this in the introduction. Rather than facing the anger, sadness, and frustration we might feel toward a partner for how unheard, uncared for, or disregarded we might have felt, we act it out by being financially controlling toward them. We might start by making harsh comments about what they spent on; move on to limiting how much of our (or the jointly held) money they can access for recreational purposes; things might escalate and money becomes just an object we withhold to protest about the more significant withholding we have felt from them (withholding of affection, sex, or emotional availability).

The psychology of the controlled

It is hard to comprehend why some people stay in (or frequently end up in) dynamics that are so damaging for them. As I mentioned previously, there is often a repetition taking place of past emotional experiences which they might be seeking rescue from: a hope that this time it will turn out differently.

Psychoanalyst Bernhard Berliner[12] described the process through which a child might identify with the hateful and rejecting parent and manifest this against themselves, meaning that a part of us becomes mean and punishes the masochistic part of us. Suffering therefore becomes the price one needs to pay to feel loved. Experiences of aggressive or emotionally abusive parenting might have shaped a belief that love and suffering are inevitably interlinked. If in our minds we have a fused idea of love and suffering, suffering might be how we preserve love. We don't do this consciously of course, we don't seek it out knowingly, but end up in it partly because it is familiar, partly because we don't feel we deserve better, and partly also in the hope that this time it might turn out better.

Our partner's blaming us for everything that is wrong in the relationship hooks into a template already established in our minds: a narrative of self-blame, of deserving punishment, of being worthy of little. We are resigned to the idea that we'll give more than we receive. The control or the financial abuse is hard to question and challenge, and for some victims, it's so familiar that they struggle to even see that there is anything untoward with the dynamic they find themselves in.

As the *Psychodynamic Diagnostic Manual* (a diagnostic handbook) writes, some people may "subordinate their needs to those of others and appear to view suffering as a precondition for maintaining an attachment relationship. The attachment relationship may be experienced as desperately needed; fear of losing the attachment overrides the patient's concerns for his or her own safety and welfare." In other words, an abusive relationship might, in their minds, feel safer than no relationship at all. As psychoanalyst Léon Wurmser put it: "Torment me but don't abandon me."[13] So both the abuser and the abused may share the very same longing to be attached and loved yet one defends against it by controlling their loved one and the other by relinquishing their needs and being submissive to the other.

Case studies

Jonah, a client, was working as a part-time teacher and struggling to meet his financial obligations (like paying his bills and rent). He told me, "I would rather get evicted than ask my father for money." Jonah's relationship with his father was complex. There were clearly disappointments and anger that characterized the relationship. Jonah felt his father had been selfish and not empathetic toward his mother as she struggled for years with post-partum depression. The main reason for Jonah's refusal of his father's money (which was often offered) wasn't anger or pride, but the fact that his father had always used money in a manipulative and controlling way. His father tried to entice Jonah to spend more time with him through abundant gifts, which Jonah experienced as controlling. Jonah explained, "If I accepted a gift or money from him, I would see it thrown back in my face one way or another. He will repeat a thousand times how good and generous he is and wants me to agree with him and thank him. He will definitely ask for something in return like to go out with him." It never felt like a generous act, but an indirect request for an exchange. Jonah explained that his father used every encounter to talk about himself, impose his own views or needs, or to show off about his achievements, failing to express interest or to understand his son. For Jonah, the financial giving was a painful reminder of everything he had felt deprived of, all the unmet emotional needs, his longing for a dad who would be interested in him. His gifts were therefore rejected or resented. He would say, "This is NOT what I want from him. I want his love. I want him to care about what is going on in my life. I don't want his money!" Jonah felt that money for his father was a weapon for control as well as a substitute for emotional giving, which Jonah longed for.

It is hard to know what drove Jonah's father to behave in such a controlling way with money. It might have been, unconsciously, a way of coercing a desirable response from his children (gratitude, appreciation) which would reassure him that he is a good father. It might have been an effort to connect with them, without being aware of how manipulative his way of seeking their attention was. It might also have been a repetition of how his own parents received any positive attention from their children. What seemed evident was that there wasn't in his father a sense of faith that Jonah would want a relationship with him unless it was extorted or manipulated out of him. Maybe then, his controlling behavior was a defense against being rejected or denied something important. If he offered money and only then asked for gratitude, meetings, or reassurance, he minimized the chances of being denied it.

So a dynamic of financial control isn't unique to romantic relationships, and it can be subtle, like the occasional imposition (a friend that insists we all share the bill equally, leaving little room for your input into the choice), it can be less subtle, like the case of Jonah, or it can be a case of economic abuse, like the one I will present to you now.

In 2022, I participated in a podcast called *Grano* (which is an Italian slang word for money), hosted by Mia Ceran.[14] In this episode on economic abuse, an audience member volunteered to share her story of abuse as a child growing up. At the beginning of the chapter, as we looked at definitions of control and abuse, I spoke about a power imbalance and an obvious question here is how to define economic abuse between a parent and a child when the financial relationship is so unbalanced by nature. The child is financially dependent on the parents, so there isn't, like in couples, an expectation of equal power in the dynamic. But as I also explained, it isn't simply about an imbalance but also about how power is used and the impact it has on the other.

This example is undeniably one of abuse and it so vividly shows the psychological impact of this form of control, in this case from her own parents.

Paola tells us: "I was able to start shopping independently in my early twenties, once I had my first job. Before that money was inaccessible to me. What I needed was tied to my parents' wallet. I wasn't allowed to attend concerts or parties or go on vacations with my friends. I couldn't use public transport or buy shoes or clothes independently. Deodorant was an excessive ask (my parents told me that I should shower if I smell), and the only sanitary towels I was allowed to use were the very bulky ones. The thin ones were, too, an excessive ask.

"I was under the strict control of my parents. [. . .] After high school, my parents wanted me to attend a prestigious private university (as it would elevate the family's prestige), but despite my desire to go, I refused the offer. Agreeing to it would have tied me to the family in a relationship of further dependence in which I would have been allowed to attend, but on their terms and under their strict financial control [. . .] with the obligation that I delivered top marks. I was faced with shunning, verbal and physical aggression, and obstacles to living an ordinary life. I applied instead to a course that would guarantee me a job after graduation and, even though I braced myself for rejection, I was accepted based on merit. I then faced the challenge of traveling to and from the venue. [. . .] I didn't believe in my ability to cope on public transport. [. . .] I wasn't capable of doing anything, or so I felt: an incapable human being. Everything scared me, I saw every obstacle as insurmountable.

"Eventually my parents conceded a very small stipend. It was enough for basic needs, nothing else. [. . .] Managing every expense I accumulated enough to afford a movie ticket. My boyfriend had insisted for years on paying for my ticket, but I didn't want to depend on someone for my freedom. I used to always tell him, 'The day I can afford to come, I will join you.'

"[. . .] After obtaining my first job, I decided to open a personal bank account. I was showered with insults: I was just a bad daughter, an ungrateful, selfish b*tch. How could I do such a thing? My family needed that money and I had allowed myself to keep it as if mine? I couldn't stand up to them because I didn't have the conviction of being on the side of reason. I was dominated, convinced to be in the wrong. I did compare myself to others (and remember this was pre-internet) but could not consider myself a victim of economic violence. Of course I realized that I was not like the others; I did not have the same possibilities, but I always thought it was how life was in a family that isn't wealthy."

Paola was denied access to basic products; her reasonable requests were belittled and denied; communication with her parents left her feeling attacked, criticized, and unworthy; their behavior left her feeling powerless and guilty. Rather than helping their child grow into an autonomous and confident person, they left her feeling like an incapable human being and trapped.

These experiences set the stage for Paola to be fearful of dependence in her adult relationships: She wouldn't let her boyfriend buy her a movie ticket. For Paola, this innocent offer evoked the fear of ending up in a scary controlling dynamic that she was determined to avoid at all costs. A red flag popped up in her mind to safeguard her from being hurt again: She wouldn't go back into a prison of control. In those moments, when present relationships evoke fears from the past, doing a reality check is not easy. Accepting that a ticket does not condemn her to a life under control seems too great a risk to take . . . but slowly, some with therapy, some with the reinforcement of positive experiences and relationships, some people manage to build faith in relationships again, to lower their defenses and allow themselves healthier, more fulfilling experiences of relationships in the future.

As an adult, Paola carried money-related fears that created obstacles for her as she became financially independent. Later in the podcast, she spoke of a difficulty in spending with largesse. Of course, in part this is due to the real economic difficulties she faced. But it was more than that. People who grow up with narcissistic parents, like Paola, are deprived of two essential elements of healthy psychological separation and growth: the space for their needs and desires to be expressed and met in a good enough way, and real empathy. A narcissistic parent reduces everything to their own needs and feelings. This leaves the child with an inadequate sense of deservedness. The message that was reinforced at home was "your requests are ridiculous, you don't deserve." It is no surprise then that this generated a conflict in her as she grew up: an adult part of her knew that now that it was her money, her choice, she could afford to give herself more, but another part, the child part of her, still believed that she did not deserve them, that her desires were outrageous. As she says: "Because you don't have the conviction that you are on the side of reason in the end."

Exiting dynamics of control and abuse

Exiting an abusive relationship is not easy. Paola's resolute commitment to preventing the past from repeating itself and her ability to muster the courage and strength to enable that are admirable. Many victims of abuse feel stuck for the rest of their lives, incapable of changing their situation. It is difficult to convince oneself that the future will be different from the past, but allowing for that possibility is the key to change. Even though the past was your normal, it doesn't have to be like that. Paola tells of how disorienting it was, growing up, to realize that others had a very different experience of being parented. What she considered normal was not common at all. She says: "You wonder where the truth lies, the right way to live, the right way to have relationships." Paola had to find a way to redefine what normal was for her.

Exiting a repetitive cycle firstly entails accepting the reality of what is happening, which isn't easy. One victim of abuse says: "When you're in the moment, you just kind of downplay it and you just think, 'Oh, it's not that bad.' [. . .] I think I'd accepted it. I just thought, this is it. This is my life and I couldn't see how it was going to get any better." There is the denial but also the slow and gradual escalation of events that helps the denial.

Secondly, finding the strength to ask for help (from a friend, a family member, professional, or even a helpline). Help is particularly important in cases where the victim has lost all financial independence, making it logistically impossible to leave. Often in relationships of financial abuse there is also psychological abuse that includes isolating the victim from close people (making the help feel out of reach). Every situation is different but often the level of impotence (psychological but also financial) is such that only with the support of someone close can you get out of such a situation.

In some cases, it is possible to secretly save some money with the purpose of exiting the abusive relationship (and of course this is a money secret with more benefits than disadvantages).

Once out, as we saw with Paola, there is work to be done not only to process the traumatic experience, but also to ensure that we have enough psychological robustness to have a healthy relationship in the future: neither avoiding relationships altogether, nor falling into a similar dynamic again.

* * *

This chapter has shown how we can use money as a weapon of control and while cases of financial abuse are extreme (albeit more common than we might expect), there are many subtle ways in which we can enact controlling dynamics through money. The question I invite you to ask if you have recognized yourself in this chapter, is what might be driving your desire to control the other? Is it rooted in memories and experiences of money being used as the lever that exerted desired responses? Or are you responding to feelings evoked in your current relationship that you are finding no other way to address? Is controlling your partner a way of protecting you from a fear of being left, rejected, or denied what you long for? But most importantly: Can you allow yourself to recognize the detrimental impact of control and think of a different way to address whatever fears and desires you are trying to cope with?

If you are a victim of financial abuse, you can seek help by reaching out to the National Domestic Violence Hotline at 1-800-799-7233 or live chat at thehotline.org/get-help/. Note: They help victims of any gender.

CHAPTER 9

Money secrets

Paul Tournier, renowned for his work in pastoral counseling (a counseling approach that integrates spirituality/faith with psychotherapy), once wrote, "Nothing makes us so lonely as our secrets."[1] I couldn't agree more. Even though secrets are much more common than any of us would ever expect (or care to admit), they can be detrimental to our mental health. Money secrets are no exception, both in their frequency and also in how isolated they might leave you feeling and the harm they may cause to your relationships.

There are all sorts of money secrets people keep. From hiding purchases and addictions to lending money without consent, hiding a source of income or debts/accounts. You can imagine how interlinked financial infidelity might be with sexual infidelity, for example, either paying for sex or treating an extramarital partner to meals, vacations, presents. The research on money secrets is not abundant but there have been a number of surveys and polls that give us a broad idea of the frequency and type of money secrets that people keep.

According to the NEFE (National Endowment for Financial Education) poll, of the surveyed adults who have ever combined their finances, around two in five (43 percent) committed a form of financial deception, of which most hid something from their partner (usually cash or purchases) or lied about finances (be it debt, income, or other). According to research by Aviva in 2023, two out of five people in a relationship admit to financial infidelity.[2]

According to a 2021 survey, the top areas of secrecy are hidden credit cards (37 percent), personal loan (23 percent), and secret savings accounts (21 percent).[3] The Aviva survey found that 38 percent of participants admitted to having savings (on average around $2,000) which they are keeping secret from their partner.[4] Common lies found by the NEFE study were hiding purchases and lying about the price paid for something.

Despite these high figures, we seem to be in denial of how common money secrets are. One survey asked whether people kept money secrets but also whether they suspected their spouse of keeping money secrets from them. While 45 percent admitted to currently keeping a financial product undisclosed from their partner, only 23 percent of these participants suspected that their partner was doing the same.[5]

I had a client, Elly, who was considering keeping a financial secret from her husband. Elly and Liam had been together for over 15 years. Their relationship was strong, with an abundance of love, empathy, and understanding, but over the years as efforts to communicate gradually faded, and with the pressure of external challenges (career and three children), they started having trouble in their relationship.

Liam's repeated work trips kept him away from family life and responsibilities. And because of this, Elly started seeing him as selfish. She grew resentful of his absence and of his unspoken assumption that *she* would make the career sacrifices needed for the children to have at least one parent around, and of the lack of equality in the division of commitments at home. The bickering grew into bigger arguments to the point where they spent days without talking to one another. It was at this stage of the relationship that Elly (who had up until this point been 100 percent transparent with Liam about everything) started thinking the following.

- "Maybe he is not the man I thought he was." (Disappointment)
- "Maybe he doesn't deserve my unconditional trust. How far will his selfishness go?" (Mistrust, fear)
- "Does he think I am so desperate that I will stick around forever, no matter how unfair things are?" (Anger)
- "Why doesn't he see how unhappy I am?" (Sadness)

This whirlpool of emotions and thoughts was hard to manage. The couple were no longer communicating constructively, which left Elly feeling lonely, angry, and unheard. Her view of him had changed. In her mind, he had become capable of greater selfish acts, and she wondered whether he was cheating on her.

It was in this state of mind that Elly started contemplating financial infidelity: "I put my great aunt's inheritance in a new account. For a rainy day . . . I didn't tell Liam about it, I mean, if he was ever at home, I might have mentioned it . . . but also, I don't know what *he* is up to . . . and you never know . . ." Therefore, leading to the birth of a secret.

In her pondering we see her confusion: Withholding this money from his knowledge was her retaliation (he wasn't going to be the only one withholding something and being selfish in the relationship); it was also a safety blanket for a rainy day (was that a fear they'd separate?); the secret (and the money) also made her feel more powerful in a dynamic in which she had felt unappreciated and undervalued.

I have witnessed people's extended mental debates about the degree and pace of financial disclosure in relationships. Is it better to tell him the full truth at once? Or should I adopt a piecemeal disclosure strategy and wait until I reveal the more shameful aspect of my financial reality? Financial disclosures may fill us with fear and dread. Will she leave me if I tell her about my debt? Will my parents think I am a failure if I admit to quitting my job? Will we get into another fight if I tell her I went gambling again? Will he only be interested in my money if I tell him how wealthy I am?

As we explore why we lie about money, we will uncover reasons that are very much personal and linked to our own past experiences or our own self-judgment, and others that are more about how we structure relationships and particularly the emotional baggage that we bring to a relationship (which I will also cover in chapter 10). It could be insecurities about disclosing a money behavior we fear the other will disapprove of, but even more broadly, it could be a way of addressing non-financial fears about deepening a relationship or losing autonomy.

Before we can explore these in more depth, it's worth defining what comprises a "money secret." The *Oxford English Dictionary* defines a secret as something that is kept or meant to be kept unknown or unseen by others. Under this definition, any information related to our finances which we are intentionally keeping unknown from others (through lies or omission) qualifies as a secret. The key word is "intentionally," which implies first of all that we know about it and secondly that we have agency in disclosing it and are choosing not to.

The only problem with this definition is that it doesn't help us draw a distinction between privacy and secrecy. Interestingly, the same dictionary defines privacy as someone's right to keep their personal matters and relationships secret. So when we define money secrets we can't condemn all secrets because some of them fall within the realm of our privacy.

In a 2021 poll of over 2,000 adults run by NEFE, 38 percent of the respondents thought that some areas of finance need to remain private.[6] I am not advocating that couples should be transparent about every single expense they incur, or that children (particularly adult children) necessarily need to disclose their financial realities to parents from whom they are financially independent. It's all about expectations: Has there been a conversation in the dyad (whoever the two parties are) about what will be kept private and what won't? Have we agreed with our partner, for example, that $X a month will be allocated to each of us for our own personal enjoyment without having to report on each expense? Setting boundaries around privacy can help a dyad distinguish between these two in order to avoid feeling deceived or betrayed.

The term "financial infidelity" also has its limitations. Financial infidelity has been defined as engaging in any financial behavior expected to be disapproved of by one's romantic partner and intentionally failing to disclose this behavior to them. As Garbinsky et al. explain, it involves both an act and the intentional concealment of the act assuming disapproval.[7] Although that is a helpful distinction to make, it leaves out secrets that are kept for all other reasons (not just expected disapproval): Elly is the perfect example of this. While she chose to withhold the information (intentionality), this wasn't because she assumed he'd disapprove of her receiving an inheritance. Rather, it was a mixture of anger, resentment, and mistrust that stopped her from being honest.

And of course, I talk about money secrets more broadly because many money secrets are kept from people other than our romantic partners. For example, not telling our parents who still financially support us through university that we have lost $3,000 of the money they've given us on a gambling app. This clearly is a financial secret, kept intentionally, expecting disapproval.

The following is an example of a money secret kept for reasons other than expected disapproval. Someone, who I will call Rose, recently asked me, "Am I being a liar for not telling my best friend that my fiancé and I could only afford the new flat because my parents gave us the money for the down payment?" She is contemplating a secret and breaking what seems like an expectation of transparency between these close friends. There certainly is intentionality in keeping the information from her friend (she didn't just forget to tell her friend, she purposefully withheld the information). There isn't, though, an expectation of disapproval: Rose doesn't imagine her friend would ever disapprove of her parents being generous and supportive. Why then, is the fact that she had her parents' help so difficult to be transparent about? What is being avoided and what is the cost on the relationship of this information emerging later?

One reason for keeping it secret is that she wanted to impress her friend with her achievement of buying a flat, without giving the full picture. This might have left her feeling like a phony by keeping this version of reality going. Or she might have withheld the information because her friend had been complaining to her for months about how unsupportive financially her own parents had been when she asked them to borrow money for a home renovation. The non-disclosure then might have been about protecting her friend by not exposing her to such a painful contrast between parents who were supportive and generous and her friend's, who seemingly weren't. Maybe it was also about avoiding her friend's envy. Whether it was a desire for admiration and praise or a desire to protect a friend, this wasn't about avoiding disapproval.

There may be very legitimate reasons for our omissions and our lies, but we are not in court and it's not about convincing ourselves or someone else that we had reasons to lie or not be transparent. What is more helpful is to recognize which emotions might be driving the desire for secrecy so we can be in a better place to assess if the best way to deal with them is in fact by keeping a secret. Being realistic about the impact of secrecy may help us evaluate whether the scale should tip in favor of honesty for the sake of the relationship.

Social context

Dishonesty is not seen as a virtue. In most cultures and societies, it is condemned and (depending on the nature of the lie) it's even punished by law. Most religions denounce lies, deceit, and lack of transparency too. In Christianity, for example, deceit and lies are sins. The Bible writes: "What you have said in the dark will be heard in the daylight, and what you have whispered in the ear in the inner rooms will be proclaimed from the roofs" (Luke 12:3).[8] In Islam, Prophet Muhammad said: "Falsehood leads to wickedness and evil-doing, and wickedness leads to the Hellfire. And a man may keep on telling lies until he is written before Allah as a liar" (*Sahih al-Bukhari*). Buddhist teachings similarly condemn lying as it goes against what they call "right speech," which is a crucial element of achieving peace within an individual but also in their society.

Society condemns secrecy, dishonesty, and deception. People who are perceived as secretive may face social disapproval or damage to their reputation. There are laws and regulations that guarantee transparency and disclosure of information. But even though society condemns secrets, they are common. Thinking specifically of financial secrets, there are several societal trends that might have contributed to our desire to hide our financial reality and our ability to do so.

One trend that might have enabled secrecy is the move from physical forms of money dealings to electronic ones. We no longer need to be receiving letters from the bank at our home address, risking our partner finding out about the secret account we have been withholding. A secret stock trading account, supplying us with some extra income, can be managed straight from a mobile phone. We don't need to justify trips to the bank when most transactions can be done online. This is true for parent-child dynamics too: With the new generation of adolescents often being more technology savvy than their parents, there is a lot of scope for secret financial activity that escapes parental scrutiny.

Social media might mislead our perception of how common financial problems are. If we give too much weight to platforms used for showcasing professional achievements (where understandably there are more people boasting about their latest promotion rather than people talking about being made redundant or struggling to manage their debt), we might be left feeling that we are the only person who isn't financially successful. It might then be harder to disclose any financial failings to a partner or friend if our view of how ordinary financial difficulties is being distorted.

Reasons

Secrets (and the lies that often come with them) damage the most fundamental component of any relationship—trust. So why do people do it?

Some of the research has very much looked at financial infidelity as a normative conflict, namely a clash between our own financial preferences/goals/desires and those of the other.[9] This results in a situation in which we have a choice to either act in accordance with our partner's preferences or in contrast to these, and if we choose the latter, then we can either confess or lie about it. I struggle to take such a rational view of financial infidelity, because in my experience people are not always clear about their partner's views. There are a lot of assumptions and projections (we imagine our partner will be very critical because we are very critical with ourselves about our behavior), nor does hiding always happen as a conscious choice (sometimes there is an intention to confess that gets postponed in time out of fear).

I am not saying that we have no agency in lying or omitting the truth, but money secrets are often driven by much more irrational and emotional psychological processes. There are money secrets that are intended to mask our own personal fears and insecurities: It might be a fear of abandonment that makes us stash away an emergency fund we choose not to disclose rather than an expected disapproval; it could be envy of our partner's success at work that makes us overspend and feel enriched by beautiful items when we feel so insignificant compared to our successful other; or a mixture of complex feelings, like we saw with Elly in the example above. Money secrets that involve helping others, for example (like supporting children financially, or giving a loan to a close relative) may be kept undisclosed because we are ashamed of exposing to our partner how easily persuaded we are, how hard we find it to say no to people (aspects of ourselves that we struggle with in various parts of life, and that might have been criticized by our partner in the past).

For many, keeping secrets is what they are used to. Secrets might have been a feature of family life: children who knew of their parents' affairs, but it wasn't talked about or ever discussed. Families in which too many conversations happened behind closed doors, leaving the children with a sense that few things can be talked about openly. In a family where truths are hidden and maybe secrets even justified as a good way to not hurt the other, it will inevitably make hiding the truth a viable option as a coping strategy for difficult feelings.

Emma was raised by a manic-depressive mother who struggled with alcohol addiction and had fallen into a string of romantic relationships after her husband left her (when Emma was only 11). She had grown up feeling her father had abandoned her to this out-of-control mother, and the feelings of rejection were exacerbated by his moving abroad and cutting off contact with her. Her mother would regularly embarrass Emma, who attended a school in a wealthy suburb, full of good and functional families: picking her up from school in manic states and making drunken comments in front of Emma's friends. This troubled childhood had left her with a longing for more, a sense of being owed more than she had received alongside a deep sense of shame about her family history and fears of her own madness. Her lying started in school: She often made excuses for her father's absence: "He is traveling for work," she would tell her friends when they asked why her father never attended the plays and recitals. Lies quickly became a coping tool for avoiding getting in touch with her own sadness, disappointment, and anger, and also a tool to help her avoid judgment and the resulting sense of shame that this would evoke. The shame was close to the surface: Emma never felt good enough and often wondered if her father left because she wasn't what he wanted—he always wanted a boy, or so she had heard Grandpa say. All these complex and deep-seated feelings set the stage for understanding and unpacking why now, age 35, she spent compulsively and kept a large sum of hidden credit card debt from her partner. Recently married, Emma came to therapy to understand why she was seemingly sabotaging her relationship with such a big secret.

Of course there wasn't one explanation that accounted for everything but, like peeling an onion, there were layers upon layers of emotions that stood in the way of being transparent. Lying was a useful defense when she was a child. But was it helping her present relationship? What was she really afraid of if he'd find out? What was she trying to hide from her partner? It was that shame, the shame of her non-perfect past, the non-perfect family, the embarrassment of her mother and Emma's own terror that she might one day wake up to find out that she too has mental health issues. These fears were the real secret, but as long as it took on the form of hidden debt, it could be tucked away, it could give her the sense that she was in control of what was exposed and what was going to remain undercover.

The overspending (mainly on cosmetics, clothes, and accessories) could be about soothing some of her feelings, the emptiness that a mother with an addiction can leave in the child. But it was also about a desired transformation: If only she looked the part, she would feel like she fit in (the longing was to fit in back then, in school and now too, with her husband and his social entourage). The part of her that didn't feel she fit in could be kept secret as long as she dressed the part. As the therapy progressed, Emma worked on this sense of shame until she was able to stop overspending and adopt more healthy spending habits. While she didn't come clean, she slowly repaid her debt so as not to have a secret to keep any longer. Her spending and secrecy (her defenses) lost their psychological power because there was no longer that strong sense of shame to defend against.

Emma's story brings together a lot of the themes I have and will touch on and shows us how unhelpful it is if we try to find one answer, one experience that explains it all. It also shows why past experiences and feelings can influence our money choices in the present.

Defense against guilt, shame, and fear of judgment

We all make mistakes, we might have bad habits or indulge in vices, and exhibit behaviors we are not proud of. There are aspects of ourselves and our behavior that we wish we could hide from the world. With money behaviors we sometimes choose to go down that route: hiding the *n*th shopping bag from our inspecting and judgmental mother; shredding the credit card bill to hide our excesses from our partner; making up a story about where we were instead of disclosing that we were gambling, yet again. Secrets might be a defense against our feelings of guilt: partly because we don't have to admit publicly to our crime and partly because our lies, our hiding, might be part of our denial. It's like when my clients sometimes say: "If I say it out loud it will make it feel more real." Well, it's real all right, even if hiding the evidence helps you, temporarily and only in part, to pretend it isn't.

Shame is harder to manage than guilt (and as I explained, more detrimental to our mental health). We may be ashamed of being an addict; we may be ashamed of being a liar, feeling that our dishonesty will expose an aspect of ourselves that defines us; we may be ashamed of being a failure and so we still put on our suit and pretend to go to work as we can't face telling our parents that we got fired from our first job. For Bernie Madoff, the beginning of his dishonesty came after a financial loss. He couldn't face the shame of failing, so he lied to maintain the illusion of success.

A client once came to his first session looking very troubled: "I have a $2 million problem," he said. I imagined this man, who looked so distressed, had found himself in an enormous amount of debt. Was it excessive spending? Was it bad investments? I listened as the story unfolded. Robert grew up in a middle-class family, had a steady job as a software engineer, where he had been for 12 years, a wife he had met in school and two adolescent kids. Robert was a man of routine. He had lived in the same town all his life, spent his Thursdays playing cards with the same group of friends since college, consistently applied the 50/30/20 rule (spending 50 percent of his after-tax income on needs, 30 percent on wants, and 20 percent set aside as savings). Last year, when he was 48, a business that he had owned a minority stake in for over two decades was bought by a large multinational and he suddenly found himself becoming very wealthy. The $2 million was not debt, but proceeds from the sale of the company. Finding himself with $2 million had deeply unsettled him. Now, you might think: "It's not a bad problem to have," and of course it's better than what I was imagining. However, I was there to help Robert understand what was so troubling for him.

"I haven't told anyone about this, apart from my family of course, and it's becoming harder to hide. My wife has been putting a lot of pressure on me to move to a bigger house . . . I don't want things to change. I don't want my friends to behave differently toward me. We decided to take the kids to New York for Christmas . . . but when we came back, I just couldn't face meeting people answering the questions about the vacation . . . I didn't want to sound like I was bragging. I mean, I know my friends all spend their vacations locally, which is what we've always done. Will they think I am this 'big shot' now, no longer interested in going on camping trips with them? It will drive a wedge between us, I know it . . . I am afraid of what will happen to the kids too; I don't want them to be spoiled."

As Robert's example shows us, having money can evoke very difficult emotions and anxieties. For him, money unsettled a life that he was content with. It introduced lots of risks: the risk of evoking friends' envy, the risk of being alienated by his friendship group, conflict with the wife about how to spend it, fears about how it could spoil the children. In future sessions, Robert revealed that his father, a self-made man, had ingrained in his children messages about working hard and finding pride in the fruit of one's work. The ease with which this money had befallen him left him feeling as if it wasn't deserved. How could he shift this sense of shame? How could he manage his fears and worries about what the money could do to his life and relationships?

Our work was going to be about addressing the feelings first, so that he could look at this wealth not as something that happened to him, but as something he had control over and changed. Even though he couldn't control people's envy, he could control *how* he spoke about vacations. Even though he might not have wanted to keep hiding his new financial reality from everyone, he could manage *how* it was presented to the children and think about steps that might help them not feel spoiled by the family's newfound abundance of wealth. He needed to address his feelings and shift his view of money as a bad thing, a problem, to looking at the opportunities that it brought. His wife's request for a bigger house were met with a hard no by the Robert who held all those fears, but with time, as he worked through the fears related to enjoying the newfound financial freedom, joint decisions about a good enough balance of enjoying/saving/investing would be possible. Hiding it was not the optimal solution; not emotionally and not rationally either.

As we saw, wealth shame can be dealt with through a number of psychological defenses: Some people might unconsciously sabotage their success, while others might simply be secretive about it—their riches become their dirty little secret because they feel like an imposter having something they are undeserving of or, like Robert, there might be all sorts of fears about making it public. We can see why defending through self-sabotage is destructive, but the secrecy is harmful too. We may start to avoid social interactions because of how draining it feels to be inauthentic, and lie to hide the truth. It begs the question: Is it worth paying such a high price for a secret? Well, if like Robert you are crippled with fears it might feel worth it, because what you imagine will come with transparency is even worse. But once you address the fears and consider the real impact of secrecy, the balance might begin to shift: It might no longer feel worth it to lie.

There is shame that is more insidious, and more entrenched in our minds and unrelated to money. We might be ashamed of parts of ourselves and worry that we are somehow defective/ unacceptable. Hiding an addiction, for example, can also be about hiding our depression, our dark thoughts: The addiction is just helping us mask these. We might hide these aspects of ourselves from the people we care about not out of malevolence but because we want to be accepted by them rather than scare them away and risk losing their love. We might even be trying to protect them by not exposing them to our dirty secrets.

To express anger through a passive-aggressive act

In my experience, people tend to be afraid of their anger. Anger is often seen as an inadmissible emotion or one that is hard to express in a reasonable way. I have seen people come up with creative ways to avoid even naming it, as if it would be shameful to just recognize how furious they were in a particular situation ("Maybe not angry, more like frustrated," "Angry? No, more like annoyed"). Anger also gets confused with aggression and sadly, because of the families some people grew up in, they become inextricably linked, so anger is suppressed, rather than expressed. This is evidenced in the amount of times I ask, "Did you tell her how angry it made you feel?" and the response I hear is, "Well, I didn't want to start a huge fight," as if the only way to express anger is explosive, damaging, and hurtful.

No one likes to think of themselves as passive-aggressive. However, often, that is exactly what money secrets are. I have seen this with differing views on money, which rattle our desire to have things our way. Consider two parents who disagree on whether they should help their 19-year-old son purchase a car:

Sarah: "I think we should help Philip with his car purchase, maybe offer to pay for half?"

Joseph, Philip's father, doesn't like the idea.

Joseph: "He is an adult now and can be responsible for his own financial decisions; let him figure it out on his own."

Of course Sarah is free to give money to her son. However, having asked and heard Joseph's disapproval, going ahead with it would be passive-aggressive. She is angry Joseph didn't agree and giving the money in secret would be a sign of her protest.

I am often asked what to do when, like with Joseph and Sarah, we differ in our views on money. In most cases people test the waters and give up at the first sign of resistance from their partner. What about having a deeper discussion about why Sarah wants to help Philip? Joseph might actually help Sarah see that she is struggling to give her son the autonomy and independence he needs to develop the skills and confidence needed to be an adult managing his finances. Or Joseph could see that sometimes he takes a very harsh and unsupportive approach toward his son in an effort to toughen him up (which is similar to how he was parented). And ultimately, out of discussing and understanding oneself and the other, a solution might emerge with either party changing their opinion, or maybe the couple coming to a compromise on the amount to contribute.

Fear of conflict

It is a fact that money is one of the most common causes of conflict in relationships. It is no wonder, then, that if we suspect our partner will be disapproving of our money behavior, keeping it secret may feel like a good way to avoid an argument. Of course, depending on the secret, you might be avoiding a small short-term conflict but risking a bigger fallout down the line (where the rupture in trust might be an even greater cause of conflict than the behavior).

Our fear of conflict and arguments may be grounded in the reality of how much we have argued on money issues, or it could be rooted in our experience growing up watching our parents have endless money arguments. There are several possible explanations as to why the younger generations (Gen Z and Millennials) are significantly more secretive about money matters. According to a Bankrate.com survey of 2,500 adults in relationships, 64 percent of Gen Zers and 54 percent of Millennials confessed to financial infidelity, compared to 29 percent of Gen Xers and Baby Boomers.[10] One explanation is that these younger generations are more likely to have had divorced parents, a process that is much more likely to expose children to the nasty side of money arguments, influence their sense of durability of relationships, and maybe instill in them a need for financial autonomy. It is also the case that, as the new generations get married later in life, they might not have confronted a lot of the money differences that inevitably come up with time, and so shame, or expected disapproval, might be more present in their minds and holding them back from full disclosure.

Fear of closeness/intimacy

Money secrets then can be a defense against a fear of being depleted or taken advantage of. The same way that separate bank accounts, for some, may be just an expression of their fear of closeness and merger with the other, secrets may also psychologically give us a sense of relief that we haven't given the other everything. It's a symbolic way of withholding and regulating emotional distance.

Similarly, having felt emotionally smothered by a parent, or overburdened by their needs and desires, might have left us longing for relationships that don't have those qualities: We might value our boundaries and independence. A sense of anxiety might begin to emerge if we feel too much closeness and so, afraid of ending up in that psychologically suffocating state, the secret acts as a boundary, a barrier in our mind that reassures us that we are still separate, autonomous, and free.

* * *

In Italy there is a saying: "Lies have short legs." The truth often catches up with us and the damage can be irreparable. I found it personally quite shocking that only about 10 percent of victims of financial infidelity find out by confession (according to a 2023 survey by US News & World Report).[11] The rest is discovered in other ways . . . you spot a large purchase on the joint statement, you find a statement for an account you don't recognize, you notice your partner being secretive with their phone, or maybe a comment slips out inadvertently.

Secrets isolate us and this goes against our very nature as humans, it goes against our need to connect and be understood. Michael Slepian, an associate professor of leadership and ethics at Columbia Business School, who studies the psychology of secrets, says that secrets interfere with our human desires to relate, connect, and be known.[12] He articulates the internal conflict that this generates in us and which is a cause of deep discomfort: A person's need to connect with others directly clashes with their desire to keep their secret to themselves.[13]

We learn about ourselves by talking to people. Talking to others and sharing what is troubling us, our worries and concerns, are ways in which we try to make sense of our actions, understand them, look at them differently. Sharing with a trusted other our shameful habit or a financial difficulty is also a way of experiencing relief, of feeling a weight being lifted off our shoulders. Keeping secrets, we don't get a chance to learn nor to feel relief.

If we have gone as far as telling lies to hide it, then we might have to manage feelings of guilt. At some level we know that we are hurting the relationship (even if the lie is meant to protect our partner, we know that hiding, if discovered, won't be well received).

Shame is the most damaging side effect of many secrets. We have seen how shame can be a reason for keeping something from our partner in the first place (it's the actual secret that we are ashamed of). However, shame can also be a consequence of keeping a secret from someone we care about (shame about being a liar). The gap, in our minds, between the person we would like to be and the person we are widens because of our secrecy. Slepian found that the more often you think about your secret, the more detrimental it is to your well-being.[14] In his research, Slepian and his colleagues also discovered that secrets linked to shame are more harmful to our mental health than those linked to guilt.[15]

Secrets also cause a sense of psychological discomfort as they are often experienced as being inauthentic. In fact, the more inauthentic people felt they were being as a result of their secrecy, the lower their sense of well-being.[16] As I discussed in a *Women's Health* interview, in the social media world we live in, some can spend a lot of energy keeping up appearances or even building a public persona that's more akin to who we would like to be rather than true to how we really feel (or what we actually have or can afford).[17] That consumes a great deal of mental energy and feels inauthentic. In this context, we shouldn't just consider the impact of big secrets and lies. Take the example of the friend who bought the flat: She *knew* that her parents helped her pay for it, but she took full credit for the compliments received. What she projected into the world was not a picture congruent with the reality, so it became a burdensome inner conflict to manage.

Transparency can help others as much as ourselves. In a world where people often Photoshop and hand-pick the best version of themselves to portray on social media, it can be quite liberating to hear that people have vulnerabilities, especially if we can identify with them. It is tempting to scroll through and conclude that everyone is successful, everyone is achieving. Hearing that others too might take shortcuts (like using their parents' money for a deposit) or have limitations (be on a tight budget, for example) can help us feel less lonely if ever we felt financially vulnerable or in dissonance with where we would have liked to be.

Is financial transparency always recommended? I have read surveys citing varying statistics about how honest/dishonest parents are with their children about finances. I am not sure that full disclosure in a parent-child relationship is appropriate nor does it guarantee that this will result in an adult that isn't secretive about money (quite the contrary actually—I have seen people grow up exposed to so much detail and anxiety about finances that they take the opposite approach to money in response to that: clamming up and denying, repressing, or avoiding money conversations). Transparency among adults I would recommend, but of course full disclosure on a first date might be unnecessary (even though people have started posting their credit score on dating apps).[18] What I can advocate are money conversations between partners that create a shared understanding of the boundaries of privacy and secrecy. You might come up with a scenario in which transparency is not the best strategy. However, what my experience as a therapist has taught me is that secrets are consuming and cause havoc when they come to light.

CHAPTER 10

Couples and money

The longest study on happiness, conducted by Harvard Medical School, found that the number one, most important determinant of happiness in life is not (as they expected) financial and career success but, rather, having good quality relationships: ones in which we feel connected to the other, we feel warm toward them, and feel we can count on them. The study started tracking the lives of 268 men in 1938 (and has since expanded to include their families) and has regularly and extensively measured all aspects of their lives (career, health, wealth, relationships, family). Some became successful businessmen, doctors, and lawyers, yet others ended up with schizophrenia or addictions, but the number one factor that determined whether they were happy in life was close relationships.[1]

Our blueprint for relationships and our expectations and behaviors when we are in one are morphed by two important experiences: the experience of relating to our parents (as I have discussed in previous chapters) and the experience of watching our parents relate to one another.

Our parents' example is a point of reference: For most people it becomes a model they consciously/unconsciously, at least in part, replicate (because we are drawn to the familiar and are predisposed to repeating). Some, with a lot of conscious effort and determination to avoid ending up like their parents, manage to establish different dynamics in their future relationships. Whatever our circumstances, the reality is that we are not fully aware of the myriad of expectations, hopes, and fears that we carry as a result of exposures to the parental couple, but enhancing that awareness can be beneficial.

The challenge of coupling is significant: Our own complex web of influences that shape how we approach relationships collide with those of our romantic partner. Our partner brings their own experiences of being loved (longings, fears, desires, and attachment style), their own internalized parental couple, and their own adult views of how a couple should operate. It is no easy pursuit to negotiate and manage those differences.

Money conflicts abound in all kinds of relationships: romantic ones, friendships, and business partnerships for the following two reasons.

1. Money is part of living a life, so it comes up a lot and our different views on money might clash and trigger conflict.
2. Money can be a symbol that we use to act out emotional issues that actually aren't about money, but pertain to other aspects of the relationship.

In this chapter I will focus on romantic couples who face the challenge of combining their financial worlds as the relationship progresses.

I was listening to a couple recently having a conversation about their holidays:

Jason: We really cannot repeat what happened this year and spend all this money on our vacations.

Vera: "Why?"

Jason: "It's too much! I added it all up and we have spent $3,000 on vacations! That's outrageous!"

Vera: "Is it? We can afford it now."

Jason: "I know . . . But still . . . it just doesn't feel right . . ."

Not an uncommon interaction for a couple that faces growing income and has to make the choice of what to do with the extra funds coming in. Do they increase how much they spend on lifestyle (so-called lifestyle inflation)? Or use it to address other financial objectives (like grow their savings pot, invest in their pension, buy a first property/car)? If they ride the wave without thinking about whether increasing spending on lifestyle is in line with their values and financial objectives, they may end up unhappy about their choices and full of regret. And what to do if their partner has different views on what's best?

It sounds like what Jason considered overspending on vacations, to Vera was a rational choice in line with their new purchasing power. But there is a lot we don't know, and which the partner should not assume to know either. Does the amount clash with Jason's values about what money is for and what it should be spent on? Or does he think it is interfering with other financial objectives that the couple had decided to prioritize? Does he feel guilty indulging in a trip his family or friends wouldn't be able to afford? Or does he carry a narrative from growing up that money is wasted on expensive vacations and should be saved or invested? There could be several reasons why it doesn't feel right, and unpacking these would be beneficial for Jason and help Vera to better understand his point of view.

What about Vera's nonchalance about it? We could assume she is being rational and comfortable with her vacation budget, but that might not be the case. Has she thought through the implications of lifestyle inflation? Has she considered the financial realities and priorities of the couple and concluded that $3,000 is a reasonable amount to spend on vacations? She could have her own unconscious forces pushing her to spend more (maybe a desire to impress her friends and family, or fears that financial abundance won't last so best to enjoy it while it's there). It's also worth exploring the relationship dynamics in this couple: has Jason been cast into the role of the accountant or voice of reason while Vera has checked out of thinking about finances?

When approaching money differences in a relationship, it is worthwhile to step back and consider the following.

- What emotional baggage do we each bring to the relationship when it comes to money and beyond?
- How can you understand your partner's attitude to money in greater depth and negotiate the differences that will inevitably be there?
- Are your money conflicts about money or is money just the language you use to express feelings about the relationship?

Couples often argue about money

Money arguments are common. Depending on which research you read they are either the main or one of the main sources of marital conflict. A 2019 YouGov poll found that over a third (37 percent) of people in a relationship have argued about money.[2] In a 2023 study, run by wealth and retirement solutions provider Aviva, a quarter of respondents in a relationship admitted to bickering about money at least once a week.[3] In the National Survey of Marital Strength, conducted in 2000 and including over 21,000 married couples, they found that even for happy couples, money is a topic of disagreement more so than any other.[4]

Money attitudes and behaviors

Couples come up against their different views on what money is, what it represents, and what it should be used for. Each will have a view on how much debt is acceptable, what flat size is reasonable, how much to spend on a friend's wedding gift, whether lending money to friends is a good idea, and so on. Leading an ordinary life involves countless choices that are made by tapping into these internal compasses and it is rare to coincide on everything with our partner. When there are sizable differences in beliefs, values, and behaviors, conflicts are expectedly more likely. If enhancing our own Financial Emotional Awareness is hard, there is an extra challenge in understanding what drives someone else's money behaviors.

What adds to the muddle is the fact that sometimes our excesses and restraints or our appetite for risk are in conflict with what we actually believe and value. We may be more risk-averse than we'd like to be because of financial trauma, or splurge to show off because of our narcissistic nature, or resist eating out because spending is guilt-evoking. As we have seen throughout this book, even once we decide how we want to act with money, we face limitations, so even if our values and attitudes to money are in line with our partner's, our irrational behavior might be what causes friction.

How financial decisions are made

Should we join bank accounts or keep them separate? Who has the final say? Is it OK for one partner to delegate all responsibility to the other? What is the right balance between a partner's freedom to be impulsive versus the need to consult the other? Where do we draw the line between privacy and secrecy when it comes to our money behaviors?

The National Survey of Marital Strength asked couples about their top stumbling blocks regarding finances: Half of the couples felt their partner was trying to control the finances.[5] This indicates a real difficulty for couples to find systems that allow each party to have sufficient autonomy and voice in financial decisions and this difficulty has been exacerbated by the growth in dual income families. The dynamics of two working partners raises many questions about power and freedom, and I will come back to this later in the chapter.

Couples have to reconcile different views on transparency and privacy, on fairness and equality, on trust and intimacy. These are not just money conversations, but topics that capture a wide array of beliefs and maybe even insecurities that may be reflected in many aspects of the relationship (parenting, sex). The partner who avoids money conversation may avoid any topic of conflict and delegate a lot of other responsibilities to the other; the partner that is secretive about their finances may be generally withholding; the one that is insistent on equality might want that reflected in both finances and parenting responsibilities, for example.

The National Survey of Marital Strength found that 89 percent of happily married couples agree on money issues versus 41 percent of unhappily married ones, which I imagine is not because they are a perfect match in terms of expectations, fears, and desires related to money, but rather they found a way to manage the inevitable money differences in a way that doesn't lead to big arguments and damaging conflict. In fact, happy couples in this study cited good communication and creativity in resolving differences as strengths of their relationship: These are probably crucial in shaping their sense that they agree on money issues.[6]

Money as a hot topic

I believe the following are the four main reasons why money is a hot topic for couples.

1. Money is still a taboo, and couples often delay conversations about money until they face conflict.
2. We wish differences weren't there and are not great at dealing with them.
3. Many modern-day couples are experiencing a financial dynamic they have no blueprint for.
4. "Money fights" are often not about money at all, so the couple might actually be arguing about issues that are very emotional under the disguise of a financial conversation.

I will explore these in depth in the following sections.

1. Money is still a taboo

For starters, there is the simple fact that money still remains a taboo, and that people are more likely to reveal their views on religion, politics, and sex before they open up about finances. According to research by Fidelity, 29 percent of the female population would rather share details of their dating history than talk about the state of their finances.[7]

For many, it is a topic of conversation that is stressful, boring, or simply unromantic. When couples enjoy the relaxed daydreaming of the early phases of their relationship, discussing future travel destinations, food preferences, or sexual positions, they are less inclined to bring up a topic that seems both mundane and potentially emotional and wrapped up with shame and fear. Yet money will insidiously make an appearance on most first dates, as the two parties are faced with the decision of who pays for what, how much to spend on wine, or whether to take an Uber or public transport to head to the next venue.

Money might also still be a taboo because of our lack of Financial Emotional Awareness. Finances might simply be an area of life that we haven't thought about in great depth and we ourselves are in the dark about. We might have heard a friend comment on how easily we just bought that new coat, or our visiting mother suggesting we are stingy with food shopping, or even a friend joking about how reckless it was of us to invest $1,000 in Bitcoin. But we might not have analyzed and come to grips with how we make our financial decisions and so we leave the topic in the shadow, unthought of and unexposed.

Avoiding the topic has its dangers too. The same way we might want to know that our new partner has an ex-wife, problems with intimacy, or is a hoarder, we might also want to know that they have a five-figure credit card debt, or that they have a history of gambling. Pretending that finances are unimportant is both naive and shortsighted, since money is part of living a life.

It's important to find a good enough moment to bring up the many topics related to finance with a partner. I am not advocating asking for their credit score on a first date, but waiting until we are engaged to tell them about our spending addiction might be detrimental to the trust-building process that accompanies a deepening relationship.

2. We wish differences weren't there, and we are not great at dealing with them

Finding out that our partner doesn't fully align with either our own beliefs and values or maybe with the expectations we had for a partner is a painful process. Having to learn to tolerate and negotiate differences is, in my experience supporting people with relationships struggles, one of the hardest things to do in a relationship.

How can he not be anxious about the future of our finances? How can she struggle to enjoy money; isn't that what money is for? Why does he take so much risk with his investments? Why does she avoid the topic; shouldn't we get on the same page on finances? These differences often catch us off guard when what we really hoped for at some level was to find someone that saw eye to eye with us on everything. Doubts arise about our choice of partner, and some of us fall in the trap of confirmation bias, finding evidence that all other couples seem to be happy and in harmony, living happily ever after.

Take Aaron and Stella. Stella has always been more indulgent than Aaron when it comes to spending. In the relationship, Stella and Aaron have been trying to reconcile Stella's desire to enjoy money with Aaron's frugality, but at the same time Stella is internally torn by a conflict between the part of her that wants to enjoy their new financial freedom and another part that feels guilty when she spends because she grew up in a family where thrift was praised. Aaron, meanwhile, while visibly comfortable with his frugality, faces a conflict about a part of him that prides itself on his financial prudence and another part afraid of taking it too far and becoming a miser, like his dad. You can see the challenge: how hard to reconcile different attitudes about money when our own views might be contaminated by ambivalence, fears, or psychological conflict.

What sometimes adds to the struggle in romantic relationships is polarization. With time, when differences aren't understood and managed, the two partners might become increasingly entrenched in their opposing viewpoints. Stella had a desire to spend more and was testing her ability to do so more freely now that she could afford it (despite her own inner voices telling her that thrift is a good thing and excesses are wasteful). However, after repeated clashes with Aaron, her view of "we could spend more" became "we should spend more." What started as a suggestion became entrenched into a stubborn viewpoint in which she was in the right and he was simply wrong and too frugal. If this couple had communicated more successfully when their different behaviors and desires manifested themselves, they would have been able to fruitfully explore the common ground that was there, like the fact that they both grew up in families where parsimony was a virtue; they both wanted to enjoy the money they had more and both struggled with guilt when it came to spending (even though Stella avoided her guilt while in Aaron's mind the guilt reinforced his view that spending is wrong).

But that missed opportunity and continued clashes on money choices made Aaron even more entrenched in his view that spending is bad. The little room for change that had developed in his mind as their financial situation improved, disappeared as he armored himself with debate ammunition for the next argument with Stella on why frugality is what's best. Polarization shifts the purpose and dynamics of the dialogue: Instead of sitting next to our partner searching for a good enough compromise, we are sitting opposite them trying to be right. Instead of listening, we are fighting. Instead of resolving the issue, we are competing. It is a very difficult dynamic to move away from. Who will put their armor down first, making themselves vulnerable, and dare take a new stance?

So the partner with a moderate risk appetite might slowly become risk-averse in conflicts with an impulsive and risk-taking other. The person who is generally a bit anxious and avoidant of finances might end up delegating all responsibility to their partner who then begins to feel entitled to all decisions and takes all financial matters in their own hands. In all these examples, you see the tragic missed opportunity: A couple that could have become complementary has now become incompatible.

I find incompatibility to be a tricky concept. On paper, a couple is incompatible when their differences make it too hard for them to have a healthy and functional relationship. However, in my experience, people often decide they are incompatible prematurely, without having really tried to understand each other, to step into the other's shoes and look at the world from their perspective, to experiment with new ways of doing things, out of their comfort zone.

When it comes to money differences, looking at our partner's opposite view might reveal advantages to their frugality, or their ability to enjoy what money can buy; there are advantages to risk taking and to risk aversion. What this means is that actually, having two partners with different views on money can either be a deal-breaker or a great opportunity to shape a complementary approach to managing finances as a couple.

Two people who want to be together could find imaginative ways to negotiate a compromise, but that's not easy for everyone. Most people, faced with difference, either sulk and give up, or insist that the other changes, and then give up. People might feel unable to manage conflict and have the difficult conversations needed to move forward.

3. Many modern-day couples are experiencing a financial dynamic they have no blueprint for

According to Michael Aitken, the chairman of Magus Wealth, a financial planning company, it is not uncommon for only the male partner to attend a scheduled appointment for financial planning assistance requested by a couple. "I now insist that both partners attend the meeting," he tells me.

Traditionally, men have been responsible for handling financial matters, while women have typically focused on raising children and managing the household. The average modern-day couple is quite different. First of all, in that a couple no longer necessarily comprises a man and a woman but also because societal changes have made dual income households the norm, which means that the way in which financial, house, and childcare responsibilities were traditionally divided would need adapting in light of these changes.

In the past few decades, there has been a significant rise in the number of women and mothers who are employed, in part due to gender roles being challenged, a desire in women to have fulfillling careers, and an increase in the cost of living, but also greater career opportunities for women and flexible working arrangements. In the US in 1968, men were the sole breadwinners in 35 percent of households compared to 18 percent in 2018.[8] In OECD countries, the majority of couples have both partners engaged in paid work, as indicated by statistics (these couples are commonly referred to as dual earning or dual income couples).[9] While there are differences between countries in terms of how this is divided as far as full-time/part-time work, the fact remains that many more women are now working and earning money and more mothers are in employment than ever before.

This new earnings structure generates all sorts of conflicts and dilemmas. If we both had a stay-at-home mother who was given an allowance for groceries and other items while our father earned all the money and handled most financial obligations (bills, debts, investments), both we and our partner might find it challenging to adapt our expectations of one another in light of our new and different reality, in which we are both earning an income. These changes introduce dilemmas in our minds as we try to build a relationship under potentially very different circumstances than the model we grew up with. We have no blueprint for a couple that divides household responsibilities, negotiates childcare commitments, or shares accountability for contributing to the shared income of the couple.

Are we then both equal participants in financial decision-making? Should we be equal participants if one only works part-time and the other works full-time? What if one of us earns a higher salary than the other? How do we split responsibility of bills/debts, etc.? What do we do with debt that a partner brings into the relationship? Can we allow/do we want a greater degree of autonomy with finances now that we both can support ourselves financially or should we still subscribe to "what's yours is mine?"

If we are both on a successful full-time career path, how do we decide who will make the career sacrifices to take on childcare responsibilities? These (and many more) are difficult decisions to navigate, particularly when partners have different views on the answers.

Role reversals can be more challenging. It is still the norm that men provide the majority of income in dual income households, but that too is a changing trend. The number of heterosexual couples in which the woman earns more than the man is growing (28 percent in 2017 compared to 12 percent in 1990).[10] This dynamic is so difficult for many couples because it tends to be unfamiliar to both. While on the surface both parties are fine with it, the emotional discomfort brought up by the dissonance between the couple we have internalized and our current situation begins to show signs of impact. I have seen male clients who struggled sexually with their higher-earning female partner, feeling emasculated by the dynamic. They couldn't see themselves as a potent man, in part because the financial dynamic was so in contrast with their internal idea of a man as a provider. And of course, this message wasn't just conveyed by one's own family experience, but it's a society-wide expectation that men should succeed economically.

Claer Barrett, in her book *What They Don't Teach You About Money*, writes of her experience having been married to someone with whom the fact that she was the main breadwinner created many difficulties. In her next marriage, her experience was very different and she says that in part, this was because her second husband had grown up with a single mother who sustained herself. For him, a woman taking on the role of a main earner didn't raise an internal conflict.

The manageability of a new and unfamiliar dynamic depends on many factors, like the couple's desire to be together, how competitive both partners are, the higher-earning partner's acceptance of the salary imbalance or, as Turkel adds, the extent to which the man derives his sense of self-worth from money, and the extent to which other assets he may have brought into the marriage even out the imbalance.[11] If she is frustrated by his lower income or interprets it as a lack of ambition, it is more likely to become a contentious topic and constant source of irritation.

In some cases, successful women, who at some level, conscious or unconscious, want their husbands to be at par with them (or maybe even at par with how successful they viewed their own fathers to be), might find that the husband's success in other areas (even if not financially equivalent) offers that sense of equality they sought: They can still be proud of them and relax in the comfort of a dynamic that doesn't seem awfully unfamiliar. In other cases, that desire for equality might not even be there and so, if a woman who doesn't long for a successful man meets a man who doesn't need money to validate their worth or masculinity, it works out fine.

Even though financial realities are shifting, it seems like some gender stereotypes are hard to let go of and adapt to the new reality. Research still shows that while the majority of couples make large financial decisions as a team, in most cases, it is still women who manage the household budget and men who manage the couple's investments.[12]

Every couple is different. In some cases, it's women who haven't developed the confidence to feel able to manage investments and therefore happily delegate that responsibility to their husbands. While in other cases, it's the husband who appropriates the responsibility of managing investments because it matches both their expectation and greater confidence about managing investments. In short, both parties might become complicit in keeping things familiar.

Ultimately, when we link all this back to the idea of financial well-being, the question we need to ask is, "Are we consciously choosing the status quo or have we ended up in it because of a whole set of unconscious fears, stereotypes, and pressures?" If we have delegated all investment decisions to our partner, is it because we believe they are better at it and have more education/information on the matter, while we are not particularly interested in taking on that responsibility? Or is it because our partner expects to be in charge, while we fear we might be bad at it and have resigned to being powerless in the relationship?

It is important to understand *how* we have landed in a particular status quo and whether we feel we had a say in it. Feeling like we are in an equalitarian relationship (meaning a relationship in which both parties feel equal) seems to be key to a happy marriage. In the National Survey of Marital Strength, they found that most (81 percent) of the couples in which both spouses perceived the relationship as equalitarian were happily married, while most (82 percent) of the couples where both perceived it as traditional were mainly unhappy. Which doesn't mean we need to split investment decisions 50-50 but that we feel at some level that the split we have landed on as a couple is one we had an equal say in.

Even though the statistics I cite above are about majorities and averages and limited in their cultural representation, what I invite you to think about is how your internalized expectations of gender roles related to money have been influenced both by the society you live in and by the couple you were raised observing. Both of these will have shaped how you feel and what you expect from a relationship dynamic in the present. Who had the financial decision-making power? Who made more money? Who looked after the home and the children? Who managed the family's investments?

4. Money fights are often not about money
Arguments about money are rarely just about money. They are

often about much more and unpacking what may be behind the conflict is crucial for resolving it. What does it represent? Does it get used to act out issues that belong to the wider relationship?

Clara and Thomas had recently started dating. While Thomas (age 40) had had a handful of long relationships in his past, Clara (age 37) hadn't. She had grown up in a dysfunctional family where her parents had both engaged in extramarital affairs. Her father had left when she was a teenager. Clara avoided relationships. Even coming to therapy was something she did reluctantly (you have to have some faith, at some level, that something good can come out of a relationship in order to come to therapy and Clara was very ambivalent). But she had met Thomas and with him something felt different. She wanted to give it a try but was afraid of messing it up. Some of the initial clashes the couple had were related to money, and it's such a good example of how money gets used as a medium for communicating something that is hard to put into words.

The relationship started slowly, reluctantly. On their one-year anniversary, Thomas gave Clara an expensive pair of earrings. Clara came to the session and started telling me about them. She could barely finish the sentence when her eyes welled up with tears. "I feel so guilty. I don't know why . . . I looked at them and felt awful." A month later, returning from a work trip at the airport she found a pre-booked (and paid for) car waiting to take her back home. She was so angry with him. She struggled to explain why she had found the gesture so triggering. A pattern began to emerge, any kind of giving from Thomas had the same effect: It made her uncomfortable, angry, and guilty. Their arguments about how much he'd spent on the earrings or the car service could have been mistaken as a clash over spending habits/values, but it wasn't about that at all. Thomas struggled to understand her; he was just trying to be nice, so why were his gestures not appreciated? Were her feelings obfuscating her view of these acts of kindness for what they were?

The reason why Clara found these acts of generosity from Thomas so uncomfortable were rooted in her fear that she couldn't give a relationship what it needed. In part there was the fact that Clara felt (at least at times) undeserving of love. She lived in fear of one day finding out that she was incapable of having a relationship and that her past had damaged her in an irreparable way. Thomas's ability to give, to please, to love, made her angry because in her eyes it highlighted how good he was and how bad she felt: A part of her wished he were less giving, so she wouldn't have to be in touch with her sense of inadequacy.

This is an example of a money conflict that was about relational insecurities. The next example is of a couple (a cisgender woman and a transgender woman) who at one level were arguing about how to share household responsibilities in light of their different work circumstances, but the conflict underneath was broader: It was about power and entitlement.

In one episode of the BBC series called *Couples Therapy*,[13] in which real couples speak to a couple's therapist, Sarah and Lauren are talking to Dr. Orna Guralnik. Sarah is expressing her frustration to the therapist about Lauren's demands of physical closeness when they are in bed, which Sarah experiences as overwhelming. But a complaint about Lauren's demands in the realm of affection quickly turns into a conversation about a broader relationship dynamic. Sarah says: "She wants what she wants, and she doesn't give a shit where I'm at or what I want . . . I mean, it's indicative of a bigger problem . . . this is how a lot of things operate, in our relationship . . . there has been, like, this sense of entitlement in the past, that has been at the core of our problems . . ."

And this relationship dynamic, it turns out, is played out in the arena of money too. Lauren was the breadwinner in the relationship and Sarah (who was not in full-time employment) felt there was an expectation that she be the one doing the housework, making dinner, etc., but interestingly, this wasn't about Sarah having more free time on her hands.

Sarah: "Let me ask you this: If you and I are working the same amount of hours, whose responsibility is it to clean the house [. . .]?"

Lauren: "Ideally, we should both split it."

[. . .]

Therapist: "And can I just ask, and I know it's not a PC* question to ask, but . . . and does it matter how much money each person is bringing in?"

Lauren: "I think . . . [long pause]. In my gut I feel like, yeah . . ."

Lauren believes that her higher earnings entitle her to less housework, which Sarah disagrees with. But when we step back from the narrative about money, there seems to be a general frustration in the couple about Lauren's greater sense of entitlement, even emotionally. You can see that there are two levels of conversation taking place: One is about real beliefs about money and power, but the other is about a broader desire or expectation that her needs are met and prioritized over her partner's. As the couple's therapist rightly points out, Lauren didn't invent the paradigm of money = power. It is therefore not a coincidence that money is the chosen object used symbolically by Lauren to express her sense of entitlement.

With the help of their therapist, they can decipher the subtext of an argument seemingly about space in the bed or division of household chores and see it as a narrative about power dynamics. Money was just one arena in which this couple clashed on unspoken assumptions about whose needs get prioritized: relationships dynamics can be pervasive, and money is just one aspect of the relationship in which the same dynamics get acted out. Understanding both the money

---

* PC = politically correct.

conflict (and different views on what is fair in an imbalanced dynamic of earning) but also the conflict about emotional needs can help this couple build a stronger relationship.

There are many examples of money arguments that aren't really about money, or where money is just one arena in which more general dynamics manifest themselves. A couple's insistence on splitting every bill may be about a couple's ambivalence about deepening the relationship. A couple with submissive-dominant power plays may act these out with finances but in the bedroom too. A couple with trust issues may keep money secrets or separate accounts. Of course, there isn't a relationship issue at the core of every money conflict: Sometimes we simply disagree.

Why are money conflicts important to address?

Money conflicts are detrimental to relationships. Having had the same fight a million times may cause a couple to lose faith in their ability to live harmoniously, to negotiate differences and have more good than bad moments together. Anger, disrespect, and secrets related to money drive a wedge between the couple and create ruptures in love and trust that they may feel are irreparable.

There are a number of reasons why I believe it's important to address money conflicts in the most constructive way possible. First of all, because couples who repeatedly argue about money are more likely to divorce. According to one study of over 5,300 couples in Germany, couples who disagree about financial matters are twice as likely to divorce as those on the same page about their finances. Differences in risk preferences (of any sort like career, sports, driving) were the biggest predictor of marital separation in the long run, but *financial* risk differences were the strongest predictor of divorce. According to the study's authors, people who differ on savings and investment decisions are less likely to own a home together or renovate a home if they did purchase one.[14]

In my experience, money arguments are often just a symptom of a couple's difficulty with communication, resolving differences, or addressing conflict, which is why finding a constructive way to discuss money differences can have a positive ripple effect on other areas of the relationship.

The second reason to address money issues is that understanding them can help unearth other underlying issues in the relationship that might be getting expressed through money. It is easier to fight about the concrete, in this case money, than to verbalize some of the emotional frustrations and dissatisfactions that need addressing. It might be easier to say, "You don't give me enough money" than to say, "You don't show me enough love." It might be easier to say, "You spend too much on your nights out" than to say, "I wish you invested more in our relationship," or to say, "I think we need to keep our finances separate" than to say, "I don't feel I can trust you."

Finally, and most importantly, finding ways to resolve differences about money can set a good precedent for the couple: It can become a model for how other differences (not money-related) can be addressed and resolved.

How to resolve money differences

I will give you ten tips to improve how you address money differences and even prevent conflict.

1. Don't avoid it
Many couples don't even give themselves much of a chance to enter the conflict resolution phase because their strategy is avoidance.

Not talking about something doesn't make it go away. Money is part of living a life and the more conscious we are of the choices we make with it, the more in control we'll feel of our finances. Avoiding money conversations with our partner because they are awkward or difficult will simply keep us stuck.

In the National Survey of Marital Strength they found that the vast majority of people wish their partner were more willing to share their feelings and discuss problems.[15] They admit to having trouble vocalizing their needs, and that they don't feel understood by their partner. Spouses in happy marriages are significantly more likely to feel understood by their partners, and they find it much easier to express their true feelings than their unhappy counterpoints. Understanding each other's different money attitudes, but also the wider relationship dynamics, can help bring two people from conflict to reconciliation.

2. Change your perception of conflict

People think of conflict as a negative thing. "I don't want to start a fight." Especially if conflict in your family of origin meant carnage: insults, shouting, disrespect, and pain. However, this need not be the case: Couples can grow stronger by facing their differences, if this is done with respect and without judgment. It's all about how things are talked about. Conflict means your differences have clashed, but could this be looked at as an opportunity to learn about and from your partner?

In a negotiations class at Wharton Business School, I distinctly recall a case study that proved seriously challenging for most of the bright students attempting to achieve the best possible results.[16] The task was to negotiate a deal. We were divided into groups of four where two people were in Team A and two in Team B.

Team A represented a biologist from a pharmaceutical firm researching methods to combat enemy uses of biological warfare. Because of a transport accident, chemicals had leaked, risking the lives of many, and the synthetic vapor the researchers had developed could neutralize this damage. The vapor was made with a chemical taken from the rind of ugli oranges (a very rare fruit of which only a limited number were produced). What Team A needed (3,000 oranges) was in the hands of Mr. Cardoza, who, however, was also approached by Team B, representing a competing pharmaceutical company. Team B needed the ugli oranges to develop a drug that combats Rudosen, a disease impacting fetuses and resulting in blindness. Team A and Team B met to negotiate a deal in order to avoid the risk that either would strike a deal with Mr. Cardoza and be left with nothing. Teams were given details on production processes, authorized bid size, potential human risk if they didn't strike a deal, etc.

We were given 30 minutes to negotiate the best possible deal for our company. The murmur of negotiations swept the room, and quickly you began to hear all sorts of conversations: "My cause is more time-sensitive than yours"; "Our product will save a greater number of lives in the long term"; "Let's split it evenly as that would be fair"; offers and counteroffers, heated arguments and the occasional bang on the table. When time was up, each group revealed the compromise reached. Most teams landed somewhere in the middle, dividing the oranges evenly, or close to evenly. Except one team. They were each going home with 3,000 oranges. How?

They had listened to each other. Instead of competing about whose cause was more valuable, more important, and who was offering more money, they had listened and understood each other's needs with interest. It turns out, Team A needed the rind of the orange to produce the vapor, while Team B needed the juice of the orange to produce the medicine, so they could both get what they wanted out of the 3,000 oranges.

This example shows how easily we can misunderstand difference and turn it into a zero-sum game, where someone wins and the other loses. To solve this case study requires the participants to ask, "How can we both get what we want?" rather than participate as if in a tug-of-war.

3. Think of the couple as a "third"
The priest at a friend's wedding cited the following proverb: "Every problem has three solutions: mine, yours, and the right one." I found it quite pertinent to the challenge faced by many couples when looking to resolve conflict: how to think of a solution not in terms of "what I want" versus "what you want" but in terms of "what would work best for the couple?" In psychotherapy terms, we are talking about what psychotherapist Stanley Ruszczynski called the marital triangle, which he describes as the ability of a couple to reflect on their own needs, the needs of the other, and on the needs of the relationship. Often and inevitably, these various needs will be in conflict and require reflection, possible relinquishment, and tolerable, though ambivalent, resolution.[17]

In the ugli orange case study, a situation that could easily turn into a conflict, if approached by the two sides as sitting on the same side of the table, looking for a mutually beneficial solution, can turn into a win-win situation. It's not about who is right, but about what is the best solution for this couple's financial well-being.

4. Be creative and flexible when it comes to compromise
When we approach negotiations with a creative mindset, we can find innovative ways to settle differences. Partners that disagree on risk aversion could end up with a portfolio wholly invested in medium-risk assets. Or they can each have a pot they invest in accordance with their risk appetite. Or they can set a maximum amount to be spent on high-risk assets (thus limiting risk exposure). If you are fighting endlessly with your partner on whether to spend $1,000 or $2,000 on your eight-day stay in Mexico this summer, the

answer might be to find a $1,500 house instead, but it might also be to go camping this year and do a luxury stay next year. Many people approach these topics from a right/wrong and black/white angle, which only allows for binary solutions. You'll find better solutions are found when two minds meet with a creative mindset.

5. Be curious

The ancient philosopher Zeno of Citium said, "We have two ears and one mouth so that we can listen twice as much as we speak."[18] People's listening skills can be quite poor, even more so when they are feeling angry and under attack. This is why trying to resolve a disagreement in the heat of the moment is never a good idea.

In order to understand what is happening between us and our partner we must listen and do so in a non-judgmental way, otherwise our spouse will feel discouraged from exposing their feelings and making themselves vulnerable to us.

Approach the conversation with a desire to understand both yourself and your partner. If you are in a relationship with an overspender, for example, how often are your comments on the topic complaints and reprimands rather than genuine attempts at figuring out what is driving this behavior? "You went shopping AGAIN?" "Why don't you just stop throwing our money away like that?" "Did you really need another pair of shoes?" "At this rate we'll never have enough for that down payment."

If you are just trying to convince the other that you are right and they are wrong, you will end up in a stalemate. Talking about money issues is not just about getting something off your chest and telling the other to change. If you listen to your partner you might be more instrumental in helping them curb a behavior they are struggling with, but also they might have something helpful to say about your attitude to money that will further your understanding of yourself.

6. Look at the two dimensions you were avoiding

When you think of your money attitude and that of your partner, there are four dimensions that you need to consider. Undoubtedly, both yours and their money attitude will have pros and cons (even if they are not evident at first). What tends to happen is that one focuses on what is good about their attitude and wrong about their partner's. However, for the purpose of finding a compromise, it is important to consider the two dimensions that people naturally avoid thinking about. You need to ask yourself: What are the downsides of your money attitude? And what are the advantages of theirs?

Every coin has two sides (to use a money metaphor!). If you face the trade-off in your money attitude, it will help you improve it too. Fine, you are great at watching every penny, but maybe you envy how generous your partner can be. Yes, you take pride in how little time you spend worrying about money, but you also recognize that sometimes you avoid the topic a little too much and miss out on opportunities (unlike your partner who is anxious about finances and worries about them all the time). You take pride in your cautious approach, but your partner made twice the return on their investment last year by taking on higher-risk investments.

It isn't until we own up to the trade-off in our attitude to money and acknowledge the benefits in our partner's that we can begin to find grounds for understanding and compromise. And by the way, this applies to conflict on any difference, not just money ones.

7. Recognize your role in the dynamic

We have looked at some of the unconscious processes that sometimes drive how we set up relational dynamics. We can't put all the blame on our partner and hope a dynamic will change if we don't face the fact that we are complicit in it: It takes two people to set up a dynamic. Did we slowly relinquish control instead of standing up for ourselves? Did we give up the reins to our finances because at some level it was too scary to hold on to them ourselves? In relationships, unconscious forces within us and our partners might act as a pull that casts us, like characters in a play, in a particular role. What role have we taken? Did we do so willingly? If Jason acknowledges that his taking on the role of the voice of reason when it comes to finances in the relationship might have actually enabled Vera's lax attitude toward money, it will be helpful for him to think about handing some of that responsibility back to Vera.

It's easy to say to a partner, "Why can't you be more involved with our finances?" but if we then continue to perpetuate the dynamic by taking it all in our hands, when do we create the opportunity for the other to step in?

We looked at polarization and how this can entrench our partner further in a behavior we dislike or disagree with. Can we face the fact that it might be our slow sliding away from a middle place that has led our partner to slide away in the opposite direction? The more we take the role of the responsible one, the more they act irresponsibly?

8. Pick the right time for money conversations

You'd be surprised how many people start difficult conversations by blurting out something impulsively at the worst possible time. Clearly if your partner is about to walk out of the door to go to work, or is exhausted and about to fall asleep, these are not the best times to bring something sensitive up with the hope to be heard or to get an empathic response. The excuses I hear are "but there is no other time" and that is simply untrue. Keep in mind that what you are hoping for is to be heard and understood, not to get it done, so you need to set the stage for this to have the maximum chance of happening.

9. Mind your tone

How you say something matters just as much as what you say. Tone makes a difference, and this is something to keep in mind when you are communicating, especially when it's a sensitive topic. Acknowledging negative feelings like anger/frustration without shouting will be much more effective than putting the other on the defensive from the outset.

10. Phrase your message carefully

A basic principle of communication is that offering a first-person point of view is much more likely to get a good response than starting your sentence with a second person accusation (which will just rile up the listener). Let's say you want to confront your partner about his excessive spending on nights out with friends. If you start with "I feel angry when," your partner will immediately clock how you are feeling in response to their actions and can't argue with that. It is different from starting the conversation with "You are an idiot for . . ."

After the "I statement," you state a fact (not an opinion or a judgment). So, "I feel angry when you spend $250 on a night out with your friends" is better than "I feel angry when you act like a spoiled and irresponsible child." Again, your partner will get a clear idea of what they did and how it made you feel rather than feel attacked and confused.

* * *

At the time of writing (2023), we are facing a "cost of living crisis," as it has been called in the media. Economic crises are an obvious external stressor that can fuel money conflict in couples: uncertainty, job insecurity, and rising costs can generate all sorts of anxieties in the individual and make any money conversation more stressful. It might also introduce difficult compromises and choices that the couple might have differing views on. Which costs to cut? How to save more? To help out family more affected by it? For middle-class families it might introduce compromises they never had to consider before, while for working-class families the choices might become even harder as they mean choosing between basic needs. In the Aviva study cited above, a third of respondents attribute an increase in money conflicts to the cost of living crisis.[19] It is bills and debt that are the leading causes of conflict in couples, which of course become more stressful when the state of the economy threatens our finances.

Whether it's external stressors or differences that were always there, learning to talk about money in a relationship and to manage differences is an important challenge. Unless we think of the third angle, the relationship, then we might not reach solutions that work. There is no denying that money can be an emotional issue, one that hooks into insecurities, fears, and desires. This means that every person's individual experience will be different and so trying to combine those of two people, with the resulting complexity this generates, means that there isn't one solution that is right for every couple. But the best question that a couple can ask themselves is, "What's best for *us*?"

CHAPTER 11

Money and other relationships: friendships, families, and the workplace

A frustrated parent whose child keeps using them as an ATM. A baffled entrepreneur whose business partner seems in denial of the dire financial state of the venture. A worried sibling who fears their brother won't ever repay them for the expenses of a joint vacation.

It is worth being curious about how we deal with money with anyone we have financial dealings with, as there may be meaning to be uncovered or irrationalities that we could benefit from exploring. Money in these relationships can become a hot topic as we try to reconcile our different views of money, or as we unconsciously try to express feelings related to the relationship. Awareness of what money means in these interactions, and how our differences impact the relationships, can help us better manage it and defuse the heated nature of the conversations.

Parents and children

The struggle for separation

Money can embody multiple meanings in a parent-child relationship. In this book we have explored a few examples: We have seen how parents can use money as a tool to control the children (as with Paola in the financial control chapter); we have considered children whose financial self-sabotage was an expression of their fears of separating from their parents (as with the young woman who overspent to avoid financial independence in the self-sabotage chapter); we have seen how parents may use money to express concern and offer support to a child they perceive as vulnerable (like with mother Sarah who wanted to help her son Philip purchase a car in the money secrets chapter).

It is the parents' job to supply their children with the resources needed to eventually get out into the world and thrive without their support. This is a gradual emotional process. The financial relationship between parents and children (at least in Western societies) generally mirrors the process of separation. Children go from being financially dependent on their parents to slowly becoming equipped with the tools needed to achieve financial independence. In the process, parents might still be providing some level of support to help them make ends meet until they become self-sufficient. The gradual nature of this approach is aimed at supporting the children while gently pushing them along the path of independence.

Many families manage to achieve this progressive financial separation successfully. However, in many cases the process doesn't go nearly as smoothly. Young adults who resist and postpone getting a job; parents frustrated and resentful of their children's continuing dependence or repeated pleas for financial rescue; parents who, out of a desire to hold on to their children, continue to give generously without facing the disservice this might be doing to the child; parents' refusal to give more cash misinterpreted by the children as being unloving rather than as an expression of the parents' desire to motivate them to strive for self-sufficiency. Money plays a crucial role in the process of separation and independence where the challenge is concrete and symbolic at once, and the acting out that often creates conflict and frustrations can be a representation of either the child's or the parent's (or parents') emotional struggle with separation.

In an episode of the podcast *The Money Clinic*, a mother and son explore their money conflict with a relationship counselor.[1] Fiona is critical of 20-year-old James's attitude to money, which he feels unable to change. "I am terrible with money," he says, explaining he is not very boundaried with his expenses and often ends up asking his mother for money, having exceeded his budget. With things he doesn't like spending on (gas), he takes a passive approach and hopes his mother will intervene (which she does, refueling the car). Fiona gives examples in which she had rescued James from risking a criminal record because of unpaid fines. She voices her frustration: He seems to be stuck in these behaviors because "it doesn't have consequences, because I pay it. He is reliant on me to sort it out."

But in speaking with the therapist, Fiona can begin to ascertain that there are emotional barriers that prevent her from becoming a catalyst for change in her son's behavior. First of all, what is unearthed is her sense of guilt with regard to James. Fiona admits that the family couldn't afford to give him the designer clothes he wanted (and his friends had) when he was younger. She acknowledges that James suffered from that, but he also suffered from his parents' divorce when he was age five. She can see that her desire to support James financially is, at least in part, addressing her guilt about those earlier deprivations.

She is also helped to see that following the divorce, when James was acting out at home with difficult and challenging behavior, he was labeled "the naughty one." Interestingly, James has a twin sister who has a very different approach to money. It's a good example because it shows us that even despite having been parented by the same person, at the same time, the role that we take on in the family may be quite different. A whole family could be complicit in casting us and then keeping us in a particular role (the naughty boy, which incidentally James says is "like Dad," indicating too that there might be an identification with Dad driving James's behavior). Mother and daughter often laugh about James's mischief, and family friends wait for the next story of what trouble James got himself into. Fiona admits that maybe "we all have responsibility of not treating it with the seriousness it deserves." James still often hides his financial difficulties until they surface, "like a naughty toddler," explains Fiona, wondering to what extent he is seeking her attention with his behaviors, as he did back then.

Finally, they discuss Fiona's feelings about the upcoming transition. As James is preparing to move out of the family home, Fiona's anxieties about no longer being needed or losing regular contact with her son might be fueling her desire to connect with him, albeit in the role of the financial rescuer. "While he is bailed out, he'd have a reason to come back," she says. There is therefore an inner conflict for this mother. While on the one hand she wants her son to be financially independent, on the other hand this could feel threatening as she hopes to keep connected with him at an emotional level.

As the podcast concludes, Fiona says: "I [realize that] we are in the relationship we had when he was six or seven." It is yet another example of a relationship in which we can quickly jump and place blame on the one doing it wrong without realizing our role in preserving or even fueling that dynamic. It would be limiting to look at James's behavior with money outside of the relationships it's taking place in. This isn't just James's overspending problem; it's a mother and child's struggle to separate. On both sides there are emotions linked to the relationship that need to be understood before the money behavior can change, and they both have a role to play for this change to happen. It sounds like Fiona could play a part in changing James's behavior: She needed to let go of this narrative of him as a naughty boy, which kept him stuck in this role; she also needed to manage her guilt linked to the past so that she didn't act it out by repeatedly rescuing him instead of helping him become more responsible; and finally she needed to recognize that empowering him to be autonomous would involve her mourning a loss (the "feeling needed," which in a way was a disincentive to helping him change). James, on the other hand, needs to be conscious of how he is interfering with his desire for autonomy (expressed by his moving out) by continually keeping himself dependent on his mother. For him, there is an emotional process of acknowledging his desire to still be looked after, which he can in part find healthier ways to express and in part slowly let go of as a trade-off for allowing himself to feel empowered and independent.

Parents can forget that children need to be taught financial independence. These are not skills we are born with. Even wealthy families, where it doesn't feel like a priority because money seems like an unlimited resource, are not immune to problems related to financial separation. In some cases, access to unlimited financial freedom, without the adequate emotional support that comes with the gradual approach to financial independence, can leave children feeling insecure about their ability to manage financial responsibilities as they grow older. Children might be burdened prematurely with large financial responsibilities (like managing a business) which could be a sign of the parents' generosity, or their desire to empower or recognize the potential of their child, but which might be experienced as an imposition and come wrapped with expectations these adult children feel dwarfed by. For these parents too, the question that needs to be asked is, "What process will build my child's emotional robustness so they are confident and skilled adults when it comes to financial management?" The emotional robustness is, I would argue, as important as having the business degrees and management experience (which they usually have easy access to). I have seen many adult children of wealthy families daunted by the prospect of stepping into big roles because they often jump from being the passive recipient of everything to having big responsibilities, without the gradual empowerment. It's expectedly overwhelming.

Difficulties giving and receiving

Sometimes parents are generous and giving, but when they are met with a refusal to receive, it can easily be misinterpreted. In family businesses, there is often an expectation that children will take over at some point, and when children choose to pursue their own career path, outside the business, they are sometimes seen as ungrateful. It is difficult for parents to manage their desire for the continuity of the family business in a way that isn't experienced as shackles limiting the child's freedom. Those strong desires can obfuscate the parents' ability to hear what the children are telling them, to think about what's best for their children. Aren't we being great parents, they ask me, by offering them a safe career route on a silver platter and preventing them from squandering money in acting school only to be met with a decade of failed auditions before they come back asking us for a job? Well, "offering" is the keyword. Expecting, demanding, pushing will feel like shackles and, in my experience, gets the parents the exact opposite result of their desired one.

There are those parents too who cut their children off financially. Sometimes because children are not complying with expectations. Other times because they want to teach them a lesson. In some cases, that's how they themselves had been parented. Now, does that justify their behavior or negate the child's feelings of frustration or even betrayal? No, but making that link can help both the parent and the child understand that something is being repeated in the family. Is this a repetition that feels beneficial? Or do the parents maybe want to reflect on giving their children a different experience from the one they had? Sometimes, in fact, financial cutoff might be what is most needed, but the key is in having thought it through and reached that conclusion rather than acting out anger, taking revenge, or blindly repeating history.

These are just examples. There are, of course, parents who allow their children the freedom to carve their own paths and make their own choices. They invest in their financial education and, in the cases of very wealthy families, they sometimes even employ teams of experts, mentors and therapists to support their children as they take on greater financial responsibilities. And there are children who, rather than refuse what's on offer, embrace it and grow up longing to be like the admired successful parents one day and willingly take on greater responsibilities.

Difficulties in giving and receiving in parents and children could be a reaction to past painful dynamics. Some examples include children who steal from their parents (by taking the occasional dollar bill or misusing their credit cards for unauthorized purchases, for example) because they felt emotionally robbed by them. Or parents who steal from children not out of need, but out of spite, envy, or a sense of entitlement (the thinking might go: "Why do *you* get to have so much, when I didn't at your age?"). Sometimes the resentment these parents hold toward their own parents mixes with the envy of watching their children receive in an abundant way (and not just financially: They receive opportunities, support, guidance in a way that the parent didn't have access to) and it gets acted out in such ways.

We have seen examples of children left burdened by debt because of the parents' choices (or mismanagement of finances). Of course these are difficult circumstances to deal with emotionally, but when they occur in the context of an already strained relationship, the debt becomes symbolic of a lot more than a financial failure: It becomes a representation of everything the parent didn't give, didn't do, could have done better. In these cases, mismanagement of the debt or deterioration in the relationship may be about more than just the anger attached to the parents' *financial* choices. Has the debt taken on a symbolic meaning and been burdened with all the negative affect that is now attached to it? What are we really angry about? Can we separate what belongs to the relationship so we can take control of the management of the debt from a more rational point of view?

Other examples of ghosts of the past being acted out between parents and children are those cases in which parents try to compensate for their absence by giving generously. They give more than feels right/appropriate, but it seems an unstoppable urge to do so because it comes from a place of guilt and reparation rather than a rational choice about what's best for them and their children. Their children might resent these gifts, and might even learn to dislike money as it becomes a representation of the emotional lack (money never compensated, after all). In an effort to push away these parents who only knew how to give financially, children sometimes adopt a contemptuous attitude toward money (and financial success), which often backfires. Yes, it allows them to rebel and to upset the parents, and it might even supply an inner sense of triumph that they didn't turn out like them, but it excludes other important elements they might want to take into consideration when making choices in life. Have we chosen something because it's aligned with our desires, likes, and talents? Or have we defined ourselves in antithesis to our parents, choosing something that we know our parents will dislike and disapprove of? We might find out that alongside the triumph, there is discontent and frustration because our choices have foreclosed a lot of opportunities and possibilities. Would facing the frustration feel like admitting they were right? Admitting that money was important after all?

Supporting our parents as they age

As children grow into adults and parents age, questions then arise in many families about supporting parents financially through retirement or illnesses. The so-called sandwich generation, referring to middle-aged adults who find themselves having to care and support financially both their own children and their aging parents, can find themselves under great financial (and emotional) pressure. A Pew Research Center survey found that with people living longer and young adults struggling to gain financial independence, close to a quarter of adults are now caring for a parent age 65 or older as well as at least one child younger than 18 (or providing financial support to an adult child).[2] But even before retirement, parents might ask their successful adult children for money (be it a loan or an act of solicited generosity).

How each family negotiates those boundaries, what is expected, what is given with joy and received with gratitude, or given resentfully and received ungratefully, will depend on the quality and evolution of those relationships in time. I have seen adult children working hard to obtain wealth they long to share with their parents either to show gratitude, or to help a parent they saw as a victim of an abusive relationship, or because they learned that this is what happens trans-generationally. Yet others work tirelessly to extrapolate themselves from a toxic family environment and end up either refusing to support aging parents, deferring to other siblings, or footing the bill regretfully and resentfully.

It cannot be anything other than an emotional decision when it comes to a child giving money to a parent, but the question is, Have the emotions been understood and thought about? Or are we unconsciously complying with or denying a request without being aware of the complexity of the decision? Giving money to our parents because we have been, once again, guilt-tripped in a way that was all too common, which pains us and we resent, is very different from giving because we are grateful and have always felt supported by our parents. Rejecting their request because we are angry toward our self-interested and exploitative parents is understandable, but have you considered all aspects of the decision? If you say no, will you feel relieved and proud of having successfully placed a boundary, or will you be consumed by guilt? The answer might be both, but giving yourself a chance to weigh up all the emotions involved in such a choice places you in a position of managing them better. After many sessions weighing up the pros and cons of giving her historically manipulative mother (who struggled with overspending tendencies) $4,000 toward a new car, a client decided: "I know placing the boundary was the right thing to do. If I feel guilty it's because that is how I was always made to feel when I didn't comply with their requests. But I am an adult now and I can make my own choices and what feels best this time is to say no."

I couldn't possibly cover every scenario of how money can be managed from an emotional place in a relationship between children and parents. However, what I invite you to do is to apply the same curiosity and depth to understanding how money might be used/misused in your relationship with your own parents or children.

The hidden message in your inheritance

It is important to consider what message you might be inadvertently sending to your family (or the world) through your estate planning choices and to wonder whether your message will be understood in the way it is meant. What do we want the world to think about us (praise our generosity in our church community, remember us as influential in our university, consider us fair, etc.)? What impact do we wish to have after our death (help family members, contribute to a worthy cause)? These are much more than logistical matters; they are expressions of feelings and meaning, and they can be forms of communication.

Consciously or unconsciously, as we age we begin to become preoccupied with the idea of legacy: What will we leave behind? What impact will it have? Of course, legacy doesn't need to be linked to finances, but for many people money is an important part of it. An estate planning process done with Financial Emotional Awareness can be a positive experience: It allows us to focus on the bits we can control in the face of the unpredictability of our fate and to feel a sense of agency in making choices that will have an impact on other people's lives or on causes dear to us.

Yet not many people have these conversations. I am not particularly surprised by this: As if money wasn't enough of a taboo, imagine a conversation that involves money AND death. Discomfort, shame, and fears often plague both topics. Thinking about our mortality is distressing enough, but inviting our spouse or children to consider it might go against our desire to spare them pain. As potential recipients of an inheritance, we face the additional fears of being perceived as insensitive, or even worse, greedy in bringing up the topic, even if our intentions are positive. Family culture around money can add to the difficulty: On one end are families where money isn't spoken about at all, and at the other end are families where money may have been a regular source of conflict, thus making one apprehensive about initiating a conversation about money.

Avoidance of the topic comes in many forms: Many people postpone and never quite find the time to address estate planning.

They may make jokes and change the subject when it's brought up or make rushed decisions to avoid the discomfort of staying on topic. According to Caring.com's 2023 Wills and Estate Planning Study, only one in three Americans have an estate plan. About a third of respondents say they don't have an estate plan because they do not have enough assets to leave to anyone, while others blame not knowing how to create one (15 percent) or the cost of creating one (14 percent) as reasons not to have it. The latter statistics flag some misconceptions about estate planning: Many believe they have no estate (not realizing that any possession, and even their life insurance or bank account counts as an estate) while others imagine it is a tedious and expensive process (unaware that there are now online tools that make it easier and more accessible).[3]

Most of us have a sense of how infantilizing it may be to reunite with family and how quickly we all fall into old dynamics, almost as if no time had passed. In my experience, family discussions on estate planning can also trigger early dynamics as they quickly transition from adult and rational conversations about financial assets to lively exchanges about how typical this is of them, how selfish the other can be, how insensitive their choices are. Sibling rivalries awaken, insecure attachments are tested, feelings of rejection and betrayal relived and revisited. Even in less passionate conversations one can detect, in between the lines of the money narrative, messages about disappointment, favoritism, respect, envy, fear, etc. Not all families find these conversations so tragically difficult, but many do, and when that is the case, the question to ask is, "What is really being talked about?"

Since each person will attach a different meaning and make different choices when it comes to money, it is helpful to verbalize and share the thinking around estate planning with the family so as not to leave people with assumptions and unknowns. I have spent countless hours supporting people who were left to decipher the meaning of their parents' or spouse's choices. When things aren't discussed in advance, all that heirs are left with are doubts and assumptions about the deceased's choices. If a rationale for an unequal distribution among children isn't explained, for example, children are left with their own phantasies about why parents made that choice, and phantasies are often colored with our fears. Something meant as a benevolent action to help a child in financial need might be interpreted by the siblings as a preference for that child. The result of unexplained wills can be a lifetime of having to sit with not knowing, on feeling unfairness, disappointment, and even betrayal without a chance to ask questions.

Imagine parents who pass away leaving a surprisingly large inheritance to children who had, up to this point, been unaware of the extent of the parents' wealth. Even though parents might have meant for this to be a pleasant surprise for the children, the children may feel betrayed in some way: Could they not have been trusted with the information? What about the sacrifices or denied requests from the past: What was the real reason if financially their requests could have been granted?

If you are considering bringing up the topic with your parents or spouse, it is important to be aware of the reasons for raising the matter. Is the intention positive and constructive (like a desire to ensure their wishes are adequately fulfillled) or is it about our own curiosity or reassurance that you will be treated fairly or recognized?

In a conversation with Francesco Baccaglini, a wealth manager who helps families with estate planning, he tells me that often when parents think about how they will hand down their wealth to the next generation, they approach the topic with a strong focus on tax savings rather than considering the pros and cons of handing down their wealth in lump sums to a generation that might be unprepared to manage it. In other cases, he says, a desire to control *how* the wealth is passed down and distributed obfuscates considerations about the most efficient vehicles for the handing down of inheritance. These are important considerations to address. One cannot treat estate planning as solely a rational financial matter and it would be naïve to underestimate the importance of values, fears, and desires in the process: Emotional barriers around trust and relinquishing control often influence the choices his clients make.

But even in those best-case scenarios in which plans have been drafted and communicated, after the passing of a loved one, discord in the family might prevail. In my experience, financial greed is only a secondary driver of such disputes. With mourning in process, and grief evoking anger, sadness, and a sense of emptiness left by the deceased, we might be using disputes about money and possessions as a vehicle to rid ourselves of some of these difficult emotions: Easier to be angry with our brother about them wanting Dad's car than to recognize our anger toward Dad; easier to feel robbed by our sister who wants to sell the summer house than to recognize how robbed we felt of a childhood by our mother who just passed away; maybe easier to say, "It's not fair that you get more money," than to ask, "Why did she love you more?" As people find themselves having to process incredibly difficult emotions related to the loss of their loved one, the anger that they might feel (which is a natural part of the grieving process) might get projected on to those around them. How do we prevent this? Well, we are human and maybe it's OK to be emotional and irrational after losing a loved one. An awareness that this is possible and maybe even likely can help us step back from the argument about the vase or fridge magnet or the proceeds of the sale of their belongings and think about what it is that is upsetting us so much, and whether it is reasonable to fixate on the object when really the pain and anger belong elsewhere.

Siblings

As adults, we might have money dealings with our siblings in different ways: jointly managing assets or involvement in a family business, but also in the day-to-day (shared expenses, small loans). Money conflicts among siblings can be the cause of rifts and estrangements. They can become so heated that they end up being lethal for the relationship. Why? Well, despite the fact that in psychoanalytic literature, sibling relationships are talked about probably as little as money, our relationship with our brothers and sisters can be among the most passionate relationships we have in a lifetime. In the Bible, the first murder in human history is a fratricide (the murder of a brother): Abel, son of Adam and Eve, was killed by his own older brother Cain out of jealousy and anger toward God's preference for Abel's offering over his own.

Siblings are there often early on in our lives (if not at the start) and have a profound impact on our expectations and fears in relationships. They can impact our experiences of competition, power, loyalty, love, support, difference, fairness, equality, etc. and because money can stand for some of these, it can become a tool we use to make statements on these topics.

Our ability to share is not just tested when we learn to share mother with father, but it is very vividly tested with our siblings (sharing our parents with them, sharing our toys with them). There is no doubt that sibling rivalry for parental attention is at the core of most sibling relationships and that jealousy and envy are feelings that are intensely evoked by them. Commenting on the murderous content of some children's dreams and the intensity of sibling rivalry, Freud wrote: "Hostile feelings toward brothers and sisters must be far more frequent in childhood than the unseeing eye of the adult observer can perceive."[4]

If we feel our sibling(s) received more attention from our parents, it can leave us with a bedrock of jealousy that is quickly evoked in present circumstances. We might feel angry with them and betrayed by our parents if there is any sign of unfairness in how finances are handled, or crossly protest to our parents or lash out at them if they receive, say, a more expensive birthday gift. Small irritants become big symbols of past injustices. But we might carry these dynamics elsewhere, like in the workplace where relationships with peers and bosses are impacted by our need to feel equally treated: We might be particularly annoyed seeing colleagues receiving more praise or money than us.

In families where parents modeled competition (by being competitive in their business lives, or even with their spouses) or fueled it (plenty of parents willingly or unwillingly foster competition among siblings), children might struggle to act sensibly in the running of joint ventures. Children might become more focused on prevailing over their sibling, evoking their envy, impressing the parent (whether alive in the flesh, symbolically represented by a boss or shareholder, or even simply the parent in their mind who they want to show off being the best to), rather than attending to business priorities. They might, in their careers, strive for financial success because ultimately, it's all about beating their sibling and attracting the admiration and validation of the parents.

Never are feelings of envy, jealousy, and competition more evident than after the death of a parent, when children quarrel over a will. Money becomes mistakenly consecrated with the power of making one feel valued, loved, and so siblings fiercely fight for it (only to find out that even when obtained, it falls short of expectations). Depending on how deprived we felt of parental recognition when we were young, we might secretly hope that our parents' financial arrangements would finally give us the recognition we always longed for. If you have followed in the media the succession feuds common of large family businesses (or watched the popular series *Succession*), you get a sense of the emotional and symbolic nature of these decisions. The jobs, stocks, or board seats that siblings fight for are representative of approval, parental endorsement, and triumph over other siblings. Business negotiations among siblings can evoke feelings of greed that are almost primal and visceral, even when there is enough financial wealth for everyone, exactly because it's not about the money. We hope, at some level, that money can correct the emotional injustices and deprivations of the past.

We might be afraid that our siblings will take on the qualities that most irritate us from our parents (which is very much possible). "She is just as irresponsible as Dad," we might proclaim at the first sign of carelessness. It is difficult to manage these fears and not let them get in the way of how we manage finances with our siblings: We might be reluctant to lend money to them if they have been a bit chaotic with their finances, like our father; we might spend little on their present, expecting them to be as miserly as our mother; we might be alarmed if they suggest a casino night, because father had a gambling problem. What we need to be mindful of is that even though they might remind us of our parents in some of their attitudes and behaviors, that doesn't mean that they will duplicate their behaviors (like overspending, miserliness, avoidance of money conversations); casting them in a role that doesn't quite represent them can be harmful. With siblings we are rarely as measured in our responses as we are with other people in our lives: We sometimes blurt out exaggerations in an unfiltered and often hurtful way.

Our assumptions that they will be bad at saving, avoidant of money, and overspenders like our parents might actually set up a potential self-fulfillling prophecy. It also interferes with understanding them better and relating to them in a more realistic way. We saw how labels and assigned roles in families can be a real barrier to change (like the example of Fiona and James). Repeating to our brother that he is "as stingy as Dad" might just convince them that this is true, rather than feeding something back to them, giving them a chance to learn something. If said in an empathic way, you can ignite their curiosity about their behavior and even their desire to do something differently next time. Imagine, instead, saying something like: "I was a bit disappointed by your present . . . it made me feel unimportant to you," and you might even add: "It reminded me of how we felt when Dad gave us socks for our birthday." You might be drawing a comparison to Dad, but it's with a view to help them reflect on how their action made you feel and help them relate to that. It's not an attack and certainly not a statement lacking in hope, like declaring they are a lost case, like Dad. Even if you can't control how they will respond to you (they might ignore you or just see it as an attack), you have a choice about how you feed something back to them and doing it in a way that is considerate can potentially be helpful (to them but also to the relationship).

Rifts between siblings or dynamics of preference and exclusion can repeat trans-generationally. A parent who felt less loved by his own father might end up inadvertently giving more (love/recognition/money) to one of his children. A mother who watched aunts and uncles break off contact after feuds related to grandmother's will might find it so stressful to think of her own will that she postpones it and ends up leaving her own children in an ambiguous mess causing the next generation of money conflict. We need to be aware of what examples run across generations so we can ask ourselves: Are we unwillingly allowing an undesirable history to repeat itself? Are we playing a part in creating the same conflict/rifts that we witnessed in our parents' generation?

Being the youngest of a string of siblings has an impact on one's development. Growing up in a household in which everyone can reach the top counter, is more able at sports, can already recite the seven times table, inevitably has an impact. Some of it can be positive: Youngest siblings might have learned to be patient, to share, to fight for resources and attention, but they might also carry insecurities that get acted out in adult settings. Eldest siblings, on the other hand, having had to manage the experience of potentially feeling dethroned by a younger sibling, could find jealousy quite triggering as a result: They might be on the lookout for situations that feel unfair. If that early experience of losing mother's undivided attention left them with the anticipatory anxiety that what is available today might be unavailable tomorrow, they might be anxious and greedy. However, these are massive generalizations that capture only one of countless dimensions and experiences that shape a person. It would be wrong to make assumptions: This is not about that. This is about trying to understand the nuances of certain dynamics that may be at play between us and our siblings: Maybe the fact that we never let them win is why they so proudly shove their big salary in our face at Christmas dinner.

So in dealing with money matters with your siblings, before you act, it's worth taking a step back and reflecting on the relationship as a whole so that you can stop yourself from making choices driven by emotions and old dynamics: Was it always the case that you felt pushed around and taken advantage of by your sibling? Well, when you deal with them financially, it might be important to put measures in place that leave no room for that (whether it's clauses in a contract or clear rules about who will pay for the card, and wrapping of the gift you are jointly buying for your father). Is there a history with your sibling that put you in a position of privilege (maybe you got the big room, you got the private education and your sibling felt unheard and unseen)? Well then, you might want to watch that you are not complicit in perpetuating that dynamic in the present and assume, for example, that you will get the bigger office/hotel room/share of the business. You might also want to be more aware of the potential, in your sibling, to feel unheard or unseen by you as you negotiate financial matters. Do you leave space for them to speak first when you have a call to discuss how you should set the renovation budget for the jointly owned property? Or do you jump in pushing your view? Whatever the background, the point is that money conflict is rarely about money, it's about the roles we cast ourselves and others in, and what those roles evoke in us. If you are mindful of that, then maybe you can take a more detailed and nuanced approach in your money dealings.

Business partnerships and the workplace

Our ability to compete for an account, to feel deserving of a higher salary and ask for it, or our demeanor in negotiations with a business partner, are influenced by the emotional relics of past experiences. Even our career choice might have been influenced by our desire for money, or rejection of it. We saw that people with high potential can end up sabotaging their careers or fail to ask for adequate pay, while others invest great effort to achieve their financial objectives only to feel fraudulent and unable to take pride in their accomplishments. We bring ourselves and our emotional blueprint of how the world works, how people interact and respond to us and to one another in our professional lives too. When it comes to financial transactions, there is room for money to become a magnet for meanings and dynamics that are not fully within our awareness.

If, in dealing with your business partner, you feel you are not happy with how you are handling the finances, try to understand what is behind your behavior: Does your partner have the slight patronizing demeanor your father did, and so you end up inadvertently positioning yourself as inferior to them making unwanted concessions in negotiations? Or are you finding you are unusually lax about what counts as a business expense, because you are exploited by your business partner? Maybe you are growing anxious about having enough cash flow as a result of polarization, sensing that your business partner's complete disregard for its importance is pushing you to compensate? I could go on with endless examples.

Sibling dynamics are one of the many ghosts of the past that affect our relationships in the workplace and in business partnerships. We might find we are experiencing our partner or reacting to them in a similar way to how we did with our bossy older sister or entitled younger brother. We might not be consciously aware of the fact that the present interactions are evoking in our minds a familiar dynamic from the past. However, when (in the therapy room) we begin to explore why our partner gets to us or irritates us so much or why we tend to often overreact or misinterpret their actions, it's often because we are using a lens to look at the situation that is 20, 30 years out of date. It's possible that our partner is, for example, bossy at times or more assertive and insistent than us when they express their views, but are we slipping into our role of the younger sibling whose toys were snatched or who was shushed by their elder brother, or can we inhabit the adult place we are in and respond to them appropriately? Can we separate what belongs to the past from the present situation?

Starting up a business with friends, they might feel insecure about what *they* have to bring to the party: They might experience others as always being more capable than them, or fear that they will be elbowed out of situations or underestimated. Money is often used to compensate for those fears and insecurities: They might accept lower pay, give away too much equity, or even end up pumping their own money to rescue the business in the hope of being taken seriously and being valued by the others.

Experiences of being bullied by siblings could profoundly shape one's confidence and trust that others (like colleagues) will be supportive and not critical or aggressive. If parents have been oblivious or passive to this dynamic, this might set us up for constantly searching for others who will stand up for us or leave us resigned to the fact that no one will. How could this get in the way of our relationship with money? Well, I have met people who go through life with a defeated attitude: If there have been more experiences of being the kid with the fewest sweets at the end of a piñata than experiences of us getting our fair share, we might go through life (and in our dealings with money) in a reluctant, hesitant way, expecting to be beaten by bigger fish. It is hard, then, to compete for a commission at work; it is hard to walk into their boss's office and demand that their salary is matched to their peers. Their choice to start their own business might in part come from a lack of trust in organizations; joining a company could be fraught with anxieties about being part of another bad family that won't protect and look after them.

They might adamantly refuse to partner with someone else in a start-up venture, even if beneficial for the success of the business, because the idea of sharing evokes uncomfortable fears: Best to try and be self-reliant than risk feeling in competition with or even risk being robbed by a partner.

Or they might join a company secretly hoping *this* pseudo-family will be fairer, but walk in with their anti-bully antennae perked up, cautious of any warning sign that they might be walked over. The way our mind works is that there isn't one experience that will lead to one outcome, but when we find ourselves in a salary negotiation, unable to utter the words, it is worth understanding what it is that is stopping us. Tracing it back to a lack of trust that we'll be given our fair share because this isn't what happened at home empowers us to ask an important question: Is this a reality of the present situation or are these just fears belonging to the past?

The breadth of workplace behaviors that might have been driven by sibling dynamics that left an imprint, a longing, a fear in us is so broad. I have seen the sibling of twins whose experience of exclusion and longing to pair up with someone led him to fiercely fight and argue that his spouse have a seat at the board table of the family business, partly because she had skills to contribute, but most importantly, it seemed, because of his longing to have a twin on his side of the table and put an end to that feeling of two against one.

Sibling dynamics are just one example of a constellation of past experiences that add up to an inner script about how we will be treated in the world. They can guide our behavior in various areas of life, including workplace relationships (transactions, negotiations, issues of rights to and feelings of entitlement about money, board seats, bonuses). So if you are unsettled by how you are managing financial issues at work, try to be inquisitive about how it is that you feel in these situations. What is it reminding you of? When else in life have you ever felt like that?

When colleagues compete for a commission as if their life depended on it, it's worth wondering what, in their minds, the bonus stands for. Maybe the ferocious contest is just a result of two competitive personalities sparking off each other? But its intensity might suggest that in their minds it has taken on a symbolic meaning: Maybe they were trying to prevail over the ghost of a sibling? But it could also be an attempt to win the approval of a ghost parent. It could also be about proving to themselves that they *could* achieve something having heard one too many times that they weren't good enough. There might be more than one answer, but we can only put things in perspective if we understand what they are *really* about.

Friendships

Money is a common reason for fighting with friends, with polls showing that, for example, one in five Americans has lost a friendship over a money dispute.[5] Have you ever found yourself resenting a friend for ordering the most expensive item on the menu, then expecting to split the bill evenly? Or lending money to them never to be repaid? Or maybe you always volunteer to buy the joint present, but then some never pay you back for their share of it? Money comes up in friendships, inevitably, and most times, one hopes, money dealings go smoothly. But when they don't, it can interfere with the harmony of the relationship (or be an expression of a disharmony simmering beneath the surface).

Money-related rifts in friendships are usually avoidable if things are brought up and talked about, but that often doesn't happen because money is an awkward subject to raise, and mostly because people fear confrontation and conflict. However, feeling trapped in a dynamic that unsettles us might end up in an explosive confrontation that causes irreparable damage to the relationship if the feelings (like frustration, anger, and resentment) build up until they become unmanageable.

As discussed in other parts of this book, understanding the role *you* play in a money dynamic you are unhappy about is vitally important before you seek to address it. It is easy to place the blame on the friend who is not paying you back, who keeps expecting you to treat them to dinner, who assumes everyone will share the bill equally (even though they always order the most expensive thing on the menu). What have *you* done to enable this behavior? What has stopped *you* from speaking up in the past? What about this particular friend makes it difficult to bring something up? What about your expectations of relationships or how you see yourself has acted as a barrier to saying something?

No one likes feeling exploited and taken advantage of, but sometimes those are the feelings evoked by a dynamic you might have helped enable because you are caring, generous and like looking after others. Your desire to please and give has led you to be loose in your boundaries around giving. It might start with "I don't mind helping a friend out" but when the help stops being met with gratitude, your feelings might begin to shift. It's easy to place the full blame on the now seemingly entitled friend, but recognizing your role in the dynamic is important because it might help you understand the other side. Your friend cannot know what is going on in your mind, and at what point you have begun to resent the giving if you have never verbalized any negative feelings about their behaviors or reactions.

Our views, fears, and expectations of others are intensely evoked in friendships. The accumulation of millions of life experiences of exchange and generosity will shape the internal pathway of our expectations from others: We might pay for takeout this time because we trust that our friend will get it next time, because in the majority of our experiences relationships are balanced. If, on the other hand, our internal pathway tells us that people tend to be exploitative and selfish, we might feel more anxiety and reluctance to pick up the bill.

If we were marked by a highly competitive environment (at home, and then mirrored in school), we might find it extremely challenging to admit to our friends that we can't afford to join that expensive group trip they are planning, or that we think the contribution for the group gift is expensive: Would it make us feel like we are losing in our internal theater in which everyone is constantly competing for greatness? That same emotional imprint could unconsciously make us choose a group of friends in which we can prevail financially and never feel lesser.

"Brokefishing," a new term used by the media, is a good example of a complex dynamic that friends may end up in. Brokefishing refers to when friends present themselves as being in financial need, when in reality this isn't the case. This can manifest itself as a friend who always asks others to cover their part of their bill and never pays them back or asks to borrow money (seemingly for essential items) and spends it on luxuries. Brokefishing may leave others feeling betrayed, angry, and unwilling to continue the friendship. It can be a one-off event or a recurring pattern of behavior.

Why does one ask for money from a friend if they actually have enough themselves? As I discussed in a recent contribution to *Women's Health*, one potential reason is that asking someone to give something up for them makes them feel looked after, taken care of.[6] Some people go through life seeking that, possibly out of an early lack of nurture. It could also be a way of avoiding giving something up; for example, if they want to save toward a trip or a luxury object, they might have to make sacrifices to do that. Rather than facing this and being honest with themselves (and their friends) about it, they present as not having enough money. They might even convince themselves that they don't have enough, whereas the truth in fact is that they don't have enough money *for everything they want to do*. They just don't want to compromise.

A set of childhood experiences that leaves one feeling short-changed by life could also explain how brokefishing, for some, might be about a search for justice (like stealing): a way to address the envy and the sense that others have more than we do, a desire to make things fair. The person brokefishing is at some level aware of the deception they are setting up, but it is (consciously or unconsciously) justified ("It's not so bad because our friends have more than we do"). There is a certain sense of triumph if they manage to obtain some of what the other has (in this case represented by money).

It could also be a way of projecting on to others feelings they haven't been able to manage within themselves. Unconsciously, they are acting in a way that makes the other feel manipulated and deceived, which could be because they themselves have felt manipulated and deceived in the past and they keep unconsciously placing these feelings onto others rather than confronting them within themselves. It's a classical psychological defense, a projection, and a way to rid ourselves of painful feelings.

As I always say to my clients, it takes two people to create a dynamic. So what is going on for the person who ends up giving them money and subsidizing their activities? It's worth looking at both sides of this dynamic, especially if it's not just a one-off situation but a pattern (which in many cases it is). One would find it hard to brokefish a second time if they were met with a confident, boundaried, and assertive friend who had been burned once before by them and said no thereafter. But they find an accomplice in people who struggle, for example, with a chronic sense of guilt and go through life seeking reparation. For them, saying no to a friend asking for money is too hard, and saying yes gives them hope that they have redeemed themselves somehow. The accomplice could also be someone who, through this dynamic, acts out unconscious phantasies of rescuing others.

Before confronting a friend who keeps brokefishing it is therefore worth asking yourself: Is this the price you feel you need to pay to keep a friendship alive? What sin are you constantly seeking to redeem yourself for? Is this the part of you that is seeking to always please others (and where does this part of you date back to)? Who is it that you actually wish you could rescue? Or is this about avoiding conflict at all costs (easier to say yes than to face a potential conflict)?

Whatever the reason, rather than having any positive emotional outcome, you end up feeling deceived and lied to. You often conclude that there was something malicious and intentional in what the friend did. Disappointment, sadness, shock, anger. These are a very painful set of feelings to deal with and an ordinary response to this situation.

Another topic that is important to address in friendships is that of difference. In friendships, our ability to cope with difference is expectedly tested. In a group of friends with different views on money, different financial realities, different values about what it should be spent on, it is easy to have disagreements. When this happens, we are confronted with multiple choices: Do we stand up for what we believe in and tell everyone that we could pick a decent hotel instead of camping again? Do we tentatively voice that we feel $30 is too much for a group contribution for a child's gift? Or do we say nothing and go along with it because, for once, it's OK if we go with what everyone else wants to do? What we decide to do will be influenced by a myriad of very personal factors that shaped our pathway to this choice, like how safe we experience groups (and this particular group) to be. What happens when we speak up for ourselves? How able are we to compromise our needs for others? Or to accept that people see things differently from us? And many more.

Sophie confessed to a journalist how frustrating it was to live on her first salary in New York City trying to be financially independent, while her friends were still receiving financial support from their parents. Her paycheck barely covered her basic expenses, but her friends insisted on making plans that involved spending more money than she could afford in trendy restaurants. She says: "I found myself turning down invitations. From their perspective, I wasn't putting much effort into the friendship. From mine, they were valuing their need to go out over spending time with me. It definitely sparked some fights, but it wasn't so much the money as the fact that we couldn't understand each other's perspectives. [. . .]"[7] It sounds like Sophie's friends struggled to adapt to her changing circumstances, both because it wasn't their own financial reality that changed but also because they had never been in a situation of such scarcity that it meant compromising on the lifestyle they were accustomed to. The friendship survived these dynamics, Sophie explained, for a combination of reasons: She was clear and honest with them about why she wasn't joining their outings without making excuses ("I only have $30 to spend this week"); her friends' circumstances changed too and as they began to make attempts at their own financial independence, they could relate to the desire to cut down spending and choose the occasional "staying in and cook" option; but also because Sophie was upfront about alternatives that would allow friends to meet without blowing the budget. Not all such stories end this way, mainly because of the shame that is often present when we have to admit to not having as much financial bandwidth as others, which leads to murky communication: lies, evasive answers, or a reticent retreat.

* * *

In this chapter, I have invited you to reflect on money dynamics in your wider relationships. We can let money be an expression of positive thoughts and feelings: "I value you," "I want to leave you my wealth," "I want to pay you what you deserve." But it can also become a symbol of negative messages: "They loved him more: Look how much more money he received"; "He is as entitled as Dad: How can he expect more shares in the business?"; "They won't pay me what I am worth: They are selfish, like everyone I know." How do we interpret money messages? What different money behaviors manifest themselves in our various relationships and what about those relationships do we think is driving that? If we were to put into words what is being communicated through money, what would it be? If we were to take the word "money" out of the argument we just had, what was the argument *really* about?

With a wider perspective in mind, try to pick up on patterns in your behaviors. Do you find that in more than one relationship (for example, both at work and in friendships) you end up worried that the others will take advantage of you one way or another (you might worry that everyone is getting better pay or bigger bonuses at work, or that your friends are free-riding on your resources)? Or maybe you end up in more than one setting (with your siblings and with flatmates) taking charge of finances only to find that people are blaming you when things go wrong? Whatever the scenario, if you find that a dynamic repeats itself in more than one area of life, it's worth wondering what *you* are bringing to it, allowing it to unfold.

I have also invited you to wonder about the underlying causes of a financial dealing that just doesn't feel right. If you are finding yourself in a situation that feels uncomfortable, where there is external conflict (as in you are arguing with someone about money matters) or there is internal conflict (you feel unease, uncomfortable about what is happening in your financial dealings with someone), it's worth taking a step back to look at the bigger picture.

Ask simple questions like: How do I feel about this? Is this how this person generally makes me feel? If this is the case, something about our dynamic *with them* is being manifested in money too. Ask yourself, Is this somehow typical of how you feel with this person in general? For example, they always present themselves as a helpless victim and you are always compelled to give them more (more support, more attention, more money). Do you want to continue to engage (and be complicit) in this dynamic of victim and rescuer? Do you maybe want to try and take on a different role in the relationship (and not just the one you feel you end up being cast into)? You could start the new dynamic with any interaction, including your money dealing. You could respond, this time, by saying something like: "I wonder if we could think about why you often ask to borrow money from me?" They might not have the answer, they might make up excuses, but that's not important. If you are hoping to shift the dynamic, then saying something different in a kind and open way will accomplish many things: You are holding up a metaphorical mirror so that they can confront what they are doing; you are telling them that you want this dynamic to be addressed; you are expressing your curiosity (and do listen to the answer they give); and finally, hopefully, you might have ignited their curiosity about it. But you can't *make* people change. You can only change your half of the dynamic and by saying something different rather than, once again, handing over the $10, something already shifts. You can't control whether they will be angry, feel rejected, never ask again, or continue to ask, but you have a choice about what you say and when and how you say it (as we saw in the previous chapter on how to have money conversations).

If a conflict or money dynamic feels uncomfortable, you might also want to ask yourself: Is this how *someone else* made me feel in the past? In which case the person in front of you might be triggering responses that are tainted by relics of the past. Ask yourself, Am I overreacting? Am I being paranoid? Am I responding to the person in front of me? Or, for example, because they used language that made me feel slightly manipulated, I am reminded of my father, so am I responding in an out of proportion way in the present out of fear I will end up feeling like I did in the past? The challenge here is to separate what belongs to the reality of the conversation you are having from what are essentially fears that history will repeat itself. The flags that are raised in your mind as you pick up on that manipulative tone/word are there for a reason: They are there to protect you from feeling hurt again. However, we need to engage the rational parts of us (sometimes with a conscious effort) in order to reality check.

You've probably heard the sayings: "Family and money are like oil and water; they don't mix," or "Before borrowing money from a friend, decide which you need most." Well, often we cannot avoid financial dealings with friends and family. The reason why these often end badly is that we allow all the emotions that color those relationships to get acted out through money and, of course, as symbolic as money is, it's also very real and has real consequences that can have an impact on our financial well-being. Money is supposed to be a medium for exchange of goods and services. However, what ends up being exchanged goes well beyond that.

CHAPTER 12

Understanding and shifting your attitude toward money

As a psychotherapist, I don't apply the same framework to every person. My focus is on understanding the individual as best I can in their complexity and helping them identify, name, and understand their feelings so they can alter the behavior they wish to address. There is nothing structured or linear about the journey because that's not how the mind works.

I won't try to condense a hundred years of psychoanalytic literature in a "how to change" chapter, but I hope to at least point you in the right direction by offering you guiding principles that can help you start the journey of self-exploration with a view to understand and potentially break from the stuckness you might be feeling with regard to your relationship with money.

There are three key principles that I would like to explore.

1. Approach self-exploration with a curious, not critical mindset.
2. Gather information with depth and creativity.
3. Reassess and expand your choices.

1. Approach self-exploration with a curious, not critical mindset

It's important to see the process of self-exploration as an opportunity to better understand yourself rather than to beat yourself up for everything you don't get right when it comes to money. Critical blanket statements, such as "I am terrible with money" or "I am useless with saving," won't get you far. If your inner critic is active and eliciting consuming, self-deprecating thoughts, the process will feel too defeating and lead nowhere. Be as kind in how you speak to yourself as you would be in trying to speak to someone else.

If you are not curious, you won't ask the right questions. I remember one of my clients who struggled with overspending asking herself: "What would I do if I didn't go shopping on the weekend?" I let silence fill the room. She started to cry. She had allowed herself to ask the most difficult and important question that helped us see that shopping was a defense against her feelings of loneliness: It was there to fill a painful gap of solitude.

Another client, who was an investment banker working tirelessly to amass more and more wealth, was telling me how "it's all good," because it's all part of his plan to retire early. "Yet here you are," I responded (suggesting that if he was seeking therapy, it wasn't because it's all good). To which he replied, "A part of me wonders if I will be happy once I have all the money to retire?" Aha. That was the question he hadn't dared ask himself. Once he did, we could begin to reflect in an empathic and curious way about the choices he was making in the present and the fears he held about the future.

A few questions for you to start with are as follows.
- Which chapter rang the most bells?
- Which example did you identify with the most?
- Did any of the fears or desires mentioned in this book trigger a thought/feeling in you?
- Did you feel unexplainably emotional reading any vignettes?

2. Gather information with depth and creativity

Considering how little most people think about their attitude toward money, even a bit of self-exploration might go quite far. As a therapist, I can help clients ask themselves the right questions, but before I do that, I gather some facts. In other words, I gather "the knowns" before I try to help them get to the "unthought known": what we know at some unconscious level.

The aim of this book has been to help people take the first steps in understanding their money attitudes and behaviors to uncover (or bring to consciousness) the hidden forces driving these. By decoding the encrypted messages that get communicated through money we can begin to think about more adaptive (or less harmful) ways of communicating with others or new ways of coping with the emotional challenges that lie beneath our money behavior. To navigate closer to the unthought known we can start with what we know about ourselves and our behavior, gathering information that is relevant and can direct our journey of self-exploration.

Facts and patterns

Facts often matter. If someone came to see me and told me, "I live in fear that I will run out of money," I would acknowledge their feelings but also gather information about the reality of their situation (I have heard this sentence from people with $1,000 in their bank account but also from people with $1,000,000). If the fear is reality-based (they only have $1,000 left in their account), then we might need to wonder if this has always been their financial reality and what, in the recent past, has made the feelings more overwhelming. We might wonder if this situation is a result of a cycle of self-sabotage that needs to be better understood. If the fear is more irrational (as is the case with the millionaire), then we might wonder about what the fear is *really* about.

If you were concerned about your excessive spending, for example, you might want to start gathering facts about the following.

- When do you spend carelessly? Is it at night before going to sleep, in the morning, or throughout the day?

- Identify the feelings at the various stages of the process. What are you feeling right before? How do you feel after the purchase? Or when the item arrives? What about when you try it on? For some people the pleasure is in the moment of purchase (the adrenaline rush, the soothing effect of shopping), yet for others it is about the object, the item they have allowed themselves to buy, treasure, and maybe even show off.

- Do you return any of the items you purchase? How do you choose what to keep/what to send back? What is the ratio usually? How does that make you feel?

- What is it that you spend excessively on? Is there a pattern in the sorts of things you purchase? Is it cosmetics and surgeries? Or is it gadgets? Or food? Where could the desire for these particular things be coming from?

- Are there situations that make your spending spiral out of control? Are these social situations? Or situations in which you feel particularly anxious? If so, what do you seem to be anxious about?

- Do you spend on yourself or on others? If so, who? Is there a pattern?

If it isn't a money behavior that you are struggling with but, rather, a feeling—for example, a paralyzing anxiety that causes you to effectively neglect your finances, then you might want to gather facts like the following.

- When did you start feeling this way? Has something changed recently to trigger the anxiety?
- How often do you feel this anxiety ? Is it daily/weekly? How intense is it? Is it closer to an easily dismissed negative thought or to a state of panic?
- What times of day/month/year do you feel the anxiety more intensely? Is it in the evenings when you think about the future? Is it in the middle of the month when pay day seems far away? Is it at the time of year when you need to file taxes?
- Where in your body do you feel the anxiety? (So you can be faster at catching the emerging feeling when it comes up next time, your body giving you a clue about what is happening in your mind.) Do you experience this feeling in other areas of life? (When thinking about an exam or a work presentation, for example.)
- Has this anxiety changed in the context of a relationship? (For example, you have become more anxious ever since you moved in with your girlfriend or ever since you started trying for a child.)

Expanding the investigation: open questions and exploratory tools

Try asking some very open questions first in relation to your relationship with money, and then specific to the problem you are trying to address. Allow images, memories, dreams, and thoughts to flow into your mind as you think of this topic. Acknowledge them and hold them in mind as you try to understand yourself.

Some of the open questions or memories you might want to retrieve could include the following.

- Money for me represents . . .
- When I think of money, I picture . . . I feel . . .
- The first words that come to mind in relation to money are . . .
- The first money memory I can remember is . . .
- Think of your early experiences related to money and reflect on how these might have shaped your attitude in the present. Was it talked about at home? Was it a cause of conflict? Were your wishes easily granted? Was money handed unconditionally or tied to performance? Did you receive an allowance, and if so, how did it feel? What did you do with it?

Open questions regarding the feelings or behaviors related to money that you are trying to address can be helpful too. Building on the overspending example could include the following.

- If I didn't spend money when I have the urge, I would feel . . .
- What I love most about my money attitude is . . .
- What I like least about my money attitude is . . .
- I envy people who can be . . . with their money
- In my family, overspending is/was viewed as . . .

In relation to money anxiety, these could include the following.

- My biggest fear with money is that . . .
- In my family, growing up, money was a source of . . .
- The most frightening experience related to money I have had (or witnessed) is . . .

Whatever your struggle with money (too much spending/too little, too much risk/too little), try to formulate questions that broaden the scope or take your thinking further. Saying "I don't ask for a raise because I am shy and find it uncomfortable" might be only half of the story and won't help you get past the emotional blocks that make salary conversations such a hurdle in your financial well-being. Allowing yourself to ask: "What else stops me from asking for a rise? What is the worst-case scenario? What would it feel like? Why might it feel like that? When else did I ever feel like that?" could help you admit that "I don't ask for a raise because I am afraid of rejection, which I think is because in my family all my requests were shut down, my sister got her way, but I never felt I did." Questions might help you see that you are using in the present a set of expectations shaped in the past and that might not be relevant in the context of your job. The fear might be felt and present in the here and now, but as an adult, you can recognize that there might be more relevant information to gather before you ask for a raise than basing your choice on out-of-date and out-of-context expectations.

Uncovering resistance to change

If you have a desire to change your attitude to money, it is helpful to acknowledge that the current attitude/behavior is often there for a reason, fulfilling a psychological objective. Think of everything you are gaining through this behavior—directly and indirectly. Through your symptom (in this case the symptom could be your overspending, your hoarding, your financial risk-taking), you gain relief from the feelings that drove you to it (loneliness, envy, anger).

- Look for the motives behind your behavior. What do you think is the upside to your current money behavior? For example, if you are hoarding money, it may be protecting you against a fear of running out of it. If you are delegating all financial decisions to your partner, it might be saving you from having to worry about any of it. If you are gambling, you might be escaping the real world and numbing painful feelings.

♦ Another way to ask this question is, "What benefits will you have to give up in order to change the present behavior?" For example, giving up on your overly generous gifting might mean potentially losing the "wow factor" you evoke in people. Or giving up your shopping might leave you with no shared activity you and your daughter can engage in at the weekend. Or giving up gambling will leave you having to face the pain of your loneliness.

Identifying both the motive for your behavior and the potential sacrifices needed for change (the benefits you need to give up) can help you understand why you are stuck, and partly resisting change. It's hard, for example, to fear giving up the one plan (shopping) you can do with your teenage daughter on the weekend. But if you figure out that this is the real reason why you find it so hard to give it up, how about looking for a substitute plan? Could that lessen the resistance to changing a behavior you are hoping to address?

Resistance to change often comes from fears, in which case it's worth reality checking these and trying to separate what feelings belong to the past and are still relevant in the present.

♦ How realistic is it that I will run out of money, now that I have put a sensible financial plan in place, have a substantial amount of savings, and are careful at budgeting?

♦ How likely is it that I will be laughed at and ridiculed if I asked for a raise?

♦ Do I *really* think my friends will be offended if I explain why I can't attend the expensive trip they've organized?

You might find that some of the outcomes you expect are unrealistic (and that you tend to catastrophize). You might even consider opportunities in them too: If you *are* ridiculed by your employer, is it a good place to work? If your friends *are* critical and unforgiving when you explain you can't contribute as much to the group gift, isn't it helpful to see this aspect of them, albeit painful?

I fully acknowledge that fears don't just disappear when you see how irrational they are: A part of you knew they were irrational already. In therapy, we often have to visit and revisit the memories attached to fears, and work through some of the feelings before the fear can lessen its grip in the present. But being conscious of our tendency to catastrophize (to think of the worst-case scenarios) can be a helpful start in trying to manage our anxieties.

In other cases, resistance comes from ambivalence: A part of us wants or feels something and another wants the opposite. We are both proud and frustrated by how thrifty we are. We are both calmed and unsettled by our gambling. We are both reassured by our risk avoidance and envious of risk-takers. Ambivalence is a result of the inherent complexity of our minds and can lead to a state of uncertainty or indecision, of feeling stuck.

Acknowledging the cost

You might have a vague sense that what you are doing is not optimal, but have you really thought through the consequences (both financial and psychological)? Think of the impact of your current money behavior on the following.

- Your finances: For example, how much money are you spending on shopping/gambling/going out? (You'd be surprised how many people deny the cost of their behavior by avoiding these basic calculations.) Think of the opportunity cost—what *could* you have saved/gained if you had acted differently? If you had saved $X a month for the past five years, you would have saved $X; if you had cooked instead of eaten out at least half the times, you would have saved $X; the point of this is not to beat yourself up with it, but to see that there are real financial repercussions to the choices you are making.

♦ Your financial well-being: Avoiding finances might be harming your financial well-being by leaving you feeling anxious (rather than in control and confident about your finances); your tendency to hoard money might be getting in the way of you enjoying the money you have.

♦ Your own feelings about yourself ("being this way with money causes me to feel . . ."): Be honest about the shame/guilt/anxiety that you have to manage as a result of your current choices. That might be a high price to pay to address the feelings you are avoiding.

♦ People's feelings toward you: Relationships with others might be suffering as a result of your current attitude to money.

3. Reassess and expand your choices

Often when people feel they have no way out, it's because they can't see (or don't allow themselves to see) the choices in front of them. Sometimes we quickly dismiss options before even considering them, because we don't like the trade-offs that come with them. If you find yourself with no choices, think, what haven't you considered? What were you avoiding thinking about?

One way to see more choices is to reframe the issue, trying to be specific. Rather than "I am a pushover when it comes to spending," saying: "I always spend more than I want to when I am out shopping with my children," is a better starting point because it flags the behavior or situations that you want to address, opening up a space to think about options like going out with a pre-established budget in mind. You could also go out less frequently, bring cash only, or just say no when they pressure you to buy them one more thing. Each of these options will have its trade-offs that you will need to accept (you might have to tolerate watching their disappointment; you might have to put up with a tantrum or feel like the withholding mother you don't want to be like; you might have to face feelings of inadequacy or insufficiency, or you might feel frustrated having only brought cash). Reframing may also point you to the feelings that drive your behavior. If overspending happens mainly when you are with your kids, it could be about your desire to be a generous mother or your fear of experiencing through them a disappointment that you are all too familiar with because of your own past experiences.

Another way to expand the breadth of your choices is to shift the focus from a personal weakness to a skill that you can work on. Rather than saying, "I am bad at saving," you might want to say, "I would like to learn how to save more effectively." The first statement might leave you short of ideas, the second can quickly turn into "How can I learn how to save more effectively?" from which a brainstorm may generate a few options to try (ask a friend how they do it, sign up for a financial literacy webinar, download an app/tool to help you).

Include options you were not considering because they seemed too hard. For example, instead of "I can't help but be generous," think of it as a trade-off: "If I were to show up with a small gift instead of my usual big gift, or no gift at all, I would feel shame/guilt/inadequacy." Whatever the answer, we are now unpacking the primary gain of your generosity (addressing shame/guilt/inadequacy) while helping you see that while you might feel stuck and that you can't help it, you are still making a choice. It's a choice that is serving a psychological purpose, defending you from those painful feelings, but acknowledging it as such (a choice) offers the freedom to ask yourself the two important questions.

1. Can't I find a different way to manage the emotions I am avoiding through my defense?

2. Is the price I am paying to employ this defense worth it? (Being overly generous comes with both a financial cost and an emotional one too, as guilt and regret sometimes follow the generous act.) Just rephrasing the issue can begin to widen your thinking.

Feeling like you have choices is a better place to be than resigning oneself to something feeling inevitable and unchangeable. But making choices is not easy. We need to overcome various obstacles to do that. First of all, let go of the idea that there is a right choice, but just options and trade-offs. Secondly, you need to be ready to mourn the loss of what you are giving up as a result of the choice: If you choose to stay home to save some money, you will have to give up the fun you might have had with your friends; if you choose to finally spend on a coat you will have to let go of the money. And all of these losses will bring up feelings in you that you will have to sit with and get through (and try not to act out elsewhere).

Accepting vs. changing

Psychoanalyst Carl Jung said, "I am not what happened to me, I am what I chose to become." It's a strong statement that reminds us that as painful as our past experiences might have been, we still have agency in shaping our future choices. If the self-exploration has led you back to painful events in your past, which help explain why you hold on to things so dearly, why you fight so much for fairness, why you feel so scared and insecure about finances, then an important part of the process is to acknowledge the degree of choice you have in the present with regard to what you do and how you act. You can decide that you won't address your loneliness by mindlessly shopping online in the evening. You can adopt safety measures to avoid the financial losses that your parents incurred unexpectedly. You can decide to call a gambling anonymous helpline instead of clicking on an online casino. The past doesn't have to repeat itself.

Having said that, I acknowledge that change is not easy. It takes time (and sometimes years of therapy) to achieve. But sometimes what is most needed and most effective, rather than change, is acceptance. Accepting who we are and what we value is very freeing because it can guide our choices and avoid inner conflict. If you accept, for example, that there is a materialistic part of you that will indulge in and enjoy having the beautiful objects you couldn't have when you were younger, you might find a way to allow yourself to still have some of that indulgence in a more measured way.

Accepting doesn't mean resigning yourself. It's about landing in a place in which you can recognize your weak spots, but also give yourself an opportunity to work on them—if you wish to do so. It is very different to be unconsciously repeating behaviors that we see in our parents versus accepting that our parents found it hard, for example, to enjoy their money, and that is something we can't change about them but can work on in ourselves. As you try to trace your attitude and behavior to money back to what you learned in your family or your past environment, part of the process in fact is to accept the parents, caregivers, and teachers you had. Trying to understand their point of view (what might *they* be repeating of their own experience) helps in that process. They made their choices, but these don't have to be yours. You can disagree with whoever's voice you have internalized, you can give yourself the chance (no matter how anxiety-provoking) to try something different, and you can redefine what success or self-worth means *for you*.

* * *

It all sounds so simple, written down in the pages of this book. Dig deeper, explore the past, consider the trade-offs. I want to be clear: It isn't simple. The mind is still largely a mystery and because we can't be studied in a lab manipulating variables, there are no formulas that can answer the whys and hows.

You might have known from the outset what aspect of your money behavior you wanted to tackle, and hopefully now you understand more about what has kept you stuck, engaging with that behavior for so long. Or you might be among the many people who just feel lost when it comes to money, who lack an inner compass, a sense of what they should do with their money and who come to therapy hoping I will tell them. Although I don't tell them what to do, I can help them establish their inner compass based on their values, beliefs, hopes and aspirations. You can begin that process yourself by identifying your feelings, fears, and desires constellating around money. You can become more aware of inner conflicts: like parts of you that want opposite things or that contradict one another. You can think of choices and trade-offs and how you feel about them. All of these insights amount to having Financial Emotional Awareness and empower you to make more conscious and grounded choices with your finances.

CHAPTER 13

A closing message

This book has been about the individual, about helping you reflect on how your unique experiences and your internal world shapes how you feel and act with money. I hope to have broadened and deepened your Financial Emotional Awareness so that you feel more conscious and in control of your financial choices. This will improve your financial well-being. Through the lenses I have used you might have more clarity on why you make the money choices you make, and why you sometimes feel stuck and unable to change bad financial habits. You might have understood some of the internal conflicts that paralyze you and sit behind your inaction or you might have uncovered that there are fears and desires unrelated to money that you sometimes act out through money. Maybe now, the hidden messages that you might be trying to convey to others in your financial conflicts are becoming easier to decipher.

I hope to have helped you understand your relationship with money and sparked some curiosity about the meaning it holds in your mind. We live in a world in which we can't escape its presence in real life and so being thoughtful about its presence in our minds can guide our financial choices.

We can't deny that money is often fetishized in our society, and that it is imbued with powers over and above its transactional value. But we can distance ourselves from the phantasy of what money could get us and be more reflective about what we want it to enable in our lives.

Money is full of meaning, but what it stands for, along with all the parameters that we set around what's enough or not enough, what's risky or not risky, and what's excessive or frugal, vary from person to person. Since there is no consensus, we are left in the dark about what others think of our money situation/behavior and so it feels risky to bring it up: We could be exposing ourselves to judgment. If we fear that others see it as a sign of success, achievement, or worth, then we might be ashamed to disclose our low salary or a recent loss or debt. If we fear others see accumulation of money as greedy, we might avoid a conversation about how big our bonus was this year. We might not just be afraid of being seen as greedy but we might also fear people's envy or exploitation (will they expect us to pay, now that they know we earn more?). It's a fear of not knowing what is in the other person's mind, not bank account, that is the biggest barrier to talking about money.

Management of money is not an innate skill. Imagine what our eating habits might be like had we not been taught about healthy habits and table manners. We need to be taught the basics and we need to be taught the more complicated lessons too: that if we don't manage our feelings appropriately, we are at risk of eating or spending to self-soothe, or we might act out our rebelliousness by pushing away food or taking on too much financial risk. This is why financial education is crucial, but something that also incorporates Financial Emotional Awareness because we are not (at least not always) rational when we make choices.

In this book, I haven't addressed every complication in our difficulties with money, nor could I cover every possible explanation for the ones I did cover. Such an attempt would be nonsensical: What makes psychotherapy so incredibly interesting (and challenging!) is the complexity of the human mind and the diversity of our experiences.

If you feel you discovered, by reading this book, the one experience that explains it all, or the one reason behind your behavior, then you might be jumping to conclusions. We are shaped by multiple factors and experiences over time, some that might be in our conscious awareness and many that won't. Becoming more aware of and piecing together the influences that have shaped your feelings, thoughts and behaviors related to money will help you learn more about yourself even after you put this book down.

Therapists are trained to look in difficult places with you and within you, helping you confront truths that are hard to face, and go back to painful memories until they stop having a stronghold on your behavior. But even ten years of studies don't equip you with a road map because the terrain to explore is different for each person. It also means that even with a therapist we might never reach truths that keep themselves buried deep within us. A friend once told me that if we think of our mind as a room, as a therapist you might only be allowed to see what is visible from the keyhole, sometimes because that's all the client allows you to see or allows themselves to access.

So don't be concerned if you find that you have gone through the questions, gathered all the information you could, and then look at it like a 1,000-piece puzzle scattered on your table and scratch your head. What does it all mean? How does it all link? That's why we say that two minds are better than one. Talking about it with a partner, a dear friend, or a parent can help us sort things out in our minds. They might help us put pieces together.

Sometimes patterns, links begin to emerge, or a narrative even that explains how you ended up here in a more coherent way. There are no guaranteed outcomes when it comes to self-discovery, but we won't know more about ourselves if we don't at least attempt some self-exploration.

Bringing money out of the shadow into clear light, and exploring and analyzing our relationship with it can be helpful in setting realistic expectations about what it can buy and what it can enable. It can help us enjoy more of the money we do have, making choices in the present and for our future that are aligned with our values, and we feel in control of.

Whether you have decided to look at your relationship with money on your own, or through therapy, think of the potential that money holds beyond its utilitarian value. This book has been rich in examples of how money is sometimes misused, and how it can become an obstacle in our journey of self-fulfillment and get in the way of our mental health and our relationships. There is no denying the fact that poverty and debt deprive many people of the opportunity to reap these benefits. But those who have money beyond that needed to cover necessities can use it as a life-enhancing tool: It can enable goal fulfillment, pleasures, and the expression of our values and beliefs. It can be a medium through which we express positive feelings, like gratitude and love. Money can offer freedom and choice. We can use it to improve our lives and the lives of others.

Using money in such a positive way is not an easy pursuit. We may struggle to know how to use the money we have or struggle with feelings related to the money we don't have. Many people who come to see me are afraid of sounding shallow or materialistic because they are thinking about money. However, the questions they are actually asking themselves are deep and important: They are questions about their longings, their worries, their relationships, and, ultimately, about their pursuit of love and happiness. Questioning our choices is an important part of growth. Being conscious of what drives them is a sign of maturity. Managing our feelings is fundamental to our financial well-being.

If money is on your mind, start by asking yourself, "What does it stand for?"

Acknowledgments

Before anyone else, I would like to thank my clients who are a continuous source of inspiration and learning. If it wasn't for their courage, this book wouldn't exist.

I would also like to thank my therapist who has helped me establish and follow my inner compasses. Her constant and gentle support throughout the years has helped me ride internal and external storms. And my supervisor whose astonishing intuition and experienced insight has enriched me profoundly. Thank you for your generosity in reading every page of the long first draft and for your important feedback.

I also want to thank everyone who was part of my journey at WPF, where the foundations of my practice were established, particularly Stephen C., and my peers Yanni M. and Lola B. for their support.

I am indebted to all those who have gifted their time to reading chapters: like Connie, Eric, Sami, and Simone, and most of all to James for going through the whole manuscript and giving me the most spot-on feedback, drafted in the most considerate way.

Thank you to my friends whose love I felt in many ways in this adventure. Sara, for dreaming bigger than I ever could. Bree for supporting me and letting me use her home office. Ciara, whose lovely afternoon tea rescued the book and much more when things got tough. Eva, for keeping me in mind and sharing all those relevant articles. Yaprak, for our Mondays. Richard J., for our Thursdays. And La Banda, for always checking in.

I can't thank my editor Madiya Altaf at Bonnier Books enough: This book would have come in tomes if it wasn't for her. You have my admiration for your ability to offer structure and clarity. And my agent Jason for his guidance and reassurance throughout the process.

Thank you to the team at The Experiment for helping to bring this book to a US audience.

To my family of origin: for their unconditional love.

Last, but certainly not least, to my treasure chest: Alexandros, Matilde, and Ale.

Notes

Introduction

1. Freud, S., "On beginning treatment (further recommendations on the technique of psychoanalysis)," in *The Standard Edition of the Complete Psychological Works of Sigmund Freud*, Vol. 12 (London: Hogarth Press, 1913/1958), 121–44.

2. "Religion, sex and politics? The M word is Britain's biggest taboo," Lloyds Banking Group, 2019, lloydsbankinggroup.com. (Accessed November 30, 2023.)

   Loudenback, T., "A survey of 2,000 Americans found they're more likely to talk about politics and relationships with their friends than money," *Business Insider*, 2021, businessinsider.com/data-americans-dont-talk-about-money-with-friends-2021-6?r=US&IR=T.

3. Hillman, J., "A contribution to soul and money," in Lockhart et al. (eds.), *Soul and Money* (Dallas, TX: Spring Publications, 1982).

4. "Religion, sex and politics?," Lloyds Banking Group, op. cit.

5. "Shame, Burden, and Upbringing: Why 29 Million UK Adults Don't Feel Comfortable Talking About Money Despite Feeling Worried About It," Money and Pensions Service, 2020, moneyandpensionsservice.org.uk/2020/11/11/shame-upbringing-and-burdening-others-why-29-million-uk-adults-dont-feel-comfortable-talking-about-money-despite-feeling-worried-about-it. (Accessed December 7, 2023.)

6. "Global financial wellbeing research 2023," Nudge, 2023, nudge-global.com/resources/news-blog/financial-wellbeing/global-financial-wellbeing-research-2023. (Accessed February 6, 2024.)

7. Richardson, T., Elliott, P., and Roberts, R., "The relationship between personal unsecured debt and mental and physical health: a systematic review and meta-analysis," *Clinical Psychology Review* 33, no. 8 (2013), 1148–62.

8. "Credit Card/Debt Stress Study," *Associated Press*, 2008, surveys. associatedpress.com/data/SRBI/AP-AOL%20Health%20Poll%20Topline%20040808_FINAL_debt%20stress.pdf. (Accessed February 6, 2024.)

9. "Financial wellbeing and productivity in the workplace," Cebr, 2021, cebr.com/wp-content/uploads/2022/03/Financial-Wellbeing-report-v1.2-1.pdf. (Accessed February 6, 2024.)

10. Diener, E., as quoted in Myers, D. G., "Wealth and Well-Being," davidmyers.org/uploads/WealthAndWellBeing_FaithMedicine.pdf. (Accessed December 1, 2023.)

11. For example, see Killingsworth, M., "Experienced well-being rises with income, even above $75,000 per year," in Wilson, T. D. (ed.), *Proceedings of the National Academy of Science* 118, no. 4 (2021): e2016976118.

12. Hasler, A., Lusardi, A., and Valdes, O., "Financial Anxiety and Stress among U.S. Households," Global Financial Literary Excellence Center with Investor Education Foundation, 2021, gflec.org/wp-content/uploads/2021/04/Anxiety-and-Stress-Report-GFLEC-FINRA-FINAL.pdf. (Accessed February 6, 2024.)

13. Klapper, L., Lusardi, A., and van Oudheusden, P., "Financial Literacy Around the World," Global Financial Literary Excellence Center, 2015, gflec.org/wp-content/uploads/2015/11/3313-Finlit_Report_FINAL-5.11.16.pdf. (Accessed February 6, 2024.)

14. According to survey by Greenlight Financial Technology, as cited in Oliveros, F., "3 in 4 Teens Lack Knowledge and Confidence in Personal Finance," Value Penguin, 2021, valuepenguin.com/news/teenager-finance-knowledge-2021. (Accessed February 6, 2024.)

15. Bhutoria, A., Jerrim, J. and Vignoles, A., "The financial skills of adults across the world. New estimates from PIAAC," 2018, johnjerrim.com/piaac. (Accessed February 6, 2024.)

16. The poll of 4,000 UK adults was carried out by Opinium on behalf of the Centre for Social Justice, a think-tank, as cited in Barrett, C., "Half of UK adults need 'urgent help' managing their money," *Financial Times*, 2022, ft.com/content/b54d48e8-e82a-4734-bb3d-d548aa19d2d0.

17. OnePoll survey of 2,000 American parents with children between 8 and 14, as cited in Melore, C., "Are you financially literate? Most parents wish they knew more about money growing up," StudyFinds, 2021, studyfinds.org/financially-literate-most-parents-wish-they-knew-more-about-money-childhood. (Accessed February 6, 2024.)

18. "Young Person's Money Index 2021–2022," London Institute of Banking and Finance, 2022, libf.ac.uk/docs/default-source/financial-capability/young-persons-money-index/young-persons-money-index-2021-22-final.pdf. (Accessed February 6, 2024.)

19. OnePoll survey of 2,000 American parents, op. cit.

20. "Beat the blues by focusing on financial wellbeing," Money & Pensions Services, 2022, moneyandpensionsservice.org.uk/2022/01/17/beat-the-blues-by-focusing-on-financial-wellbeing. (Accessed February 6, 2024.)

21. Thompson, A., "How can government and business improve the UK's financial literacy?," Confederation of British Industry, 2022, cbi.org.uk/articles/how-can-government-and-business-improve-the-uk-s-financial-literacy. (Accessed February 6, 2024.)

22. Lusardi, A., "Financial literacy and the need for financial education: evidence and implications," *Swiss Journal of Economics and Statistics* 155 (2019).

23. Hasler, Lusardi, and Valdes, "Financial Anxiety and Stress among U.S. Households," op. cit.

1   How past experiences influence our relationship with money

1. Cline, A., "What Does the American Flag Symbolize?," ThoughtCo, 2018, thoughtco.com/the-american-flag-as-symbol-249987. (Accessed February 6, 2024.)

2. Winnicott, D. W., "Transitional objects and transitional phenomena," in *Playing and Reality* (London: Tavistock, 1971).

3. Murdin, L., *How Money Talks* (London: Routledge, 2021), 171.

4. Fonagy, P., and Target, M., "Attachment and reflective function: Their role in self-organization," *Development and Psychopathology* 9, no. 4 (1997): 679–700.

5. Lee, J. R., Marchiano, L., and Stewart, D. C., "The Money Complex: Incarnating our Dreams," *This Jungian Life* podcast, episode 126.

6. Ibid.

7. Ainsworth, M. D., "The development of infant mother attachment," in Caldwell, B. M., and Ricciuti, H. N. (eds.), *Review of Child Development Research*, Vol. 3 (Chicago, IL: University of Chicago Press, 1973), and Bowlby, J., "Attachment and Loss," *The American Journal of Psychiatry* 97 (1969): 1158–74.

8. Holmes, J., *The Search for the Secure Base: Attachment Theory and Psychotherapy* (London: Routledge, 2001), 121.

9. Mikulincer and Shaver, as quoted in Wallin, D. J., *Attachment in Psychology* (New York: Guilford Press, 2007).

10. Freud, S., "The Neuro-Psychoses of Defence," in *The Standard Edition of the Complete Psychological Works of Sigmund Freud*, Vol. 3 (London: Vintage, 2001), 41–61.

11. Dodes, L., "A general psychoanalytic theory of addiction," in *Beyond the Primal Addiction* (London: Routledge, 2019), 5.

12. Ibid.

13. Turkel, A., "Money as a Mirror of Marriage," *Journal of the American Academy of Psychoanalysis and Dynamic Psychiatry* 16, no. 4 (1988): 525–35.

2 Overspending and its many drivers

1. Hines, S., "Who Needs 103 Dresses?," *Daily Mail*, 2022, dailymail. co.uk/femail/article-11239255/SOPHIE-HINES-reveals-radical-steps-took-love-shopping-spun-control.html.

2. Torre, P. S., "How (and why) athletes go broke," Vault, 2009, vault. si.com/vault/2009/03/23/how-and-why-athletes-go-broke.

3. Hankins, S., Hoekstra, M., and Skiba, P., "The Ticket to Easy Street? The Financial Consequences of Winning the Lottery," *The Review of Economics and Statistics* 93, no. 3 (2011): 961–69.

4. Thaler, R. H., "Mental accounting matters," *Journal of Behavioral Decision Making* 12 (1999): 183–206.

5. Aviv, W., et al., "Compulsive Buying," *Journal of Drug and Alcohol Abuse* 36, no. 5 (2015): 248–53.

6. Christenson, G. A., et al., "Compulsive buying: descriptive characteristics and psychiatric comorbidity," *Journal of Clinical Psychiatry* 55 (1994): 5–11, as cited in Koran, L. M., et al, "Estimated Prevalence of Compulsive Buying Behavior in the United States," *American Journal of Psychiatry* 163, no. 10 (2006).

7. "Why we shop and how to stop," The Priory Group Media Centre, priorygroup.com/media-centre/time-to-checkout-your-addiction-why-we-shop-and-shop-and-how-to-stop. (Accessed February 6, 2024.)

8. Knutson, B., et al., "Neural predictors of purchases," *Neuron* 53 (2007): 147–56.

9. Raghubir, P., and Srivastava, J., "Monopoly Money: The Effect of Payment Coupling and Form on Spending Behavior," *Journal of Experimental Psychology* 14, no. 3 (2008): 213–25.

10. Devaney, T., "Nearly 40 percent of millennials overspend to keep up with friends," Intuit Credit Karma, 2018, creditkarma.com/insights/i/fomo-spending-affects-one-in-four-millennials#methodology. (Accessed February 6, 2024.)

11. Orr, P., and Hughes, T., "Sylvia Plath on Her Early Influences and Why She Became a Writer," The Narrative Art, youtube.com/watch?v=gbNcRhxfF-A. (Accessed February 6, 2024.)

12. Plath, S., *The Bell Jar* (London: Faber & Faber, 2005).

13. Plath, S., "Last Words," *Crossing the Water* (London: Faber & Faber, 1971).

14. Krueger, D. W., "Money Meanings and Madness: A Psychoanalytic Perspective," *Psychoanalytic Review* 78, no. 2 (1991): 209–24.

15. "Arabs in Mykonos buy 200 bottles of champagne but do not drink it," *Greek City Times*, 2022, greekcitytimes.com/2022/06/28/mykonos-arab-champagne.

16. Scopelliti, I., "Why Do People Brag?" *TEDx Talks*, youtube.com/watch?v=pNTyl_nUOVo. (Accessed February 6, 2024.)

17. Spurling, L., *An Introduction to Psychodynamic Counseling* (London: Palgrave, 2009), 153.

18. Buchanan, D., "The pile of unworn dresses that buried my anguish: She spent $400 a month and once bought five ballgowns. Now, in a brutally honest testimony, this author describes the shopping addiction that masked a profound sadness," *Daily Mail*, 2021, dailymail.co.uk/femail/article-10042265/Author-describes-shopping-addiction-masked-profound-sadness.html.

19. Lee, J. R., Marchiano, L., and Stewart, D. C., "Midlife Crisis: Renewal or Stagnation," *This Jungian Life* podcast , episode 121.

20. Black, D., "A review of compulsive buying disorder," *World Psychiatry* 6, no. 1 (2007): 14–18.

21. Barrett, C., "'The dopamine is so high': the psychology of shopping addiction," *Financial Times*, 2022, ft.com/content/56232a20-acbc-4ab3-a056-970099b4451e.

22. Faber, R., "In the mood to buy: Differences in the mood states experienced by compulsive buyers and other consumers," *Psychology and Marketing* 13, no. 8 (1996): 803–820.

23. Ibid.

24. Lejoyeux, M., and Weinstein, A., "Compulsive Buying," *The American Journal of Drug and Alcohol Abuse* 36, no. 5 (2015): 248–53.

25. Harman, J., "'I'm Married to Shopping' Obsessive Compulsive Shoppers," Only Human, 2019, youtube.com/watch?v=OXf3tBnyxDo. (Accessed February 6, 2024.)

26. Black, D. W., Repertinger, S., Gaffney, G. R., and Gabel, J., "Family history and psychiatric comorbidity in persons with compulsive buying: preliminary findings," *The American Journal of Psychiatry* 155, no. 7 (1998): 960–63.

27. Grosz, S., *The Examined Life* (London: Random House, 2013).

3 Greed: when money is never enough

1. "Greed," Merriam Webster Dictionary, merriam-webster.com/dictionary/greed. (Accessed October 5, 2022.)

2. Newport, F., "Partisan Divide on Benefit of Having Rich People Expands," Gallup, 2018, news.gallup.com/poll/235439/partisan-divide-benefit-having-rich-people-expands.aspx. (Accessed February 6, 2024.)

3. Seuntjens, T. G., Zeelenberg, M., Breugelmans, S. M., and van de Ven, N., "Defining greed," *British Journal of Psychology* 106, no. 3 (2015): 505–25.

4. "Greed," Online Etymology Dictionary, etymonline.com/word/greed#etymonline_v_29933. (Accessed February 29, 2024.)

5. Kouchaki, M., et al., "Seeing green: Mere exposure to money triggers a business decision frame and unethical outcomes," *Organizational Behavior and Human Decision Processes* 121, no. 1 (2013): 53–61.

6. Kouchaki, M., et al., "Dirty Money: Mere Exposure to Money Motivates to Think Business, Cheat and Lie," Edmond & Lily Safra Center for Ethics, 2013, ethics.harvard.edu.

7. Kiff, P., "The science of greed," *TEDxMarin*, youtube.com/watch?v=OtU_nXV0i4E. (Accessed February 6, 2024.)

8. "How generous are America's rich?," *The Economist*, 2020, economist.com/graphic-detail/2020/05/06/how-generous-are-americas-rich.

9. Emerson, R. W., *The Conduct of Life* (Boston/New York: Houghton, Mifflin and Company, 1888).

10. "Greed," Online Etymology Dictionary, op. cit.

11. Robertson and Saad, as cited in Seuntjens, T. G., Zeelenberg, M., Breugelmans, S. M., and van de Ven, N., "Defining greed," *British Journal of Psychology* 106, no. 3 (2015): 505–25.

12. For examples of sources, see in Seuntjens, Zeelenberg, Breugelmans, and van de Ven, "Defining greed," op. cit.

13. Kets de Vries, M., "Is Greed Destroying Your Soul?," INSEAD Knowledge, 2019, knowledge.insead.edu/leadership-organisations/greed-destroying-your-soul. (Accessed February 6, 2024.)

14. Ibid.

15. Phillips, A., *Going Sane* (London: Penguin, 2006), 188.

16. Seuntjens, Zeelenberg, Breugelmans, and van de Ven, "Defining greed," op. cit.

17. Fenichel, O., "The Drive to Amass Wealth," *The Psychoanalytic Quarterly* 7 (1938): 69–95.

18. Ibid.

19. Klein, M., "Our adult world and its roots in infancy," *Human Relations* 12, no. 4 (1959): 291–303.

20. The Bible, King James version, New Testament, Gospel of Matthew 26:15.

21. Alighieri, D., *The Divine Comedy of Dante Alighieri: Inferno, Purgatory, Paradise* (New York: The Union Library Association, 1935) .

22. Ovid, *Metamorphoses XI*, theoi.com/Text/OvidMetamorphoses11. html. (Accessed February 6, 2024.)

23. Hawthorne, N., *A Wonder-Book for Girls and Boys* (London: Everyman's Library, 1994).

24. "Scrooge McDuck," Disney Fandom, disney.fandom.com/wiki/ Scrooge_McDuck. (Accessed February 6, 2024.)

25. Clark, M. A., et al., "Workaholism, work engagement and work-home outcomes: exploring the mediating role of positive and negative emotions," *Stress Health* 30, no. 4 (2014): 287–300.

26. "Burnout," American Psychology Association Dictionary of Psychology, dictionary.apa.org/burnout. (Accessed February 6, 2024.)

27. Baskerville, K., "I went to financial therapy and this is what I learned," *Cosmopolitan*, 2022.

28. Krueger, D. W., "Money Meanings and Madness: A Psychoanalytic Perspective," *Psychoanalytic Review* 78, no. 2 (1991): 209–24.

29. Holmes, J., *The Search for the Secure Base: Attachment Theory and Psychotherapy* (London: Routledge, 2001), 126.

30. Ibid.

31. Schroeder, A., *The Snowball: Warren Buffett and the Business of Life* (London: Bloomsbury, 2008), 703.

32. Ibid., 42.

33. Ibid., 32.

34. Ibid., 37.

35. Ibid., 38.

36. Ibid., 44.

37. Ibid., 144.

38. Ibid., 47.

39. Ibid., 49.

40. *Becoming Warren Buffett*, HBO Documentary Film, 2017, youtube. com/watch?v=PB5krSvFAPY. (Accessed February 6, 2024.)

41. Schroeder, *The Snowball*, op. cit., 703.

42. Ibid., 57.

43. Fenichel, O., "The Drive to Amass Wealth," *The Psychoanalytic Quarterly* 7 (1938): 69–95.

44. Yalom, I. D., *Staring at the Sun: Overcoming the Terror of Death* (Hoboken, NJ: Jossey-Bass, 2009).

45. Akhtar, S., "Work addiction," in Savelle-Rockin, N., and Akhtar, S. (eds.), *Beyond the Primal Addiction* (London: Routledge, 2019), 127.

46. Ibid.

4   Underspending: when we can't enjoy money

1. Levine, B., and Kellen, B., "Debtors Anonymous and Psychotherapy," in Benson, A. L. (ed.), *I Shop, Therefore I Am* (Northvale, NJ: J. Aronson, 2000), 431–54.

2. Binnes, K., "How to retire early: the Fire movement," *The Times*, 2023, thetimes.co.uk/money-mentor/article/how-to-retire-early-the-fire-method.

3. Posted on Reddit thread, reddit.com/r/fuckeatingdisorders/comments/atdq18/financial_anorexia. (Accessed February 6, 2024.)

4. Galatariotou, C., "The defences," in Budd, S., and Rusbridger, R. (eds.), *Introducing Psychoanalysis* (London: Routledge, 2005).

5. McWilliams, N., *Psychoanalytic Diagnosis: Understanding Personality Structure in the Clinical Process* (London: Guilford Press, 2011), 293.

6. Freud, S., *Three Essays on the Theory of Sexuality* (London: Imago Publishing Co., 1949).

7. Posted on Reddit thread, op. cit.

8. Niederland, W. G., "The Problem of the Survivor," in Krystal, H. (ed.), *Massive Psychic Trauma* (New York: International Universities Press, 1968), 8–22.

9. Wyckoff, P., "Queen Midas: Hetty Robinson Green," *The New England Quarterly* 23, no. 2 (1950): 147–71.

10. Ibid.

11. Wahl, C., "Psychoanalysis of the Rich, the Famous and the Influential," *Contemporary Psychoanalysis* 10 (1974): 71–76.

5 Self-sabotage: why we get in our own way

1. Jung, C. G., *Collected Works of C. G. Jung, Volume 12: Psychology and Alchemy* (New Jersey: Princeton University Press, 1992).

2. Krueger, D. W., *The Last Taboo: Money as Symbol and Reality in Psychotherapy and Psychoanalysis* (Michigan: Brunner/Mazel), 8.

3. Loorbach, D., "10 things I learned after losing a lot of money," *TEDxMünster*, youtube.com/watch?v=_8l2egORXGA. (Accessed February 8, 2024.)

4. Freud, S., "Letter from Sigmund Freud to Wilhelm Knöpfmacher, 6 August 1878," *Letters of Sigmund Freud 1873–1939* (London: Hogarth Press, 1878), 6–7.

5. The Bible, King James version, New Testament, Matthew 19:24, bible.com/bible/1/MAT.19.KJV. (Accessed February 29, 2024.)

6. "Artist Damien Hirst on 'The Currency' project, a new twist on NFTs," CNBC, 2021, cnbc.com/video/2021/07/21/artist-damien-hirst-on-the-currency-project-a-new-twist-on-nfts.html. (Accessed February 9, 2024.)

7. Richard, C., "Profit From Art Isn't Dirty. It Means: Make More Art," *The New York Times,* 2019, nytimes.com/2019/10/25/your-money/profit-art-business.html.

8. Freud S., "A disturbance of memory on the Acropolis (1936)," in *The Standard Edition of the Complete Psychological Works of Sigmund Freud,* Vol. 22 (London: Hogarth Press, 1964).

9. Turkel, A., "Money as a Mirror of Marriage," *Journal of the American Academy of Psychoanalysis and Dynamic Psychiatry* 16, no. 4 (1988): 525–35.

10. Krueger, D. W., *The Last Taboo: Money as Symbol and Reality in Psychotherapy and Psychoanalysis* (Michigan: Brunner/Mazel, 1986), 7.

11. Horner, M. S., "Toward an understanding of achievement-related conflicts in women," *Journal of Social Issues* 28 (1972): 157–75.

12. Keller, W., Molina, T., and Olney, W. W., "The gender gap among top business executives," *National Bureau of Economic Research,* 2022, nber.org/system/files/working_papers/w28216/w28216.pdf. (Accessed February 8, 2024.)

13. Miller, F., "Gender pay gap 2023: How to check your employer," *The Times,* 2023, thetimes.co.uk/money-mentor/article/gender-pay-gap-uk-2023-how-to-check-your-employer.

14. Lingiardi, V., and McWilliams, N., "The Psychodynamic Diagnostic Manual – 2nd edition," *World Psychiatry* 14, no. 2 (2015): 237–39.

15. Chester, N., "Financial domination is a very expensive fetish," Vice, 2013, vice.com/en/article/4w3ejb/financial-domination-is-a-very-expensive-fetish.

16. Ghent, E., "Masochism, submission, surrender—Masochism as a perversion of surrender," *Contemporary Psychoanalysis* 26 (1990): 108–36.

17. Freud, S., "Mourning and Melancholia," in *The Standard Edition of the Complete Psychological Works of Sigmund Freud*, Vol. 14 (London: Hogarth Press, 1953).

18. Cassidy, J., "Child-mother attachment and the self in six-year-olds," *Child Development* 59, no. 1 (1988): 121–34.

19. Fairbairn, W. R. D., "The repression and the return of bad objects (with special reference to the 'war neuroses')," *British Journal of Medical Psychology* 19 (1943): 327–41.

20. Ibid.

21. Freud, S., *Beyond the Pleasure Principle* (New York: Liveright, 1961).

22. Harman, J., "'I'm Married to Shopping' Obsessive Compulsive Shoppers," Only Human, youtube.com/watch?v=OXf3tBnyxDo. (Accessed February 8, 2024.)

23. Freud, S., "Inhibitions, Symptoms and Anxiety," *The Standard Edition of the Complete Psychological Works of Sigmund Freud*, Vol. 20 (London: Hogarth Press, 1926), 175–76.

24. Klein, M., "Some Theoretical Conclusions regarding the Emotional Life of the Infant," *Developments in Psychoanalysis* (London: Routledge, 1952).

25. Liotti, G., "Understanding the dissociative processes: The contribution of attachment theory," *Psychoanalytic Inquiry* 19, no. 5 (1999): 757–83.

26. Krueger, D. W., *The Last Taboo: Money as Symbol and Reality in Psychotherapy and Psychoanalysis* (Michigan: Brunner/Maze, 1986).

27. Turkel, A., "Money as a Mirror of Marriage," *Journal of the American Academy of Psychoanalysis and Dynamic Psychiatry* 16, no. 4 (1988): 525–35.

28. Krueger, *The Last Taboo*, op. cit., 7.

6 Generosity: from inadequacy to control and why we give

1. "Generosity," American Psychological Association Dictionary, dictionary.apa.org/generosity. (Accessed February 8, 2024.)

2. "Generosity," Cambridge Academic Content Dictionary, dictionary.cambridge.org/dictionary/english/generosity. (Accessed February 8, 2024.)

3. Amstutz, D., et al., "Reckless Generosity, Parkinson's Disease and Dopamine: A Case Series and Literature Review," *Movement Disorders Clinical Practice* 8, no. 3 (2021): 469–73.

4. Filkowski, M. M., Cochran, N. R., and Haas, B. W., "Altruistic behavior: mapping responses in the brain," *Neuroscience and Neuroeconomics* 5 (2016): 65–75.

5. Aknin, L., et al., "Prosocial Spending and Well-Being: Cross-Cultural Evidence for a Psychological Universal," *Journal of Personality and Social Psychology* 104, no. 4 (2013): 635–52.

6. Filkowski, Cochran, and Haas, "Altruistic behavior," op. cit.

7. Dunn, E., Aknin, L., and Norton, M., "Spending Money on Others Promotes Happiness," *Science* 319, no. 5870 (2008): 1687–88. Follow-up study: Dunn, E. W., et al., "Does Spending Money on Others Promote Happiness?: A Registered Replication Report," *Journal of Personality and Social Psychology: Attitudes and Social Cognition* 119, no. 2 (2020).

8. Aknin, L. B., Hamlin, J. K., Dunn, E. W., "Giving Leads to Happiness in Young Children," *PLOS One* 7, no. 6 (2012): e39211.

9. Isen, A., "Positive Affect, Cognitive Processes and Social Behavior," *Advances in Experimental Social Psychology* 20 (1987): 203–53.

10. Akhtar, S., "Generosity," in *Good Stuff: Courage, Resilience, Gratitude, Generosity, Forgiveness and Sacrifice* (Lanham, MD: Jason Aronson, 2012).

11. Klein, M., *Envy and Gratitude: A Study of Unconscious Sources* (London: Routledge, 2013).

12. Seelig, B. J., and Rosof, L. S., "Normal and Pathological Altruism," *Journal of the American Psychoanalytic Association* 49, no. 3 (2001): 933–59.

13. Freud, A., *The Ego and the Mechanisms of Defence* (London: Hogarth Press and the Institute of Psychoanalysis, 1937).

14. Saul, H., "Amy Schumer leaves bartenders $1,000 tip and tells staff: 'I've been there,'" *The Independent*, 2016, independent.co.uk/news/people/amy-schumer-leaves-bartenders-1-000-tip-and-tells-staff-i-ve-been-there-a6945421.html.

15. Green, A., "Moral Narcissism," *International Journal of Psychoanalytic Psychotherapy* 8 (1981): 243–69.

16. Freud, S., *Three Essays on the Theory of Sexuality* (London: Imago Publishing Co., 1949).

17. Lewinsky, H., "Pathological Generosity," *International Journal of Psychoanalysis* 32 (1951): 185–89.

18. Seelig, B. J., and Rosof, L. S., "Normal and pathological atruism," *Journal of American Psychoanalytic Association* 32 (2001): 185–89.

19. McWilliams, N., *Psychoanalytic Diagnosis: Understanding Personality Structure in the Clinical Process* (London: Guilford Press, 2011), 270.

20. Orgel, S. K., and Shengold, L., "The Fatal Gifts of Medea," *International Journal of Psychoanalysis* 49, no. 2 (1968): 379–85.

21. Cohn, D., "Thanks, I Guess: What Consumers Complain About When They Complain About Gifts," *The Journal of Consumer Satisfaction, Dissatisfaction and Complaining Behavior* 29 (2016): 77–90.

22. Bennison, S., "Gifting with strings attached," The Openwork Partnership, 2020, theopenworkpartnership.com/news/gifting-with-strings-attached.

7   Stealing: reclaiming, rebelling, or redemption?

1. Hughes, C., "Antony Worrall Thompson—That Sunday Night Show," youtube.com/watch?v=zbxjdv9X1cQ&t=85s. (Accessed February 8, 2024.)

2. *Diagnostic and Statistical Manual of Mental Disorders*, 5th edition (Virginia: American Psychiatric Association, 2022).

3. "Kleptomania," American Psychiatric Association, psychiatry.org/news-room/apa-blogs/kleptomania. (Accessed February 8, 2024.)

4. Nolsoe, E., "Quarter of Brits have shoplifted," YouGov, 2020, yougov.co.uk/topics/consumer/articles-reports/2020/03/16/quarter-brits-have-shoplifted. (Accessed February 8, 2024.)

5. The Bible, King James version, New Testament, Exodus 20:15, bible.com/bible/1/EXO.20.KJV. (Accessed February 29, 2024.)

6. Nolsoe, "Quarter of Brits have shoplifted," op. cit.

7. van Dijk, J., Nieuwbeerta, P., and Joudo Larsen, J., "Global Crime Patterns: An Analysis of Survey Data from 166 Countries Around the World, 2006–2019," *Journal of Quantitative Criminology* 38 (2021): 793–827.

8. Ray, J., and Briar, K. H., "Economic Motivators for Shoplifting," *The Journal of Sociology & Social Welfare* 15, no. 4 (1988): article 11.

9. Francis-Devine, B., "Poverty in the UK: Statistics," House of Commons Library, 2023, commonslibrary.parliament.uk/research-briefings/sn07096. (Accessed February 9, 2024.)

10. Schwab, V. E., *The Shades of Magic Series: A Darker Shade of Magic, A Gathering of Shadows, A Conjuring of Light* (London: Titan Books, 2017), 209.

11. Kets de Vries, M. F. R., "Doing a Madoff: The Psychology of White-collar Criminals," INSEAD Working Paper No. 2021/55/EFE, 2021.

12. Morgan, A., *The Split*, Season 1, Episode 6, BBC One, aired May 29, 2018.

13. "Interview with Annabel Scholey," *BBC*, 2018, bbc.co.uk/mediacentre/mediapacks/the-split/scholey.

14. Gelles, D., and Tett, G., "From behind bars, Madoff spins his story," *Financial Times*, 2011, ft.com/content/a29d2b4a-60b7-11e0-a182-00144feab49a.

15. Zitek, E. M., Jordan, A. H., Monin, B., and Leach, F. R., "Victim entitlement to behave selfishly," *Journal of Personality and Social Psychology* 98, no. 2 (2010): 245–55.

16. Winnicott, D. W., *Deprivation and Delinquency* (London: Routledge, 1984).

17. Winnicott, D. W., *Therapeutic Consultations in Child Psychiatry* (New York: Basic Books, 1971).

18. Freud, S., "The Ego and the Id," in *The Standard Edition of the Complete Psychological Works of Sigmund Freud*, Volume 11 (London: Vintage, 2001).

19. Freud, S., "Some character-types met with in psycho-analytic work," in *The Standard Edition of the Complete Psychological Works of Sigmund Freud*, Volume 14, via Psychoanalytic Electric Publishing, pep-web.org/browse/document/se.014.0309a?page=P0309. (Accessed February 9, 2024.)

20. Hindle, D., "Loss and delinquency: Two adolescents' experiences of prison as an external container for psychic pain," *Journal of Child Psychotherapy* 24, no. 1 (1998): 37–60.

21. Ibid.

22. Akhtar, S., "Jealousy," *Comprehensive Dictionary of Psychoanalysis* (London: Karnac Books, 2009).

23. Ibid.

24. Freud, S., *Group Psychology and the Analysis of the Ego* (New York: Liveright, 1922).

25. Boradwin, I., "New Light on Delinquency and its Treatment. By William Healy and Augusta F. Bronner. (Published for the Institute for Human Relations by Yale University Press, New Haven.)," *The International Journal of Psychoanalysis* 19 (1938): 155–56.

26. Pickhardt, C. E., "Adolescence and Stealing from Family," *Psychology Today*, 2012, psychologytoday.com/gb/blog/surviving-your-childs-adolescence/201204/adolescence-and-stealing-family. (Accessed February 9, 2024.)

27. Rizzuto, A. M., "Deprivation and Delinquency," *Journal of the American Psychoanalytic Association* 38 (1990): 811–15.

28. Worrall Thompson, A., *Raw: My Autobiography* (London: Bantam Press, 2003), 41.

29. *Armchair Anonymous*, armchairexpertpod.com/armchair-anonymous. (Accessed February 9, 2024.)

30. Dyke, S., "Review: D.W. Winnicott: Deprivation and Delinquency. Tavistock Publications, 1984," *Journal of Child Psychotherapy* 11, no. 2 (1985): 116–20.

31. Duffield, G., and Grabosky, P., "The Psychology of Fraud," *Australian Institute of Criminology*, no. 199, Trends & Issues (2001).

32. Kets de Vries, "Doing a Madoff," op. cit.

33. Worrall Thompson, *Raw*, op. cit., 27.

8   Control: a quest for power or closeness?

1. Kasperkevic, J., "Financial bullying can ruin a marriage: first-person stories," *The Guardian*, 2012, theguardian.com/money/us-money-blog/2014/aug/14/relationships-finances-bullying-abuse-dependent-equality.

2. "What is economic abuse?," *Surviving Economic Abuse*, survivingeconomicabuse.org/what-is-economic-abuse. (Accessed February 9, 2024.)

3. Butt, E., "Know Economic Abuse Report" Refuge, 2020, refuge.org.uk/wp-content/uploads/2020/10/Know-Economic-Abuse-Report-2020.pdf. (Accessed February 9, 2024.)

4. "Economic abuse and coercive control—Experiences of survivors during the Covid 19 pandemic," Women's Aid, 2022, womensaid.org.uk/wp-content/uploads/2022/10/3.-Economic-abuse-and-Covid-19.pdf. (Accessed February 9, 2024.)

5. Adams, A., et al., "Development of the Scale of Economic Abuse," *Violence Against Women* 14, no. 5 (2008): 563–88.

6. Howard, M., and Skipp, A., "Unequal, trapped and controlled," Women's Aid, 2015, womensaid.org.uk/wp-content/uploads/2015/11/Women_s_Aid_TUC_Financial_Abuse_Report_March_2015.pdf. (Accessed February 9, 2024.)

7. "Economic abuse and Coercive control," Women's Aid, op. cit.

8. Sharp, N., "What's yours is mine," Refuge, 2008, via theduluthmodel.org/wp-content/uploads/2021/12/Whats-yours-is-mine-Full-Report.pdf. (Accessed February 9, 2024.)

9. Butt, "Know economic abuse," op. cit.

10. Freud, A., *The Ego and the Mechanisms of Defence* (London: Hogarth Press, 1946).

11. Freud, S., "Remembering, Repeating and Working-Through (Further Recommendations on the Technique of Psycho-Analysis II)," in *The Standard Edition of the Complete Psychological Works of Sigmund Freud*, Vol. 12 (London: Hogarth Press, 1914), 145–56.

12. Berlinger, as cited in Akhtar, S., *Comprehensive Dictionary of Psychoanalysis* (London: Karnac Books, 2009).

13. Wurmser, L., *Torment Me, But Don't Abandon Me* (Lanham, MD: Jason Aronson, 2007).

14. Please note that this is a redacted, translated, and slightly paraphrased version of the letter, parts of which are in the public domain: Ceran, M., "Violenza economica: cos'è e come riconoscerla," *Grano,* 2024, youtube.com/watch?v=nTZCwg78iXQ. (Accessed February 9, 2024.)

9 Money secrets

1. Tournier, P., *The Healing of Persons* (London: Harper & Row, 1983).

2. "Almost two in five people in a relationship in the UK admit to 'financial infidelity,'" Aviva, 2023, aviva.com/newsroom/news-releases/2023/02/almost-two-in-five-people-in-a-relationship-in-the-uk-admit-to-financial-infidelity. (Accessed February 9, 2024.)

3. Burns, C., "Are your loved ones keeping money secrets from you?," Money Helper, 2021, moneyhelper.org.uk/en/blog/everyday-money/are-your-loved-ones-keeping-money-secrets-from-you. (Accessed February 9, 2024.)

4. "Almost two in five people," Aviva, op. cit.

5. "21 Million Money Secrets Kept From Loved Ones Across the UK," Money and Pensions Service, 2020, moneyandpensionsservice.org. uk/2020/11/09/21-million-money-scrts-kept-from-loved-ones-across-the-uk. (Accessed December 7, 2023.)

6. "2 in 5 Americans admit to financial infidelity against their partner," National Endowment for Financial Education, 2021, nefe. org/news/2021/11/2-in-5-americans-admit-to-financial-infidelity-against-their-partner.aspx. (Accessed February 9, 2024.)

7. Garbinsky, E. N., Gladstone, J. J., Nikolova, H., and Olson, J. G., "Love, Lies, and Money: Financial Infidelity in Romantic Relationships," *Journal of Consumer Research* 47, no. 1 (2020): 1–24.

8. The Bible, King James version, New Testament, Luke 12:3, bible. com/bible/1/LUK.12.KJV. (Accessed February 29, 2024.)

9. Garbinsky, Gladstone, Nikolova, and Olson, "Love, Lies, and Money," op. cit.

10. "Survey: Nearly 1 in 4 Americans in relationships are hiding financial secrets from their partners," Bankrate, 2023, bankrate. com/finance/credit-cards/financial-infidelity-survey. (Accessed December 9, 2023.)

11. Harzog, B., "Survey: 30 percent have dealt with financial infidelity," *US News & World Report*, 2022, money.usnews.com/credit-cards/ articles/survey-30-have-either-committed-financial-infidelity-or- been-a-victim. (Accessed February 9, 2024.)

12. Slepian, M., *The Secret Life of Secrets: How Our Inner Worlds Shape Well-being, Relationships and Who We Are* (London: Hachette, 2022).

13. Slepian, M., Halevy, N., and Galinsky, A. D., "The Solitude of Secrecy: Thinking About Secrets Evokes Goal Conflict and Feelings of Fatigue," *Personality and Social Psychology Bulletin* 45, no. 7 (2019): 1129–51.

14. Slepian, M., "Why the secrets you keep are hurting you," *Scientific American*, 2019, scientificamerican.com/article/why-the-secrets- you-keep-are-hurting-you/?amp.

15. Slepian, M., Kalokerinos, E., and Kirby, J., "Shame, Guilt and Secrets on the Mind," *Emotion* 20, no. 2 (2020): 323–28.

16. Slepian, M., Chun, J. S., and Mason, M. F., "The Experience of Secrecy," *Journal of Personality and Social Psychology* 113, no. 1 (2017): 1–33.

17. Dervish-O'Kane, R., "Why I can't stop talking to my friends about money," *Women's Health*, 2023, womenshealthmag.com/uk/ collective/long-reads/a44763502/cant-stop-talking-to-friends- about-money.

18. Pringle, E., "People have started posting their credit scores on dating profiles—it's winning them more matches and better dates," *Fortune*, 2023, fortune.com/2023/05/31/credit-scores-on-hinge- dating-profiles-getting-better-matches.

10 Couples and money

1. Mineo, L., "Good genes are nice, but joy is better," *The Harvard Gazette*, 2017, news.harvard.edu/gazette/story/2017/04/over-nearly-80-years-harvard-study-has-been-showing-how-to-live-a-healthy-and-happy-life.

2. "Religion, Sex and Politics? The M Word is Britain's Biggest Taboo," Lloyds Banking Group, 2019, lloydsbankinggroup.com/media/press-releases/2019/lloyds-bank/the-m-word-is-britains-biggest-taboo.html. (Accessed November 30, 2024.)

3. "Almost two in five people in a relationship in the UK admit to 'financial infidelity,'" Aviva, 2023, aviva.com/newsroom/news-releases/2023/02/almost-two-in-five-people-in-a-relationship-in-the-uk-admit-to-financial-infidelity. (Accessed February 9, 2024.)

4. Olson, D. H., and Olson, A. K., "National Survey of Marital Strengths," YUMPU, 2000, yumpu.com/en/document/read/11266980/national-survey-of-marital-strengths-prepare-enrich. (Accessed February 9, 2024.)

5. Ibid.

6. Ibid.

7. Lunn, E., "One in five women (22 percent) have a secret savings fund to provide them with financial support should their relationship end or they choose to leave their partner, according to research by Fidelity International," Your Money, 2020, yourmoney.com/saving-banking/more-than-a-fifth-of-women-have-a-secret-savings-fund. (Accessed February 9, 2024.)

8. US Bureau of Statistics, as cited in Carelock, H. (ed.), "Female Breadwinners, Money and Shame: How Financial Planners Can Help," *Journal of Financial Therapy* 13, no. 2 (2022): 61–77.

9. "How do partners in couple families share paid work?," Organisation for Economic Co-operation and Development, 2017, oecd.org/gender/data/how-do-partners-in-couple-families-share-paid-work.htm. (Accessed February 9, 2024.)

10. Parker, K., and Stepler, R., "Americans see men as the financial providers, even as women's contributions grow," Pew Research Center, 2017, pewresearch.org/short-reads/2017/09/20/americans-see-men-as-the-financial-providers-even-as-womens-contributions-grow. (Accessed February 9, 2024.)

11. Turkel, A., "Money as a Mirror of Marriage," *Journal of the American Academy of Psychoanalysis and Dynamic Psychiatry* 16, no. 4 (1988): 525–35.

12. "UBS Own your Worth report finds that only 20 percent of couples participate equally in financial decisions," UBS Media, 2021, ubs.com/global/en/media/display-page-ndp/en-20210506-own-your-worth.html. (Accessed February 29, 2024.)

13. *Couples Therapy*, Season 1, Episode 3, BBC2, Edgeline Films, aired 2019.

14. Serra-Garcia, M., "Risk Attitudes and Conflict in the Household," *The Economic Journal* 132, no. 642 (2021): 767–95. See also: Clark, C., "Differences in Financial Risk Preferences Can Make or Break a Marriage," *UC San Diego Today*, 2021, today.ucsd.edu/story/differences-in-financial-risk-preferences-can-make-or-break-a-marriage.

15. Olson and Olson, "National Survey of Marital Strength," op. cit.

16. Morrison, R. F., Evans, M. G., Kolodny, H. F., and House, R. J., "More Ugli Orange," *The Teaching of Organizational Behavior* 2, no. 2 (1976): 4–5.

17. Ruszczynski, S., as cited in Nathans, S., and Schaefer, M. (eds.), *Couples on the Couch* (London: Routledge, 2017), 51.

18. Laertius, D., *Lives of Eminent Philosophers* (Cambridge, MA: Harvard University Press, 1972).

19. "Almost two in five people," Aviva, op. cit.

11 Money and other relationships: friendships, families, and the workplace

1. "Fiona and James," *The Money Clinic*, BBC Radio 4, 2019, bbc. co.uk/sounds/play/m0007k8k.

2. Horowitz, J. M., "More than half of Americans in their 40s are 'sandwiched' between an aging parent and their own children," Pew Research Center, 2022, pewresearch.org/short-reads/2022/04/08/more-than-half-of-americans-in-their-40s-are-sandwiched-between-an-aging-parent-and-their-own-children.

3. Lustbader, R., "Caring.com's 2024 Wills Survey Finds That 40 percent of Americans Don't Think They Have Enough Assets to Create a Will," Caring, 2024, caring.com/caregivers/estate-planning/wills-survey.

4. Freud, S., "The Interpretation of Dreams," in *The Complete Psychological Works of Sigmund Freud*, Volume 4 (London: Hogarth Press, 1953).

5. Survey by Harris Interactive on behalf of CouponCabin, as reported in Kavoussi, B., "Money Ruins Friendships For One In Five Americans, Survey Finds," Huffington Post, 2012, huffingtonpost. co.uk/entry/money-ruins-friendships-survey-finds_n_1683720.

6. Ashkam, G., "Are you being brokefished?," *Women's Health*, 2022, gb.readly.com/magazines/womens-health-uk/2022-09-13/6321939c0b308a6102712cfa.

7. Kane, L., "Friends and Money: How to Handle 4 Tough Scenarios," the muse, 2020, themuse.com/advice/friends-and-money-how-to-handle-4-tough-scenarios.

About the author

Vicky Reynal, mba, is a psychotherapist in private practice and runs her own clinic specializing in financial therapy, working with clients internationally. She has been featured in the *Financial Times*, *Daily Mail*, *Good Housekeeping*, *The Telegraph*, and *Women's Health*. Her focus on financial therapy grew organically after completing her MBA as well as post-graduate studies in psychodynamic psychotherapy. She lives in London.

reynal-psychotherapist.co.uk